SHOW BIZ TRAINING

Fun and Effective Business Training Techniques from the Worlds of Stage, Screen, and Song

LENN MILLBOWER

AMACOM AMERICAN MANAGEMENT ASSOCIATION

New York | Atlanta | Brussels | Buenos Aires | Chicago | London | Mexico City

San Francisco | Shanghai | Tokyo | Toronto | Washington, D.C.

Special discounts on bulk quantities of AMACOM books are available to corporations, professional associations, and other organizations. For details, contact Special Sales Department, AMACOM, a division of American Management Association, 1601 Broadway, New York, NY 10019.
Tel.: 212-903-8316. Fax: 212-903-8083.
Web site: www. amacombooks.org

This publication is designed to provide accurate and authoritative information in regard to the subject matter covered. It is sold with the understanding that the publisher is not engaged in rendering legal, accounting, or other professional service. If legal advice or other expert assistance is required, the services of a competent professional person should be sought.

Library of Congress Cataloging-in-Publication Data

Millbower, Lenn, 1951–
Show biz training : fun and effective business training techniques from
the worlds of stage, screen, and song / Lenn Millbower.
p. cm.
Includes bibliographical references and index.
ISBN 0-8144-7157-9
　　1. Employees—Training of—Problems, exercises, etc.　2. Group
　　relations training—Problems, exercises, etc.　3. Group games.　4.
　　Experiential learning.　5. Educational games.　I. Title.
HF5549.5.T7　M535　2003
658.3′124—dc21　　　　　　　　　　　　　　　　2003000647

Printing number
10 9 8 7 6 5 4 3 2 1

CONTENTS

ACKNOWLEDGMENTS

The people responsible for my general success are so numerous that the mention of them would require a separate book. I will not, in the interest of brevity, list them here. You know who you are, and know that I am forever grateful.

In contrast, a few specific individuals are largely responsible for my show biz success. I would like to publicly thank them now: Jacquie Flynn for embracing the vision of this book; Ray Keppel for introducing me to ventriloquism; Ron Zollweg and John Miller for tutoring my magic skills; Angela Rivers for encouraging my entry into the music profession; Doris Yager for providing me with a solid stagecraft foundation; my wife Rebecca for providing steadfast support; my father for sharing the joys of jazz music with me; and my mother for introducing me to show biz. From black gum to funny costumes to pantomimes, my mother taught me that the world is indeed a stage. Mom, this book is dedicated to you.

"The mind is not a vessel to be filled,
but a fire to be kindled."—PLUTARCH[1]

TEN REASONS TO USE SHOW BIZ TRAINING

10. Your yo-yo will become a vital office tool.
9. You can behave oddly with impunity.
8. You can explore toy stores and call it work.
7. Your CD collection will be tax deductible.
6. You'll know how Copperfield does those cool tricks.
5. Wearing funny hats becomes acceptable behavior.
4. You'll be admired for your wit.
3. You'll laugh more often.
2. Your learners will enjoy themselves.
1. Your learners will pay attention, and retain your message.

I started writing this book at age five. Well, that may be an overstatement. After all, I barely knew how to write my name. I did, however, begin a trek that led to this book.

It was a late October morning in Utica, New York. As is true every fall in upstate New York, summer gives way to an early fall. Around October, winter begins fighting its way in. On this particular morning, the early morning chill indicated that the fight had begun. I was underdressed in a tee shirt and shorts. But despite my attire, I was alive with adrenaline. Today was my debut.

In my kindergarten class, to build awareness of a circus sponsored by a local charity, we were putting on our own circus, and I was one of the performers. As I entered the classroom, I saw the spectators. A large number of them had already gathered. In retrospect it was probably just class parents waiting to see their children perform. Who they were, however, was of no consequence to me. The fact that they were there to watch me is what mattered.

Our teacher functioned as the master of ceremonies, introducing the acts one by one. First the lion tamer appeared, with a staple of ferocious cats—really other classmates with painted noses, painted on whiskers, and frayed rope mains around their necks. Next came the clowns, all happy and silly. They were followed by a parade of classmates holding hands and lumbering single file around the "ring" as they bellowed like elephants. I was next.

I was to be the trapeze performer. As it turned out, I was the trapeze hanger-on-for-dear-lifer. My teacher physically lifted me through my paces, first bending me this way, and then turning me that way. This event occurred in an era before videotape recorders, and looking back on it, I am glad. I must have been the sorriest trapeze artist in the history of the Kernan Grade School.

The teacher finished guiding me through my routine. Thankful that the routine was over, I planted both of my wobbly feet on the ground. I was intently gazing at those feet and regaining my balance when I heard a strange new sound. In curiosity, I slowly looked to see what the noise was. What I saw people whom I had never met smiling, nodding approvingly, and applauding . . . ME! It was the most astonishing revelation of my life. If I could make people smile, they would praise me in return. A performance career was born.

Many people spend their lives searching for meaning, relationships, or a better job. From that day forward, I focused on reaching people through performance, and found myself drawn to any entertainment form that got a positive audience reaction.

I first performed with marionettes. Next, I transitioned into ventriloquism, and from there to magic. After a few years of practice, I joined a traveling entertainment troupe, the Rhythm-Lites. We performed in county, state, and world's fairs, at a variety of other widely known venues throughout the United States, and even at the White House. During my years with the Rhythm-Lites, I performed as a master of ceremonies, a singer and dancer, a magician and ventriloquist, a pianist and later the musical director, and show writer. Along the way, I discovered how entertainment reaches and moves people.

The late teens saw rock and roll take a hold of life. I moved into the musical arena, learned to play several musical instruments, and gained a music composition degree from Boston's Berklee College of Music. Next came an entertainment career as a musician-magician in a variety of acts over 10 years, performing in 40 of the U.S. states, in Canada, and in the Bahamas.

Many of those acts were eye catching. We named one act after our magical rabbit, Sydney. Our bass player drank a bottle of beer while standing on his head. I floated a light bulb across the dance floor. We floated the singer across the dance floor while singing the Beatle's "Lucy In the Sky with Diamonds." We burned the next singer alive. She survived but soon quit. I still wonder why.

Eventually, I put away all my entertainment toys and joined the training and development and collegiate worlds. I tried to be serious . . . really. But over time, I found myself adding entertainment elements to my classrooms. The similarities between entertainment and learning were too obvious to ignore. Both disciplines require a professional delivery. If the delivery is amateurish, the entertainer is booed, and the trainer is ignored. They both must attract attention, and fail if attention is not captured, or worse, lost after it is gained. If no one notices the selected playing card, the magician's production of it has no magic. If no one hears the learning point, that point cannot be remembered.

These similarities led me to fold entertainment elements into the learning environment. Each time I added an element, the learners responded, so I'd add another. Simultaneously, I began to notice a change in the attitudes of learners. The people entering the workforce had shorter attention spans. They did not listen well. They expected more, in less time. They were quick to begin new things, and just as quick to abandon them.

One day while teaching a college class, I heard two of these new learners praising James Cameron's movie *Titanic* (1997). Immediately, an incongruity hit me. *Titanic* is three hours long! If I attempted a three-hour lecture, they would have mutinied. To make matters more galling, they PAID to see *Titanic* again and again. None of them would have paid to repeat my class.

It occurred to me that the entertainment industry knew how to capture and maintain attention, and that if I could codify those techniques, I could too. I began analyzing the techniques used in entertainment, and aggressively looked for applications to the learning environment. As I discovered techniques and added them to my classes, I noticed that test and class evaluation scores rose. The more I employed entertainment techniques, the more effective learning became. And then, one day, a former learner approached me. She asked if she could attend a class again! I knew then that entertainment works.

In this book, I share with you a different way to think about learning. It is a combination of learning and entertainment. It is a method for increasing retention while simultaneously making learning engaging and fun. It is *Learnertainment.*

In Act One, "The Info-fog," we examine the need for Learnertainment, and the theoretical basis underlying its use. Then, in Act Two, "Lessons from Entertainment," we discover the Show Biz techniques entertainment professionals use to create their miracles, and identify classroom applications from comedy, music, and magic. In Act Three, "Stagecraft," we examine specific Show Biz stagecraft techniques that help entertainers deliver flawless performances. We then identify training applications for those techniques. Along the way, we explore several templates for placing Show Biz Training in the learning environment. Finally, we conclude by examining how one trainer put it all together and used Show Biz Training techniques to reach her learners.

With that, I conclude the overture. Please settle in, and enjoy, as we present Show Biz Training. Maestro: cue the music so we can raise the curtain.

---

[1] *Webster's Dictionary of Quotations* (1992). New York: Smithmark.

THE INFO-FOG

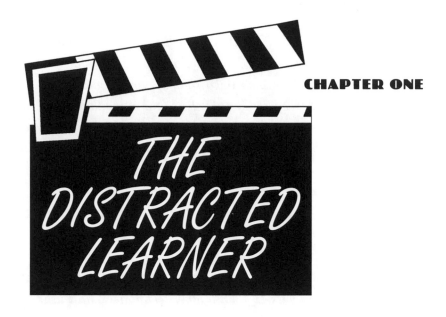

CHAPTER ONE

THE DISTRACTED LEARNER

HARRIET AND THE HOUSEKEEPERS: SCENE 1

When Harriet saw the schedule, she was ticked. Asbestos Awareness! Why? She was a soft-skills trainer, and this was NOT her area of expertise. Give her a class on communication, and she was content. But technical training?

"How could you do this to me?" she complained to her boss.

"The housekeepers requested you," her boss beamed.

The smile annoyed her, but Harriet appreciated the compliment.

"It seems you have developed quite a reputation for making dry material interesting," the boss continued. "They heard how much fun your diversity class was."

Then Harriet understood. She had recently drawn the assignment of teaching the maintenance department about diversity. They had a reputation as a notoriously difficult audience. In an attempt to win them over, she had built her instruction around music. She made the point that the African and European musical traditions had combined to create the wonderful sounds the class regarded as great music. Her kicker had been asking them to envision a world devoid of such music, and comparing that vision with the closing off of ideas that occurs when you ignore some people for super-ficial reasons. It had been a fabulous success—and apparently the word had spread. So, here she was, assigned another snoozer of a subject, all be-cause the housekeepers thought she could make the subject interesting.

"You know we've had a problem getting these employees to pay atten-tion. If they don't understand this information, we could be fined by OSHA. Besides," her boss concluded, "I'd like your ideas for revitalizing the class. It certainly needs them."

With that, Harriet was hooked. "Asbestos and interesting don't belong in the same sentence," she thought, "but what a challenge." She began to think about ways to bring the topic to life. Music worked the last time. She knew that music would have to be a component of her asbestos awareness class, but asked herself, "What other techniques can I use?"

"We live in a moment of history where change is so speeded up that we begin to see the present only when it is already disappearing." —R. D. LAING[1]

THE RISE OF INFORMATION

On January 8, 1815, American General Andrew Jackson led American troops in a battle with English soldiers, led by General Sir Edward Pakenham. It was the War of 1812, and the new nation and its former mother country were fighting again. Unlike the August 24, 1814, burning of Washington, DC, the Americans won this time, and they recorded it as a great victory. But the most remarkable fact concerning the Battle of New Orleans was not the victor. It was the fact that the battle was fought *after* the war had ended. Communi-cation was so slow that news of the Treaty of Ghent, signed on Christmas Eve, 1814, had not yet reached the combatants, and would not, until February 11, 1815.[2]

For thousands of years, the transmission of information was limited by the speed at which people could move. Vagabond travelers, merchants, and entertainers would carry news and information from village to village. As a result, information was transmitted slowly.

Some breakthroughs helped to speed the process. The railroads carried news across the countryside, and the sailing ships helped information conquer the oceans. Neverthe-less, the underlying limitations of physical movement remained. But then, in the late 1880s, humans began to harness electricity. Electricity did not, by itself, converse, but its use made new communications devices possible.[3]

One of the first electronic communications inventions was Samuel Morse's telegraph. It was cumbersome, requiring the operators to learn a complex code of electrical pulses, but with its introduction in 1844, information finally broke the restraints of physical movement.[4]

In just 30 years, the telegraph became a nationwide communicator, even spawning a national news organization, the Associated Press.[5] Certainly American President Abraham Lincoln recognized its value. During the American Civil War, he would sit for hours in the government's telegraph office hoping for quick news from the war front. The telegraph was so successful that by 1880, the number of telegraph messages traveling across America reached 30 million.[6]

When Cyrus Field laid the first Atlantic cable in 1866, instantaneous cross-ocean communication became possible.[7] Without needing to travel the ocean physically, people from America and Britain could finally update each other on happenings from both sides of "the pond."

Alexander Graham Bell's invention of the telephone advanced communications even further. It was no longer necessary to learn a code.[8] You could simply speak. Suddenly, anyone could communicate with anyone else. But even the telephone, like the telegraph before it, had a drawback. Without cable laid in advance, the device was useless.

Perhaps the larger breakthrough was the wireless. Because it did not require cables, use of the radio grew quickly. By 1920, it had spread throughout the industrial world.[9] Over their radios, people got news, information, entertainment, and advertisements. They were even able to hear their leaders' voices for the very first time.

Radio provided the auditory signal. Movies would add the video. In the 1930s, movie studios and their theater chains helped spread information through news reels. For the first time, people could simultaneously hear and see the events of the world, within weeks, in vibrant black and white.

In 1945, with the end of World War II, television entered American life. The television networks, including the Columbia Broadcasting System (CBS) and the National Broadcasting Company (NBC), created news bureaus and broadcast information directly into viewers' homes. This accelerated the speed of information transmission to the point that, in the 1960s, just 20 years later, reporters delivered videotape, delayed by only a day or two, from the Vietnam battlefields directly into American homes, much to the consternation of then American President Lyndon Johnson.

Thirty years later still, in the early 1990s, people watched live video feed of East and West Germans tearing down Berlin wall. The technology was so good, and the information so current, that the event almost seemed staged for the camera. And as 2000 became 2001,

THE GROWTH OF ENTERTAINMENT TECHNOLOGY

1909	Radio broadcasting begins
1939	Television, FM radio begins
1942	Radio/TV manufacture banned
1945	Radio/TV production resumes
1948	LP records, reel-to-reel recorders
1954	Pocket-sized transistor radios
1956	Black-and-white portable TVs
1961	FM radio broadcasts in stereo
1963	Compact audio cassette players
1965	8-track players, video recorders
1969	Research internet (ARPnet)
1972	Home video game systems
1975	Betamax, Pong home video game
1976	VHS VCRs
1977	Apple Computers, video rentals
1979	Sony Walkman, Compuserve
1982	CD players

TABLE 1-1

electronic information transmission was so prevalent that people throughout the world were able to watch each other celebrate the beginning of a new millennium (see Table 1-1).

THE INFO-FOG

This evolution from people-powered information to instantaneous electronic coverage took less than 200 years. It took 5,000 years, from 3000 BC to 1965, for the amount of information to double, and it doubled again by 1995.[10] In fact, futurist Richard Saul Wurman was reported to have claimed that a weekday edition of *The New York Times* contains more information than an average person would be exposed to in a 17th century English lifetime.[11] Depending whose prediction you believe, the amount of information available to us now doubles every seven years,[12] or five,[13] or three.[14] One prediction even claimed that information will soon double every 20 months![15]

The ready availability of information offers great benefits:

▶ Research projects that at one time required long hours of library work can now be done from the comfort of the kitchen table, as is the case with what I am writing now.

▶ Instantaneous e-mail has made it possible to keep in contact with people quickly, conveniently, and inexpensively.

1983	1984	1985	1987	1988	1991	1992	1993	1994	1995	1996	1997	1998	1999	2000	2001
Cell phones, Hi-fi VCRs, camcorders	TV broadcast in stereo, CD-ROMs	LCD portable TV	MP3 format	Recordable CDs	Multimedia PCs	The World Wide Web	Personal digital assistants	18-inch satellite receivers	Digital camcorders	CDs surpass audiotapes	DVD players	HDTV television, Recordable CDs	Napster, MP3players	Recordable DVDs	Satellite radio

► It is easy to find out what is happening in the world anywhere, at any time.

► Perhaps the greatest benefit is that it has become more difficult for crooked politicians and shady business operators to fool large numbers of people. They still somehow manage, but the glare of the spotlight is a powerful force for truth.

Unfortunately, these advances have a downside. Although this abundance of information moved in slowly, it has, like a fog, now engulfed us and is difficult to escape. The info-fog is also difficult to see through. Information, often rumors of information, or the same information repackaged, or someone's comments on that information confront us at every turn. For example, the fog that surrounded us during the mid-1990s had a name: O.J.

Former football great O.J. Simpson had been accused of murdering his ex-wife, and the entire world knew it. It was impossible not to know. The story was everywhere. For instance, approximately 95 million viewers got to watch Simpson's white Bronco as he attempted to evade police.[16] All of this occurred *before* the "trial of the century" even started. Much more was to come, ad nauseam, for another year.

We survived O.J.'s trial, and so did the info-fog. In fact, it has grown. Faith Popcorn, in *The Popcorn Report*, described it in this way: "It's as if time itself has become *faster* than it used to be. Immediate is really immediate—there isn't a chance to stop and take a breath. The speed of technology brings us the facts of life faster than we can assimilate them."[17] It has so engulfed us that separating frivolous from critical information is often impossible.

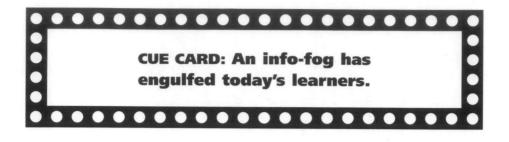

CUE CARD: An info-fog has engulfed today's learners.

Not content with the amount of information that engulfs us, we all compound the problem by strapping external sources of information to our bodies. Communications, once dictated by the speed at which people could travel, now dictates its timing to us, regardless of how quickly we move. The former carrier has become the servant. As Faith Popcorn explained: "Information technology not only makes information accessible to us at all times—it also makes us accessible to the information. We are, quite often, literally, 'on the line' much of the time. Nowhere to run to, nowhere to hide. There's just no excuse not to be reached. "18

As recently as 10 years ago, attending training would have meant being out of touch with the office for the whole day. If someone wanted to contact a learner, a note would be taken, and the learner would receive the message during a break. If the message required a response, the learner would go to the nearest pay phone, stand in line, and wait while other learners returned their messages.

As you intuitively know, none of this is true today. The office can reach us anytime and anywhere. Beepers and cell phones are unwelcome but frequent companions in the classroom. They somehow manage to interrupt loudly, with perfect timing, at the worst possible moment. It is a common sight to see learners dialing their cell phones as the instructor begins announcing a break. Some never quite make it to break. They sit in their seats, talking on a phone, only to head to the bathroom once the instructor begins again.

But beyond messaging systems, the newer communication devices provide real time news, video, and shopping capabilities during learning sessions. I have personally witnessed a hint of this new world. A group of learners with whom I was sitting decided, almost in unison, that the instructor was not worthy of their attention. They all pulled

Cell Phone Break   By Millbower and Yager

Let's Break. After that, we'll . . .

out communication devices and began writing furiously. To the instructor it looked like her words of wisdom were being recorded. In reality, the entire table was playing a round-robin card game. As our technology improves, these kinds of classroom intrusions will become more frequent, not less so. Even more technology is in the works. Bill Gates, the founder of Microsoft, claims that "the revolution in communications is just beginning."[19]

Shouting to Be Heard

> "Many a small thing has been made large by the right kind of advertising."[20]

Advertising has complicated the info-fog problem. With so much information competing for our attention, advertisers have found it increasingly difficult to be heard. As a result, advertisers have become more aggressive, and added to the info-fog (Table 1-2).

Advertising started simply enough, with two seminal events in October, 1945. The first event was the lifting of a World War II U.S. government ban on the construction of TV stations and sets, and on the licensing of new broadcast stations.

THE GROWTH OF TV ADVERTISING

1945	Television advertising begins
1947	Kraft Television Theatre begins
1948	Advertising increases 515%
1950	Sponsors switch from radio to TV
1951	The Hallmark Hall of Fame begins
1952	$288 million spent on ads
1953	FCC approves RCA color system
1954	TV becomes the leading ad medium
1955	NBC charges $4,000 a minute
1958	$2 billion spent on ads
1960	Station breaks expand from 30 to 40 seconds
1963	TV news surpasses newspapers
1964	The infomercial debuts
1977	$7.5 billion spent on ads
1983	M*A*S*H finale ads cost $450,000
1984	$900,000 Apple ad introduces Mac

TABLE 1-2

The second event was a public demonstration of commercial television (TV) at Gimbel's Department Store in Philadelphia. In a three-week time period, more than 25,000 people stopped what they were doing to watch a mix of NBC and local station content. Anything that attracts the attention of 25,000 people will draw the interest of advertisers. Television quickly became an advertiser's medium.[21]

At first, television was an addictive novelty, which actor–director Orson Welles described as follows: "I hate television. I hate it as much as peanuts. But I can't stop eating peanuts."[22] People would watch anything, including commercials. Advertisers responded by sponsoring TV shows that aggressively mixed entertainment with commercial messages.

After a while, people began to object to the intrusions that commercials represented. In 1967, 63% of those polled in a National Association of Broadcasters survey stated their dissatisfaction with commercials and said they would choose commercial-free TV. By 1973 however, the public mood had changed. *Variety* reported, by a margin of 5–1, that people regarded commercials as a fair price to pay for watching TV shows. We have somehow adjusted to the intrusion of commercials. They are now part of the info-fog. Advertisers, because the info-fog tends to block their message, have upped the amount of advertisements they broadcast:

- A typical hour of network television now features nine minutes of commercials, up from six 10 years ago.

- Americans are subjected to 254 different television commercials a day, up from seven in 1957,[23] and up 25 percent since the mid-1970s.[24]

- With all other forms of advertising included, that number rises to 3000-plus messages a day.[25]

If advertisers would limit their activities to TV, commercial relief might be possible. But unfortunately, commercials are everywhere. There are billboards on the highways, product placements in movies, ads on top of taxis, and advertisements slipped in with bills. Ads have even begun appearing on ATM deposit receipts. It's quite a racket. They take your money and you get a commercial in exchange.

The ads I find particularly irritating are the ones people experience when they call to activate a new credit card. One bank in particular makes people hold while they "activate" their cards. Of course, the length of time the "activation" takes is just long enough for the bank to pitch their other products and services. These types of actions are indicative of the continued attempts to expand the presence of ads. Be it a supermarket checkout lane, a gas pump, or a doctor's waiting room, every location in daily life is under ad assault.

To be fair, advertisers don't set out to annoy us. An ad that alienates us backfires. It's just that with so much information out there, advertisers must work harder than ever to attract attention. Otherwise, their product gets lost in the wealth of choice.

The Wealth of Choice

Perhaps the biggest driver of this info-fog is the overabundance of choice. In the early 1900s, Henry Ford revolutionized the world with the assembly line. His assembly line made one car, the model T, in one color, black. Ford used to brag that you could choose any color car you wanted, as long as that color was black. How times have changed.

▶ Deciding on a brand and make of car is a maze of confusion. At last check, more than 30 different brands of car were available in the United States, including Acura, Audi, Daewoo, Honda, Hyundai, Isuzu, Mitsubishi, Nissan, Subaru, Suzuki, Toyota, and Volvo. In addition, the flood of product choices extends beyond cars.

▶ Have you had to choose your telephone carrier lately? Several companies, whose names keep changing, advertise nightly on television.

▶ Computers are another crowded field, with a wide range of operating systems, hardware, software, and peripherals.

▶ A recent check of a medium-sized supermarket revealed the availability of 21 brands of toothpaste, 27 kinds of potato chips, and 45 different cereals. Price-Pritchett even reported that 1,000 new products are introduced to America's supermarkets every month.[26]

The multitude of options benefits consumers, but choice requires diligence, and diligence requires time. Most people are just too busy to wade through the fog of options. As a result, businesses try to educate us about their products and services, and add even more advertising.

When World War II ended, there were fewer than 7,000 working TV sets in the United States. It's probably a good thing that the viewing market was so small. There were only nine broadcasting stations: three in New York, two in Chicago, two in Los Angeles, One in Philadelphia, and another in Schenectady (Table 1-3).

The number of stations increased greatly, but the choices they presented did not. As late as the 1960s, there were only three nation-wide networks—ABC, CBS, and NBC. In most cities, reception of these stations was poor. Often, only one network would be received clearly enough to watch. Outside the major cities, reception was even less dependable.

News sources were also limited. Most Americans received their news and information from a daily newspaper, or through the nightly newscasts of the three nationally syndicated networks.

In addition to the three networks, each town had several AM radio stations, an alternative FM station or two, and, if it was a big town, a few movie theaters, each with one screen. In many locations, a cinema experience consisted of one theater, with one screen, and one choice of film during any given week.

This kind of world now seems archaic. Today, a vast sea of TV viewing choices face us, with more than 150 channels to choose from. For example, the Discovery Channel is offered in eight, and perhaps more, versions, including the Discovery Channel, the Discovery Civilization Channel, the Discovery Español Channel, the Discovery Health Channel, the Discovery Home & Leisure Channel, the Discover Kids Channel, the Discovery Science Channel, and the Discovery Wings Channel!

It is now possible to learn about everything from golf, to home improvement, to foreign language skills, to shopping, to travel, all from the comfort of your own living room. It is also possible, owing to the expansion of movie channels and pay-for-view movies, to view your choice of 30 or more movies at one of several different times.

Radio has also expanded. The narrow band of frequencies available in a simpler time has grown to include mainstream FM stations and expanded AM frequencies. Currently,

THE GROWTH OF TELEVISION

1945	1946	1947	1948	1949	1953	1954	1956	1960	1963	1965
FCC allows expansion	150,000 watch Louis-Conn fight	Meet the Press" debuts	108 stations licensed	East and Midwest linked	RCA color system approved	"The Tonight Show" debuts	Videotape introduced	Nixon-Kennedy debate broadcast	Kennedy assassination covered	NBC broadcasts in color

TABLE 1-3

we are in a transition from a world where radio transmissions fade away as we drive to global positioning satellite-based radio services that broadcast signals across the entire country.

Movie theaters have become megacomplexes, with as many as 25 screens. Some of the individual screens are so far away from the concession stand that you can devour your popcorn before you reach your seat. You can choose from a wide variety of movies, with 20 different movies playing at any given time, or the same movie playing 20 different times a day.

If all those entertainment options aren't enough, you can click onto the World Wide Web and access any of the millions of Web sites available on the Internet, on any subject you choose.

Our news sources have likewise expanded. From the original Associated Press, a wide variety of news options have opened up. In addition to nightly news broadcasts presented by the three major networks (ABC, CBS, and NBC), the Cable News Network, the Fox News Channel, MSNBC, C-Span, CNBC, radio talk shows, news flashes via beeper and phone, Internet news services and search engines, and other outlets provide news and information beyond the wildest imaginings of earlier generations.

THE DISTRACTED LEARNER

Yet with all these choices, we are still bored. It turned out that the multitude of channels merely trained us to see what else is on. With the invention of the remote control, we don't

1968	1969	1975	1977	1978	1980	1982	1987	1988	1989	1993
World watches Armstrong on moon	Sesame Street launched	Home Box Office launched	WTBS becomes cable Superstation	Showtime launched	CNN and MTV launched	Home Shopping Network launched	Fox Broadcasting Company launched	Majority of households chose cable	Pay-per-view launched	98% of U.S. households own a TV

even have to leave our chairs! So, we sit in comfort and channel surf. As a result, we often don't watch a program to its completion.

We have become so good at channel surfing that our attention span has dropped. A split focus is the norm today. We watch TV while we eat dinner, while we read work-related material, while we prepare the children for bed. The speed at which we shift our attention is visible on any music video. The average video image changes approximately every second. We've adapted to the pace; as society has sped up, so have we.

This phenomenon is especially prevalent among individuals born after 1977, the so-called Generation X and Generation Y. With 57 million of them currently in the work force, these individuals make up an ever-increasing sector of the U.S. population. And, their presence in the workplace grows every day.[27] Thanks to their away-from-home parents, they have grown up independent, self-assured, and curious about new things. Technology doesn't scare them. In fact, computers are an integral part of their lives. They have learned from computers that speed matters, and will quickly "channel-surf" people or items that don't interest them. They will try one thing, add another when the first bores them, and begin yet a third as it draws their attention.

When you combine the info-fog with the overabundance of choice, and add quick-paced, technology savvy individuals, the result is a population moving at a high rate of speed, and unable to devote single-minded attention to any one thing. There's just too much to absorb, and we don't want to miss anything. We focus less and less, as we try to do more and more. It's as if we have a collective societal attention deficit disorder. Malcolm Gladwell, in *The Tipping Point,* offers a similar point from an advertising perspective: "In the advertising business, the surfeit of information is called the 'clutter' problem, and clutter has made it harder and harder to get any one message to stick."[28] Simply put, the clutter of everyday life clogs up our human hard drive. Our brain can't compute because our memory circuits are overloaded.

Assembly Line Learning

Unfortunately, traditional classroom methods are ill equipped to navigate the info-fog. Today's classroom is a result of a long-term evolution that began with the factory system popularized in the late 1800s.

At the dawn of humanity, learning was focused on survival. People gathered food and hunted to survive. The skills considered most critical were those required to pick the fruit, capture the next meal, find water, and maintain the fire.

Humans eventually progressed to a point at which they planted, rather than gathered. Children learned how to read the weather, when and where to plant, how to care for the crops, and how to care for each other. "Book learning" was not critical to such a society.

As humans achieved success on the farms, the desire for crafted goods emerged, and those members of the community who demonstrated skills at making furniture, weapons, and other necessities of life began creating these items under barter arrangements with local farmers. This basic arrangement, or *Trades* model, was the standard for centuries.

To increase production, these craftsmen took in apprentices who, over a period of years, learned the craft. In this way, learning became a focused, local affair between a mentor and a pupil. This system began to give way in the 1780s with the advent of the Industrial Revolution. As machinery was invented, and the concept of standardized parts took hold, the trades gave way to factory-based labor. In roughly a 100-year period, 1780 to 1880, factories replaced the trades.

The factory model suggested that you could, if you distilled all the tasks required to make a product down to their simplest elements, mass-produce an item with minimally skilled workers. Henry Ford applied these techniques to the production of an automobile, the model T, and revolutionized the world.

In this new world, finely honed skills were no longer critical. The job requirement shifted to the ability to repeat a task constantly, without variation. Thought wasn't critical, repetition was. The schools of that era focused on producing factory workers capable of rote repetition. In a rote-based classroom, order and control were expected. Creativity was not. People learned their facts and figures. A focus on the meaning behind the facts was lost. Over time, successive generations were taught not to imagine, but to be quiet, not to make waves, but to do what is expected, to "be an adult."

In fairness, assembly-line learning worked. The factories gained workers, and the workers gained a steady living. Perhaps the best proof of the factory model's success is the use of this model by the U.S. military to win World War II. "Yes sir!" became both a ready reply and a call to organized, dictated action. What it was not, however, was a call to play, to wonder, to imagine.

Remnants of the assembly-line still haunt learning. Tests often focus on memorization, not comprehension. Subjects are still taught in hour-long blocks, as if reading somehow could be separated from history, and history from science. Learning has become serious business. Eventually, children learn the lessons they are taught, and grow up forgetting how to play. In speaking of the results of such a school system, Walt Disney said: "Every child is born blessed with a vivid imagination. But just as a muscle grows flabby with disuse so the bright imagination of a child pales in later years if he ceases to exercise it."[29] Michael Michalko, in *Cracking Creativity*, added:

> **"We were born as spontaneous, creative thinkers. Yet a great deal of our education may be regarded as the inculcation of mind-sets. We were taught how to handle problems and new phenomena with fixed mental**

attitudes (based on what past thinkers' thought) that predetermine our response to problems or situations. in short, we were taught 'what' to think instead of 'how' to think. We entered school as a question mark and graduated as a period."[30]

Added to that is the fear that such regimented thinking becomes ingrained in people. In their book, *The Creative Trainer,* Lawlor and Handley commented: "Most people have been conditioned by their home or school environment to believe that their memory, their creativity, and their overall ability are limited."[31]

Unfortunately, the classroom reminds many learners of boring classes, pompous teachers, punishment and embarrassment, mindless facts, and a loss of personal control. These adults are convinced they cannot learn. This lack of confidence is so ingrained that it prevents knowledgeable adults—people who have raised families, bought houses, and navigated the career world—from becoming fully engaged in the adult learning experience.

As long as the world existed within the industrial model, assembly-line learning worked. People sat down, didn't speak up, listened to the instructor, and did as they were told. Information was manageable, and the world simple.

Today, that simplicity no longer exists. As we have discovered, learners are distracted at every turn. When learners' attention is diffused, and other, more enticing possibilities command attention, rote methods feel like drudgery, and most often fail. With the amount of information available greater than the time allocated for instructors to talk, and with learners having other, more engaging, stimuli to absorb, instruction breaks down. Trying to communicate to today's distracted learners with lecture-based learning methods is like trying to be heard by an entire football stadium with a megaphone.

School Daze   **By Millbower and Yager**

Blah, blah, blah, blah, blah, . . .

In *The Entertainment Economy,* Michael Wolf explained it this way: "Merely delivering a message is no longer sufficient. *Everyone* has a message. So while the quantity of impressions remains important, the quality of those impressions is more important than ever."[32] In *Learning in Adulthood,* adult learning experts Sharan Merriam and Rosemary Caffarella, applied a learning perspective: "What is needed to overcome information overload, is to consider interaction between the quantity and quality of knowledge."[33]

It is my belief that enjoyment adds quality to the knowledge being presented, and in the process cuts through the info-fog.

In the next chapter, we examine the historical role stories have played in communicating information, as we determine how best to put fun back into the classroom. When we consider that the average person spends about 18,200 hours of his or her life in a classroom, wouldn't it be nice to focus some of that time on enjoying life?

---

[1] *Webster's Dictionary of Quotations.* (1992). New York: Smithmark.

[2] Johnson, Paul (1997). *A History of the American People.* New York: HarperCollins.

[3] Wallbank, Walter T., et al. (1970). *Civilization Past & Present: Book Three—1815 to the Present, 6th edit.* Glenview, IL: Scott, Foresman and Company.

[4] Wallbank, Walter T., et al. (1970).

[5] Johnson, Paul (1997).

[6] Ibid.

[7] Wallbank, Walter T., et al. (1970).

[8] Ibid.

[9] Johnson, Paul (1997).

[10] Pritchett, Price, and Pound, Ron (1995). *A Survival Guide to the Stress of Organizational Change.* Dallas, TX: Pritchett & Associates, Inc.

[11] Pritchett, Price, and Pound, Ron (1995).

[12] Apps, Jerold W. (1988). *Higher Education in a Learning Society.* San Francisco: Jossey-Bass.

[13] Pritchett, Price, and Pound, Ron (1995).

[14] Rose, Colin, and Nicholl, Michael L. (1997). *Accelerated Learning for the 21st Century.* New York: Delacorte Press.

[15] Whitson, Donna L., and Mstutz, Donna D. (1997). *Accessing Information in a Technological Age.* Malabar, FL: Krieger.

[16] Advertising Age's History of TV Advertising. <www.adage.com>.

[17] Popcorn, Faith (1992). *The Popcorn Report: Faith Popcorn on the Future of Your Company, Your World, Your Life.* New York: HarperBusiness.

[18] Ibid.

[19] Bill Gates in *The Road Ahead.* Quoted by Rose, Colin, and Nicholl, Michael L. (1997). *Accelerated Learning for the 21st Century.* New York: Delacorte Press.

[20] Twain, Mark (0000). *A Connecticut Yankee in King Arthur's Court.* Bantam Classic and Loveswept

[21] Advertising Age's History of TV Advertising.

[22] *Webster's Dictionary of Quotations* (1992).

[23] Advertising Age's History of TV Advertising.

[24] Media Dynamics research as reported in Gladwell, Malcolm (2000). *The Tipping Point: How Little Things Can Make a Big Difference.* Boston: Little, Brown and Company.

[25] Media Dynamics as reported in Gladwell, Malcolm (2000).

[26] Pritchett, Price, and Pound, Ron (1995).

[27] US Department of Labor Statistics data.

[28] Gladwell, Malcolm (2000).

[29] Smith, Dave (2001). *The Quotable Walt Disney: It Was All Started by a Mouse.* New York: Hyperion.

[30] Michalko, Michael (1998). *Cracking Creativity: The Secrets of Creative Genius.* Berkeley, CA: Ten Speed Press.

[31] Lawlor, Michael, and Handley, Peter (1996). *The Creative Trainer: Holistic Facilitation Skills for Accelerated Learning.* London: McGraw-Hill.

[32] Wolf, Michael J. (1999). *The Entertainment Economy: How Mega-Media Forces Are Transforming Our Lives.* New York: Random House.

[33] Merriam, Sharan B., and Caffarella, Rosemary S. (1999). *Learning in Adulthood: A Comprehensive Guide.* San Francisco: Jossey-Bass.

CHAPTER TWO

THE FIVE-FOOT BOILER

It was December 1852, and John Hay had just begun his practice of law. Cases were slow in coming, so when an older, more experienced lawyer became sick and asked for help, he gladly accepted. His task was to represent a client in Judge Davis' Chicago courtroom, some 10 miles away. The older lawyer gave Hay an overview of the case, and notes that provided the additional information necessary to win the case.

Court was to begin at 10:30 AM the next day, so Hay left very early that morning. No sooner had he begun his journey, than a snowstorm blew across the Illinois landscape. The snow, wet and icy, came down hard all through the ride. His clothes were covered with snow and his face was caked with ice. Both he and his horse were cold and miserable.

By the time they finally reached the courthouse, it was 9:30. He had made it with an hour to spare. Across the street from the courthouse, there was an inn where all the lawyers gathered. He went to the inn to dry off, and make himself presentable for the trial.

As he entered the lobby, he saw the lawyers gathered around a potbellied stove for warmth. He must look like a frozen snowman, he thought. A fellow lawyer, tall and lanky, gave him one look and asked, "Well neighbor, I thought my room was cold, but I can see I was mistaken. What room did you have?" Both men laughed as the young lawyer dried himself off.

Forty-five minutes later, a court messenger announced that court would begin shortly. That was when he first noticed the problem. Snow must have blown into his pouch. All the trial papers were ruined. He began to panic. With no supporting data, he would have a difficult time winning his case. He would be forced to try this case completely from memory.

But then he calmed down. He realized that he knew the general thrust of the legal argument. He also knew that his oration skills were excellent. He had also promised to defend the case. He decided that he would not break that promise. Determined now, he entered the courtroom and joined in the case.

When Hay's turn to speak came, he did his best. What he lacked in detail he provided in flash. His oratory soared across the room. His gestures, his vocal tone, and his posture were impressive. When he finished, the jury was in tears. He sat down pleased, and hoping that the opposing counsel would not see the hollowness of his argument.

The opposing counsel, the lawyer from the inn, stood up and began to speak. Hay was heartened by what he heard. The older lawyer's speech was high pitched, almost annoying. His accent sounded Kentucky born. His clothes fit poorly. The young lawyer thought he had little to fear.

"My friend on the other side," the tall attorney began, "is all right, or would be if not for a peculiarity which I am about to explain.

"His habit—of which you witnessed a very painful specimen, is in arguing a case of bombast without facts. But, it is not a moral fault or blemish. He can't help it. His oratory completely suspends all action of his mind.

I never knew of but one thing that I could compare to my friend. That was a steamboat. Back in the days when I was a keel boatman, a little steamboat used to bustle and puff and wheeze about in the Sangamon River. It had a five-foot boiler and a seven-foot whistle. Every time it whistled the boat stopped!"

The laughter was loud and long, and the case was lost. But in the process, a lasting friendship was born. For the tall lawyer took a liking to John Hay, and years later, would hire him to work as his secretary when the man, Abraham Lincoln, became America's sixteenth President.[1]

"Stories have always been used as a powerful tool for communicating vital information from one generation to another; they have always been used as a vehicle for the wise to educate the young. And we know that they are highly successful. If not, they would not have survived."—MARGARET PARKIN[2]

ONCE UPON A TIME

As we discovered in Chapter 1, getting any message through the info-fog is a daunting task. Even if a message is of critical importance, unfocused listeners can't absorb it. As Michael J. Wolf explained in his book, *The Entertainment Economy,* "Merely delivering a message is no longer sufficient. Everyone has a message."[3] The challenge is not in having a message. The challenge is in getting someone to listen.

There are two overriding reasons people will listen to a message: survival and pleasure.

Sometimes, a listener perceives the message being conveyed is critical to survival. This is perhaps the most powerful attention focuser known to humans. It also has limited usefulness. People can and will stay focused on critical situations, but the extraordinary level of focus required during a crisis is draining, and will dissipate at the first available opportunity.

Other times, the listener perceives that the message being conveyed will be pleasurable. When no immediate crisis is present, people invariably turn their attention toward things that give them pleasure. It's no accident that many factors critical to survival, such as food, sex, and sleep, are also pleasurable. The enjoyment they produce assures our survival. Accordingly, people choose to absorb or ignore messages based on their perception of the pleasure to be gained from the message. In other words, people self-select enjoyment whenever possible.

CUE CARD: People self-select enjoyment whenever possible.

The Storytellers   By Millbower and Yager

And they lived happily ever after.

Psychologist Abraham Maslow proposed that people have two different sets of needs, deficiency and growth needs, and that deficiency needs must be satisfied before a person can focus on growth needs.[4] In early history, survival required a constant focus on deficiency needs. Accordingly, messages not related to survival had to be pleasurable to capture attention. Most often, this meant entertaining the listeners. In an era before entertainment went big time, before Broadway, movies, television, or even books, information was made pleasurable through stories.

STORYTELLERS

No one knows when storytelling began. Although the earliest recorded example is the Sumerian epic, Gilgamesh, dating from 2700 BC, it is reasonable to assume that stories have always been with us.[5] From the beginning of humanity, stories must have entertained people while communicating critical information. Although we don't know an exact starting date, we do know that stories have helped people:

- ▶ Make sense of their world.

- ▶ Communicate with their deities.

- ▶ Join together.

- ▶ Record cultural history and norms.

- ▶ Share news.

- ▶ Comprehend difficult subjects.

Using Stories to Make Sense of the World

For our earliest ancestors, the world must have been a very strange place. Today, we have scientific explanations for most of the phenomena we experience. We even think we've figured out how the world itself was created. In contrast, our early ancestors had no knowledge of what the sun and moon were, and why they moved through the sky, disappearing only to reappear again. They would have found the weather especially perplexing. They would have wondered if their actions caused the rain to come, or the snows to fall. It is reasonable to assume that stories helped early humans make sense of the world that surrounded them.

As Walt Disney explained: "Since the beginning of mankind, the fable-tellers have not only given us entertainment but a kind of wisdom, humor, and understanding that, like all true art, remains imperishable through the ages."[6]

Communicating with God through Stories

Stories have helped people communicate with their deities. Every major religion has a storytelling tradition:

▶ Buddhism—Siddhartha Gautama, the founder of Buddhism, incorporated the Jataka or birth tales, stories of previous incarnations of the Buddha, into his teachings.

▶ Christianity—In the New Testament Jesus Christ used the parable form in his teachings, telling tales such as the Prodigal Son.

▶ Hinduism—The Ramayana, the great epic tale of India, part of the Hindu scriptures for Rama, is believed to be an incarnation of the god Vishnu.

▶ Islam—The Koran contains many stories including the creation of the world, the stories of Adam and Moses, and the explanation of the very nature of the recitations that Muslims believe God taught Mohammed.

▶ Judaism—Hasidic Jews used storytelling to introduce their rituals and beliefs to young children. Isaac Bashevis Singer is well known for his folk tales from the Yiddish tradition. One such example is the story of Zlateh, the Goat.[7]

These traditions probably began the moment that the storytellers realized that their "connection" to the community's god got them noticed, and that power and wealth followed. Soon enough, stories evolved around particular gods that explained the weather, the growth of crops, the hunt, good and bad health, and perhaps more importantly, morality as the community saw it. These stories became the legacy of each community, passed on verbally from generation to generation, until they became the myths and legends of the group.[8]

Joining People Together with Stories

The survival of early humans would have required teamwork, and teamwork required bonding. Stories provided a way to share information in a pleasurable manner. Many of us have experienced the joy of hearing a good story around the campfire. At the dawn of humanity, such experiences were the norm. Storytelling would have been the nightly entertainment.

Recording Cultural History and Norms with Stories

Early life was difficult, and death came at what would now be considered middle age. In an era of short life spans, and before the advent of writing utensils, humans were faced with a problem: how to remember the past. Memories had to be strong to ensure that basic ancestral information would pass unabridged from generation to generation. Stories filled that need. In *A Celebration of Neurons,* brain researcher Robert Sylwester explained why: "It's much easier to use a narrative format to remember several events that occurred during an experience than to try to remember the events in isolation form each other."[9]

Communities would recite their history in story form, and thus remember it exactly. Many of what we know as poems, folk tales, myths, legends, and nursery rhymes come from that oral tradition.

Tales for Training author Margaret Parkin explained: "What all these tales had in common was that they captured the imagination of their audiences in such a way that they were committed to memory; they were handed down from generation to generation and became part of that nation's culture. In many case these stories still survive today."[10] In talking about his own entertainment empire, Walt Disney added: "And out of our years of experimenting and experience we learned one basic thing about bringing pleasure and knowledge to people of all ages and conditions which goes to the very roots of public communication. That is this—the power of relating facts, as well as fables, in story form."[11]

The Shakespeare play *Hamlet, Prince of Denmark* is one example of a story's staying power. This particular story had so much relevance for people at a basic level of understanding that many of the lines remain in our language today, for example:

- ▶ "Leave her to heaven."

- ▶ "Neither a borrower nor a lender be."

- ▶ "Sweets to the sweet."

- ▶ "Something is rotten in the state of Denmark."

> ▶ "The lady doth protest too much, methinks."

> ▶ "The play's the thing."

> ▶ "To be, or not to be: that is the question."

> ▶ "To thine own self be true."

> ▶ "Though this be madness, yet there is method in 't."

> ▶ "Thus conscience does make cowards of us all."

The writing is superb, and the words speak universal truths in story form. As a result, the words have stayed with us, to the extent that even people who have never seen the play understand the everyday context of the phrases. In fact, the story keeps recurring. Sometimes it's in the usual guise of *Hamlet,* as in Lawrence Oliver's 1948 and Mel Gibson's 1990 versions. Other times, its presence is a little more obscure, as in the Walt Disney Studio's animated hit, and later Broadway stage show, *The Lion King.* As Walt Disney himself once explained: "Through historical time all the races have been dramatizing these eternal quests and conquests of mind and heart; in arenas, around tribal fires, in temples and theaters. The modes of entertainment have changed through the centuries; the content of public shows, very little."[12]

Regardless of location, every culture had its own storytellers.

> ▶ African storytellers related the tale of how Sundiata became the King of Mali.

> ▶ Tanzanians shared wisdom through the adventures of Anansi the spider.

> ▶ West African griots told the stories of their village.

> ▶ One Sumerian epic, Gilgamesh, dating from 2700 BC is the oldest recorded story.

> ▶ Persian shamans told the stories that made up the "Hazarafsaneh," which evolved into *A Thousand and One Arabian Nights.*

> ▶ In Mongolia, shamans practiced "medicine" as they told stories.

> ▶ The Scandinavian Norsemen shared sagas of their adventures.

> ▶ In the Celtic tradition, a "*bard*" would ". . . create and/or perform poetic oral narrations that chronicle events or praise the illustrious forebears and present leaders of a tribal, cultural, or national group.[13]

> ▶ In Greece, epic tales of ancient wars were told in *The Iliad* and *The Odyssey.*[14] These stories provide an excellent example of the power of storytelling. Homer

wrote them around 1200 BC. The stories where then passed largely unaltered, generation to generation, for four or five hundred years, until 700 BC when an effective writing system was created.[15]

Fidelity to the story was possible because of the importance people placed on faithful recitation of their history. Margaret Parkin explained: "Because of their importance in the community, storytellers in some cultures were actually required to take a solemn vow in which, among other things, they promised to repeat their stories faithfully and accurately, and also to show respect for their audiences and their interest and enjoyment."[16]

Sharing News Using Stories

During the Middle Ages, there was no national news service, and no way for news to travel without the physical movement of people. Storytellers served as roving reporters, sharing information, gossip, and opinions, all packaged with music, magic, and comedy into pleasurable, entertaining vignettes. For example, African shamans used magic to imply a connection with the Gods, European troubadours used music to carry their messages, and court jesters used comedy to comment on current events.

Comprehending Difficult Subjects Using Stories

Margaret Parkin, in *Tales for Trainers* (1998), explained: "It was also the traditional role of the storyteller to deal with what might be regarded as difficult truths, uncomfortable issues and complex concepts that were hard for the majority to grasp. They did this by simplifying the topics and finding ways of making them more accessible and palatable to the general public."[17]

The Jester Report   **By Millbower and Yager**

Breaking news - Taxes are up! The Queen needs shoe money!!

Jesters, because of their storytelling abilities, were welcomed at the courts of Kings. They were also the only members of the court who could criticize the Royals and escape with their lives intact. Consequently, they became adept at political humor. They would offer political criticisms in once-upon-a-time settings that made their criticisms seem benign. There would be nothing tangible for the royals to object to. In this way, entertainment became a vehicle for presenting a point of view.[18]

Throughout history political leaders have found themselves in a situation in which they were required to communicate difficult truths to their people. Some of the world's most effective political leaders have excelled at comedic storytelling.

Abraham Lincoln, 16th President of the United States, was well known for his story-telling abilities. Lincoln regarded storytelling as an essential component in his ability to communicate with and influence people. He had a huge collection of stories, and the ability to produce just the right story at the right moment to make his case. He once commented as follows: "They say I tell a great many stories. I reckon I do; but I have learned from long experience that *plain* people, take them as they run, are more easily *influenced* through the medium of a *broad* and humorous illustration than in any other way; and what the hypercritical *Few* (original capitalization and emphasis) may think, I don't care."[19]

On another occasion, Lincoln said:

> **"I believe I have the popular reputation of being a story-teller, but I do not deserve the name in its general sense, for it is not the story itself, but its purpose, or effect, that interests me. I often avoid a long and useless discussion by others or a laborious explanation on my own part by a short story that illustrates my point of view. Also, too, the sharpness of a refusal or the edge of a rebuke may be blunted by an appropriate story, so as to save wounded feeling and yet serve the purpose. No. I am not simply a story-teller, but story-telling as an emollient saves me much friction and distress."[20]**

Two excellent examples of Lincoln stories, and the situations in which he used them, follow. The first was a reply to a Union general who asked Lincoln how he coped with the challenges presented by the Civil War. Lincoln told the story of a farmer who once ploughed a rough patch of land:

> **"It (a large field laden with many tree stumps) was a terrible place to clean up. But after a while he got a few things growing—here and there a patch of corn, a few hills of beans, and so on. One day a stranger stopped to look at his place and wanted to know how he managed to cultivate so rough a spot. 'Well,' was the reply, 'some of it is pretty rough. The smaller stumps I can generally root out or burn out; but now and then there is (a large one) that bothers me, and there is no way but to plough around it.' Now, General, at such a time as this, troublesome cases are constantly coming up, and the only way to get along is to plough around them."[21]**

The second example concerns Lincoln's avoidance of political patronage:

> **"A delegation once called on Lincoln to ask the appointment of a gentlemen as commissioner to the Sandwich Islands. They presented their case**

as earnestly as possible, and, besides his fitness for the place, they urged that he was in bad health and a residence in that balmy climate would be of great benefit to him. The President closed the interview with the good-humored remark: 'Gentlemen, I am sorry to say that there are eight other applicants for that place, and they are all sicker than your man.'"[22]

Another example comes from a later president, Franklin D. Roosevelt (FDR), 31st President of the United States. In December 1940, Roosevelt was faced with a sensitive situation regarding the neutrality of the United States during the early stages of World War II. The English were running low on military supplies, and FDR was determined to aid Churchill by resupplying the British. The difficulty was that much of the U.S. citizenry was vehemently opposed to any involvement in the European hostilities. Furthermore, FDR was running for reelection on the promise of keeping the United States out of European wars. Nevertheless, FDR recognized that without resupply, England might well fall to the Nazis, and the United States would then be pulled into the war in spite of itself.

In light of the circumstances, FDR ordered the resupply. Knowing that the effort would be unpopular, FDR explained it through a simple metaphoric story. "Suppose my neighbor's house catches fire. If he can take my garden hose and connect it up to his hydrant, I may help him put out the fire. Now what do I do? I don't say to him, 'Neighbor, my garden hose cost me fifteen dollars; you have to pay me fifteen dollars for it.' What is the transaction that goes on? I don't want fifteen dollars—I want my garden hose back after the fire is over."

This story did not change the reality that the United States had decided to intervene in one side of the conflict, but the story was so simple, and made so much sense that it was impossible to argue with it. As a result, the British got their supplies and the Americans moved a giant step closer to entering the war.[23]

The 40th American President, Ronald Reagan, had a nickname: the great communicator. Like Lincoln, Reagan was adept at telling a story to diffuse conflict. For instance, at 71 years of age, Reagan was America's oldest president. His age could have been a cause for concern, but he diffused the issue through stories.

During his first state of the union speech, Reagan referred to George Washington's belief that all presidents should report directly to the American people. It was a perfectly appropriate comment and would have stood by itself. But Reagan didn't stop there. He then went on to poke fun at his own age by adding that he had personally heard Washington say those words.[24]

On another occasion, he said, "I can still remember my first Republican convention . . . Abraham Lincoln giving a speech that sent shivers down my spine . . ." He then retracted it, saying it wasn't true, that he (Reagan) had been a Democrat back then.[25]

STORYTELLING TODAY

Storytelling is alive and well today. Like all other facets of society, it has gone high tech, but, whether in the guise of TV shows, movies, books, news reports, or political speeches, the underlying storytelling form still exists. Robert Sylwester, in *A Celebration of Neurons,* addressed this subject:

> "Metaphoric forms of mass media provide us with many narrative opportunities to consciously stimulate the memories we want to maintain. So it is with novels, TV programs, songs, games, and pageants. We consciously seek out those that we hope will stimulate our memories of broad cultural issues that we consider important. It's like we're seeking out dream possibilities while we're awake. The most powerful metaphoric experiences are those that focus on important cultural needs, but define the story's characters and locations somewhat loosely, so many people can easily identify with the issues the story explores."[26]

Donald Hamilton, in *The Mind of Mankind,* added:

> "Storytelling has grown immensely in its scope and power from its simple beginning of telling stories over the camp fire. It now encompasses every facet of human endeavor. Nearly everyone has a story to tell. We are constantly being bombarded by stories both good and bad, by our family, friends and the media. Companies spend billions of dollars every year on advertising, trying to get their stories across to us, trying to influence us to purchase their products."[27]

We discuss advertising messages at great length in the next chapter, but a few quick examples can demonstrate how alive storytelling techniques are:

▶ To introduce Apple's Macintosh computer, advertising firm Chiat/Day hired film director Ridley Scott. Scott directed a storyline reminiscent of George Orwell's *1984,* in which the future was portrayed as a world of drab sameness and big brother tyranny. The commercial, much like the court jesters of old, had a target—In this instance the gray sameness and uniformity of the then dominant computer maker, IBM. The commercial ran once, during the January 1984 Super Bowl, and the Mac was born. The story was so powerful that, to this day, Mac users regard themselves as rebels against sameness, and view the worldwide predominance of Microsoft with suspicion, even calling Microsoft the "evil empire."

▶ In one heartfelt commercial, advertiser McCann-Erickson created a 1980s tale featuring a fierce football giant, Pittsburgh Steelers' defender "Mean" Joe Greene, and a little boy. The spot begins with Greene looking his fiercest, and the young boy, wanting to meet his idol, looking quite afraid. Eventually the boy offers Greene a Coca-Cola. As a result, Greene's demeanor warms, and he tosses his football jersey to the boy. The underlying message of "a Coke and a smile" comes through loud and clear.

▶ One political spot, created by Doyle Dane Bernbach for American President Lyndon Johnson's reelection campaign against Republican candidate Barry Goldwater, portrayed a young girl picking petals from a daisy interspersed with a launchpad countdown to a nuclear explosion, was a bomb of its own. It cemented Barry Goldwater's reputation as dangerous, and set off such a firestorm of protest that Johnson had the ad pulled. This ad story, which ran only once, marked the beginning of negative political advertising.

Storytelling has always served a valuable need: to communicate in an enjoyable fashion. From shamans to jesters, to politicians (is there a comparison here?!) stories have aided leading members of the community in the difficult task of getting a message out. Considering the communication difficulties we discussed in Chapter 1, stories may be more important now than at any time in history.

---

[1] Hertz, Emanuel, ed. (1939). *Lincoln Talks: An Oral Biography.* New York: Viking.

[2] Parkin, Margaret (1998). *Tales for Trainers.* London: Kogan Page.

[3] Wolf, Michael J. (1999). *The Entertainment Economy: How Mega-Media Forces Are Transforming Our Lives.* New York: Random House.

[4] Maslow, Abraham H. (1970). *Motivation and Personality,* 2nd edit. New York: Harper & Row.

[5] Wallbank, Walter T., et al. (1970). *Civilization Past & Present: Book One—Prehistory to 1500, 6th edit.* Glenview, IL: Scott, Foresman and Company.

[6] Smith, Dave (2001). *The Quotable Walt Disney: It Was All Started By a Mouse.* New York: Hyperion.

[7] Pellowski, Anne (1977). *The World of Storytelling: A Practical Guide to the Origins, Development, and Applications of Storytelling.* Bronx, NY: H. W. Wilson.

[8] Hamilton, Donald L. (1996). *The Mind of Mankind: Humorous Imagination—The Source of Mandkind's Tremendous Power.* Buffalo, NY: Suna Press.

[9] Sylwester, Robert (1995). *A Celebration of Neurons: An Educator's Guide to the Human Brain.* Alexandria, VA: ASCD.

[10] Parkin, Margaret (1998).

[11] Smith, Dave (2001).

[12] Smith, Dave (2001).

[13] Wallbank, Walter T., et al. (1970); Pellowski, Anne (1977). <www.middleeastuk.com/culture/mosaic/arabian.htm> <www.globalvolunteers.org/1main/tanzania/tanzanialegends.htm>

[14] Wallbank, Walter T., et al. (1970); Pellowski, Anne (1977).

[15] Wallbank, Walter T., et al. (1970); Pellowski, Anne (1977).

[16] Parkin, Margaret (1998).

[17] Parkin, Margaret (1998).

[18] Wallbank, Walter T., et al. (1970); Pellowski, Anne. (1977).

[19] Lincoln, Abraham, and Hertz, Emanuel, ed. (1986). *Lincoln Talks: An Oral Biography.* New York: Bramhall House.

[20] Phillips, Donald T. (1992). *Lincoln on Leadership: Executive Strategies for Tough Times.* New York: Warner Books.

[21] Phillips, Donald T. (1992).

[22] Lincoln, Abraham, and Hertz, Emanuel, ed. (1986).

[23] Davis, Kenneth C. (1990). *Don't Know Much About History: Everything You Need to Know About American History but Never Learned.* New York: Crown.

[24] Noonan, Peggy (2001). *When Character Was King: A Story of Ronald Reagan.* New York: Viking.

[25] Ibid.

[26] Sylwester, Robert (1995).

[27] Hamilton, Donald L. (1996).

LET ME ENTERTAIN YOU

THE DAILY NEWS
The News You Need

Dear Reader Reviews,

I am submitting this reader review because of a wonderful place we recently visited called "Firehouse 25."

Dad always wanted to be a firefighter. His father had been one, and his father's father too. It was sort of a family tradition, and it was his plan until the accident. While playing high school football, another player unintentionally clotheslined him. He went down hard and never stood again. Instead of fighting fires, he ended up fighting criminals from his wheelchair as a forensic pathologist.

For Dad's 65th birthday, my husband and I wanted to do something special. His health seems to have given out, and we wanted him to enjoy what might be his last birthday. We considered all sorts of options, but finally using Dad's old firefighter dream for inspiration, we went to Firehouse 25.

Firehouse 25 is a former firehouse converted into a restaurant. We thought it would appeal to Dad, and boy did it! As we approached the restaurant, Dad caught sight of the building. He started asking about it, but we didn't reply. We drove into the driveway, and a parking attendant in a firefighter's tee shirt, suspenders, and jeans welcomed us. He said, "Welcome recruits. Are you ready to put out your hunger?"

We said that we were and entered the building. A fire bell announced our arrival. On the lower floor, the old fire engine bay served as the lounge area. Dad loved all the firefighting memorabilia on the walls. The radio room had become a small gift shop, selling firefighter themed recipes, calendars, and knick-knacks. (I bought a set of salt and pepper shakers in the shape of firefighters' boots.) The slide poles that firefighters had once used were off limits to us, but we saw some of the staff using them. They sure looked inviting.

Once our table was ready, we were taken to the second floor and escorted to our table. It looked like a kitchen table. We were promptly told we needed to do our "chores," and set the table. Silverware was mismatched, and lying in wait in a plastic container. The glasses and plates were also mismatched, and the salt and pepper shakers were in the shape of Dalmatians.

The waiter (Firefighter Phil) went along with the show. He appointed Dad to be our table's fire chief. He told Dad his job was to keep the troops in line. Of course Dad said he had been doing that his whole life anyway. Phil put a firechief's hat on dad, and gave the rest of us firefighter badges to wear.

Firefighter Phil wouldn't serve our food until we stated that we had made our bunks. He asked the kids if they had washed the soot out of their hair. And one time, when my husband asked him to repeat something he just said, he commented, "You've been standing near that siren, haven't you?" He commented that we should finish our meals. "You never know when that alarm will ring, and if it does ring, it may be hours before you eat again, so eat up."

The food was good and served family style, with oversized portions, as if it was prepared for hungry firefighters. We had Captain's crab legs, Sarge's fried chicken, Stash's baked beans, Stanley's steak, and Hector's five-alarm chili.

At dessert time, all the firefighter staff gathered around Dad and sang "Happy Birthday" as they lit the giant five-alarm candle. They then presented Dad with an honorary firechief's certificate. He was beaming.

The Firehouse 25 turned out to be the right choice. We could have gone anywhere for this celebration, but we chose a location that would mean something to Dad. I highly recommend Firehouse 25. It was more than a restaurant: it was an experience.

"The buyer needs a hundred eyes,
the seller only one." —GEORGE HERBERT[1]

THE ASCENDANCY OF ENTERTAINMENT

In humans, survival and pleasure exist side by side. They are the ying and yang, the left and right, the balancing forces of our existence.

At the dawn of human history, survival was critical. Pleasure, although important, was secondary, but never absent. As noted in Chapter 2, whenever survival needs were met, even momentarily, pleasure took over. Pleasure could take many guises. Food, sex, and sleep were always pleasurable, and, for survival purposes, came first. As time progressed and survival required less attention, people began to seek out other pleasurable experiences. One such early human example would have been the sharing of stories around a nighttime fire. Out of those early stories, a whole new way of giving and receiving pleasure was born, the entertainment arts.

We know that there are scientific reasons for the development of the entertainment arts. Robert Sylwester, in his book *A Celebration of Neurons,* reported the findings as follows: "Our brain has more frontal lobe capacity than we normally need to survive because that critical-thinking and problem-solving mechanisms located there must be sufficient for crisis conditions."[2]

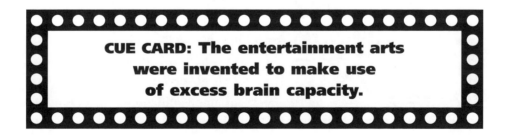

CUE CARD: The entertainment arts
were invented to make use
of excess brain capacity.

He continued by explaining that the entertainment arts were invented to make use of our excess capacity:

> **"Since our survival doesn't require our problem-solving mechanisms to operate at capacity most of the time, we're invented social and cultural problems to keep them continually stimulated and alert. The arts, games, and social organizations provide pleasant metaphoric settings that help to develop and maintain our brain's problem-solving mechanisms."[3]**

As survival became assured, we have increasingly moved toward those things that give us pleasure. Whether the forum was a nighttime cave fire, the Greek coliseum, the Elizabethan stage, the vaudeville palace, Broadway, the movies, television, or most recently, the Internet, a straight line can be traced from the receding of survival needs and the ascension of entertainment.

We have become a society obsessed with entertainment. In the United States, on average, we spend 5.1 percent of our income on entertainment. That's figure is comparable to our spending on health care (5.3 percent), and is more than we spend on clothing (4.7 percent).

What those figures don't represent is the rise in entertainment spending through the years. In 1935–36, we spent just 3.3 percent of our income on entertainment, 4.4 percent on health care, and 10.4 percent on clothing. Even more discouraging, the percentage spent on education, mostly for college and continuing adult education, has remained relatively unchanged through the years, from 1.0 percent in 1935–36 to 1.4 percent in 1999.

Where spending on entertainment is at a high, the rate of personal savings is at a low, under 3 percent.[4] After housing (32.6 percent), transportation (19.0 percent), and food (13.6 percent), enjoyment trumps all. In addition, the percentage of income spent on food is misleading, because 5.7 percent of that category is dining out costs.[5] As we shall soon see, a significant success factor in the food service industry is the entertainment value a restaurant provides.

In *The Entertainment Economy*, Michael Wolf observed, "The lines between entertainment and non-entertainment are disappearing."[6] He then continued to explain

Family Budget Cuts   **By Millbower and Yager**

We'll have to cut entertainment.

that "entertainment has found itself at the forefront of economic growth and cultural revolution,"[7] and that "we seek entertainment in activities that used to be purely work-related or at least chore-related (such as buying groceries, choosing a car, looking for a new home)."[8]

He also suggested that the implications for organizations are huge: "Without entertainment content, few consumer products stand a chance in tomorrow's marketplace."[9] Walt Disney concurred: "In my opinion, entertainment in its broadest sense has become a necessity rather than a luxury in the life of the American public."[10]

The impact of entertainment that Wolf and Disney referred to is upon us. Advertisers, news organizations, businesses, sports, and educational services have all responded to the info-fog by placing entertainment content in their products. We will examine the ways that organizations in each of these arenas use entertainment techniques to communicate. In the process, we will set up our later examination of Show Biz Training techniques.

Advertisers

Advertisers have an especially difficult task. They must make buyers out of people who have no knowledge of, or interest in, their products. They must cut through the info-fog, gain and then hold attention, and move people to favorable action. As advertising executive, Bill Bernach (Doyle Dane Bernbach), stated: "The truth isn't the truth until people believe you, and they can't believe you if they don't know what you are saying, and they can't know what you're saying if they don't listen to you, and they won't listen to you if you're not interesting, and you won't be interesting unless you say things imaginatively, originally, freshly."[11]

The advertiser's task is especially daunting when you consider that the actual difference between products is often minimal. Advertisers cannot rely on reasoning or logic to prove their point. Instead, they must associate their products with pleasure, and they use entertainment to induce pleasurable emotions. As Malcolm Gladwell explained in *The Experience Economy:* "There is a simple way to package information that, under the right circumstances, can make it irresistible. All you have to do is find it."[12]

These days, entertainment usually provides the packaging. The entertainment industry is so involved in the production of commercials that advertising is responsible for approximately 40 percent of the entertainment industry's revenues.[13]

Television commercials provide excellent examples of how advertisers package information through entertainment techniques. Advertisers start with a solid story that engages people, add comedy, use props, present gee-whiz magical effects, and play toe-tapping music to make their points. See if you can identify the use of specific techniques in Table 3-1.

ENTERTAINMENT IN COMMERCIALS

Each of the commercials listed below made extensive use of one of the following elements: comedy, illusion, props, or music. Determine which commercial relied on which element then write the appropriate word on the corresponding line. You should use each element twice. In some cases, more than one entertainment element was utilized. In those cases, select the one item that the commercial relies on most. The answers are listed below.

_____ 1. A Break Today—McDonald's staged a full production themed to clean burger machines.

_____ 2. In the Drivers Seat—People floated to earth, as Hertz put them in the driver's seat.

_____ 3. It Takes a Licking—Timex tried to destroy its own watches to prove they "keep on ticking."

_____ 4. Plop, Plop, Fizz, Fizz—Speedy Alka-Seltzer sang, water fizzled, and what a relief it was.

_____ 5. Atsa Spicy Meatball—For Alka-Seltzer (again), an actor needs relief after 40 takes.

_____ 6. That Bunny's Still Going—Eveready Energizer poked fun at commercials through a toy rabbit.

_____ 7. Museum Art—The Honda hangs on the museum wall, until one brave soul drives it away.

_____ 8. Where's the Beef?—Clara Peller looked at a hamburger as she realized she should have gone to Wendy's.

ANSWERS: 1. MUSIC 2. ILLUSION 3. PROPS 4. MUSIC 5. COMEDY 6. PROPS 7. ILLUSION 8. COMEDY

TABLE 3-1

COMEDY IN COMMERCIALS

Comedy is a major factor in ad success. In fact, approximately 42 percent of all commercials use humor to communicate their messages.[14] It may also be appropriate to say that the best commercials use humor, given that 69 percent of the commercials honored with an International CLIO award had a humorous tone.[15]

Comedic ads deliver an amazing feat: people watch for them, enjoy them, and talk about them with friends and colleagues in spite of the fact that the ads are sales pitches. Think about the number of telemarketing calls you hang up on, and you begin to see the point. Commercials dodge the "hang up" reflex by making the product being sold more appealing and therefore more likely to be marketed successfully. Advertising expert Luke Sullivan, in *Hey Whipple, Squeeze This,* explained it this way: "In all categories where products are essentially all alike, the best-known and most-well-liked brand has the winning card."[16]

In Table 3-1, we saw some likable ads, including the meatball filmshoot stuck in neutral, and a hamburger without beef. Both commercials demonstrated a sense of humor.

The Alka Seltzer "Atsa Some Spicy Meatball" commercial, from Doyle Dane Bernbach, consisted of outtakes from a fake "Mama's Meatball" company. During filming, everything that could go wrong did. As a result, the actor was forced to eat meatball after meatball, eventually finding solace in Alka Seltzer. The beauty of this commercial was the way it satirized the advertisers themselves. In the process the ad implied that the advertisers used the product too.

Wendy's "Where's the Beef?" commercials, created by Dancer-Fitzgerald-Sample, used humor to suggest that not all hamburger chains were the same, and that Wendy's had a bigger burger.

The ad was so successful that during a 1984 presidential primary campaign debate, Democratic contender Walter Mondale actually said, "Where's the beef?" when he compared the "new ideas" that fellow Democratic candidate Gary Hart was promoting to the commercial. By suggesting that Hart's "new ideas" lacked "beef," Mondale subtly ridiculed his main contender, and went on to win the Democratic nomination. (He would later lose to Republican Ronald Reagan.)

In addition to the commercials already mentioned, three others bear special attention. For in each case, humor deftly accomplished what a more traditional approach could not.

For years, California wines, and Gallo in particular, were regarded as poor substitutes for French wines. Originally, the advertising response was to hire Orson Welles to intone pompously that Gallo would "serve no wine before its time." The advent of wine coolers turned the whole idea of highbrow wines on its head. Wine coolers were intentionally designed as a more casual drink. Stuck with the limits of its own self-created image, Gallo hired Hal Riney & Partners. They created an ad campaign built around two decidedly unsophisticated down-home old timers, Frank Bartles and Ed Jaymes. The two men, completely fictional characters, would sit on the porch, introduce themselves, or rather Frank would introduce non-talking Ed, and read letters from "customers." Each commercial would end with the understated but preposterous line, "Thank you for your support." It was self-parody at its best, Gallo became low-brow, and the Bartle's and James Wine Coolers were launched.

Our second example concerns an underappreciated fruit. In the 1900s, Stan Freberg was one of the funniest men alive. He had a dry, irreverent humor that was ideally suited to the sale of Sunkist Prunes. For years, prunes were viewed as a fruit for old people. Freberg brilliantly played off this perception by creating a spot featuring an aristocratic, pompous man. In the spot, the man fussed about his dislike for prunes. He complained that they are nasty, that they have pits, and are badly wrinkled. The announcer convinced him to try a prune anyway. Much to his surprise, he liked it. He commented on its flavor and the lack of a pit. But then, in the most upper-crust manner possible, he concluded by complaining, "They are still badly wrinkled." This was the set-up for the tag line, "Today the pits. Tomorrow the wrinkles." Suddenly, Sunkist Prunes were for the non-pretentious.

Finally, there's the case of an ad that was brave enough to mock its own profession. The image of the slippery car salesman, who will say anything to make a sale, is ingrained in our society. It seems like long ago, but at one time most Americans bought their autos from the "big three:" Chrysler, Ford, and General Motors. The only exceptions were people who preferred a more reasonably priced Volkswagen Beetle, or, if really desperate, the American Motors' Pacer. Carmakers from other countries were just entering the U.S. marketplace when Isuzu, courtesy of Della Femina, Travisano & Partners, settled on a novel approach to making their name known. The ads featured David Leisure as an archetypal lying car salesman. He blatantly stated falsehoods while the correct information scrolled across the bottom of the screen.

By making fun of their own kind, Isuzu was in essence acknowledging the largest challenge in buying a car, and encouraging a perception that Isuzu salespeople were different. As a result, many sales closed, including for David Leisure himself, who became a regular on the TV show "Empty Nest." In addition, the ads have such long-term staying power that a new series of these, again featuring Leisure, reappeared in 2002.

All three ads, those for Wendy's, Bartles and Jaymes, and Izusu, overcame negative perceptions with humor. The ads captured an emotional essence that people could relate to, and told their story in an engaging manner that cut through the info-fog.

MAGIC IN COMMERCIALS

Today we live in an era of special effects. Whether you need a walking robot, a sinking ocean liner, or a full-scale battle of clones, today's Hollywood can create it. Hollywood developed this capacity because illusions fascinate people. In television commercials, illusions are an effective method for capturing attention. They force viewers to stop, look, and wonder if they are seeing what they think they are seeing.

Once illusions have captured attention, they help maintain it. For, once viewers determine that what they think they see is correct, they begin focusing on how the illusion was achieved. In the process, their focus stays on the ad.

The Hertz ads created by Norman, Craig & Kummel were especially amazing. A person, sometimes two, would, in a seated position, gracefully glide through the air and downward into the seat of an empty convertible driving itself down the highway. It was a fascinating and beautiful image to watch, and people did. The tag line of the commercial was, "Let Hertz put you in the driver's seat," and millions still do.

Another example concerns a Honda ad in which an automobile is seen on display in a museum, as if it is a work of art. One museum patron walks by the car and stops to look longingly at it. The man looks around to see if anyone is watching, and seeing that the coast is clear, walks up the wall and into the auto, and drives it away. The ad amazed. The illusion of a hanging car was so perfect that it demanded attention.

A final current example is a 2002 commercial for Propel, a fitness water drink in the Powerade family. The commercial begins with a blank space, perhaps a darkened gym, or an empty stage. Oversized water droplets fall onto this floor. As each water drop splashes on the floor, it morphs into an athlete—a tennis player, a jogger, a bicyclist, and others. The commercial ends with a person swimming up and around a Propel bottle. The commercial's effect is magical.

The size of the space being presented in the commercial poses several intriguing questions. Is it small enough to focus on a water drop, or large enough for people? How could both be true simultaneously? And, how can people appear out of a water drop? In addition, how can a swimmer float up into the air, and be small enough to swim around a soda bottle? The bottle is larger than a water drop, and much smaller than a swimmer. So, which scale is it? All these questions race through viewers' minds as they watch the commercial. In the best tradition of illusion, this ad is impossible to ignore.

PROPS IN COMMERCIALS

Often, an advertiser will use the product being advertised as a prop. In some cases, an extraneous prop is created to support the product pitch. One such example is the Energizer Bunny. The battery-operated rabbit has become so identified with Eveready batteries that it is difficult to separate the rabbit from the product.

In actuality, the Energizer Bunny is not the product. The batteries that keep the rabbit going are. The advertisers, Chiat/Day, were faced with the difficult task of portraying the moving power of a stationary product. To do so, they needed a prop that would move, and proceeded to create the bunny. The ad campaign began in 1989, and was so successful that it continues to be shown to this day. The Energizer Bunny is one prop that will keep going for a very long time.

Some ads intentionally use the product as a prop. One notable example was the Timex commercials created by W. B. Donner and Company that subjected Timex watches to all sorts of mishandling. The "torture tests" demonstrated that, as John Cameron Swayze stated at the close of each commercial, "Timex, it takes a licking and keeps on ticking."

Another example comes from the Charmin ad agency Benton & Bowles. In the ads, grocer Mr. Whipple pleaded with female patrons to stop squeezing the Charmin. The ads ended with Whipple himself caught squeezing Charmin. It seemed that Charmin is irresistibly soft, even to Whipple. These ads were repeatedly rated as the most disliked by consumers, and yet, Charmin was number one in sales. The simple, inane use of Charmin as a prop, propelled the sales.[17]

MUSIC IN COMMERCIALS

Whether the subject is the joy of fast food, or the indigestion that results from the fast food, music is a valuable advertising tool—so valuable in fact that advertisers pay exorbitant sums, known to reach four million American dollars, to use well known songs in their ads.[18]

Advertisers pay these sums because the songs work. For example, one study examined the effectiveness of music as a memory cue in an automobile advertising campaign. The results indicated that 62 percent of the people surveyed remembered seeing advertising after hearing the product's name, but on hearing a 10-second musical cue, 83 percent recognized and associated the music with the ad. The authors concluded that musical cues appear to be more sensitive than verbal cues as absolute measures of memory.[19] In another study, it was proved that people could recall movie scenes when cued by background music for that scene.[20]

Some of the music used in commercials is instrumental in nature and often functions as background information. Tony Thomas, in his book, *Music for the Movies,* describes the effectiveness of music as follows: "Music comes to bear when helping to define the meaning of the film by stimulating and guiding an emotional response to the visuals. Directly and pervasively appealing to the subconscious...It is this unique ability to influence the audience subconsciously that makes music truly valuable to the cinema."[21]

In one notable example, Benton & Bowles created a pleasing, percolator like Maxwell House theme, complete with a brewing coffee visual. The catchy audiovisual mnemonic was so powerful that it evokes the memory of the aroma coffee makes when brewing.

Other times, music used in commercials has lyrics. Songs with lyrics add an additional layer of meaning to commercials. As I explained in *Training With a Beat:* "A familiar song is as comfortable as your worn blue jeans or favorite ice cream. Songs with lyrics, especially popular hits of the last 50 years, are old, well worn, welcome friends."[22] Jeff Smith, writing in *The Sounds of Commerce,* added: "A popular song title gives any film almost immediate name recognition. In addition, a particular title may have a nostalgic resonance for certain audience members."[23]

By using pop songs, advertisers create an opening into the emotions of viewers. Consider the usage of these pop songs:

- ▶ "When I'm Sixty-Four" (The Beatles) to sell Allstate Insurance

- ▶ "Fly Like An Eagle" (The Steve Miller Band) to sell the US Postal Service mail services

- ▶ "Getting Better" (The Beatles) to sell Philips home electronics

- ▶ "Happy Together" (The Turtles) to sell Burger King hamburgers

- ▶ "Right Here Right Now" (Fatboy Slim) to sell Oldsmobile autos

- ▶ "She's A Rainbow" (The Rolling Stones) to sell Apple iMac computers

Those songs were placed in relatively normal contexts. Often, however, advertisers must discuss potentially embarrassing, extremely personal subjects. Just as court jesters delivered difficult commentary in a nonthreatening manner, advertisers use music to make the uncomfortable information pleasurable. Here are some examples:

- ▶ "Celebration" (Kool & the Gang) to sell Celebrex arthritis relief pills

- ▶ "I Feel Good" (James Brown) to sell Senakot laxatives

- ▶ "Forever Young" (Rod Stewart) to sell Pampers diapers

- ▶ "Let It Whip" (Dazz Band) to sell Tampax tampons

- ▶ "The Twist" (Chubby Checkers) to sell Platex girdles

- ▶ "Walking on Sunshine" (Katrina and the Waves) to sell Claritin hay fever medication

By providing a positive emotional musical anchor, these songs made the difficult subject matter less threatening. Instead of technical clinical discussions, these commercials entertain.

Sometimes, however, a popular song that matches the need is not available. In that case, advertisers create their own songs. From the singing Texaco gas station attendants ("You can trust your car to the men who wear the star"), to Dinah Shore singing "See the USA in your Chevrolet," to the hilltop of young people singing "I'd Like to Buy the World a Coke," original songs have effectively championed products for years.

In the McDonald's commercial listed in Table 3-1, the advertisers created a full-blown Broadway style production, full of exuberant young people, joyfully cleaning their burger machines. On the surface, a fast food Broadway musical appears to be an absurd idea.

But in reality, the music provided just the right touch. It is useful to remember that this ad appeared before McDonald's rise to supercultural status. For many people viewing the commercial, safe-to-eat fast food in a clean, friendly environment was a new concept. The musical number joyfully demonstrated that McDonald's was not a greasy spoon. It was a place to have fun. The ad worked, and McDonald's sold billions and billions of burgers.

The Alka-Selter "Plop, Plop, Fizz, Fizz" song actually told people what to expect when Alka-Selter was placed in water. Beyond that, it suggested that the fizzing sound meant relief was on the way. I doubt that are any studies on the subject, but I imagine that many an all-night party has ended with someone groping for a glass while warbling "Plop, Plop, Fizz, Fizz." In those instances, the relief was no doubt felt by both the Alka-Selter taker and the party guests who had already gone home, and thus were spared the serenade.

In summary, advertisers have packaged their commercials with pleasant emotional content that allows the information to cut through the info-fog.

Infotainment

Information providers have become infotainment presenters.

At the forefront of this change was *USA Today,* with it's one-page stories, multiple colored pages, vibrant graphics, and less-than-critical statistics. Although it was initially called the "McPaper," implying it was similar to McDonald's fast food, *USA Today* met the need for peppy, quick infotainment. It is a success with 2,241,677 average daily sales in 2001. That's roughly equal to the combined average daily sales of *The New York Times* (1,109,371), *The Los Angeles Times* (972,957), and *The Washington Post* (759,864).[24]

USA Today has had such an effect on newspapers that virtually every paper in the United States is now printed in color. Even the stogy, conservative *Wall Street Journal* finally succumbed in 2002, and began printing its front page in multiple colors. Not to be outdone, the same day that the first colorized *Wall Street Journal* appeared, *USA Today* featured, on its cover, a story with key points represented in pictures rather than in text.

LOCAL NEWS

On television, news shows have become softer, and replaced hard journalism with entertainment-like features. In the 1970s, several image consultants, including Frank Magid, developed an entertainment-based news presentation formula. Its intent was to increase rating demographics at a time when viewers were fleeing to national cable stations.

The formula consisted of a handsome/cute co-anchor team, a funny/nerdy weatherman, and an intense/likable sportscaster. Segments were kept short, one to one and a half minutes in length, and were clearly focused on sensationalistic, local human interest, stories.[25] Teaser ads would run throughout the day to hype the evening broadcast. Here is a sampling of news teasers that actually ran from February 1 through April 1, 2002 on my local stations:

- ▶ "Are you unintentionally poisoning your children?"

- ▶ "Should you know more about the school buses your children ride?"

- ▶ "Your drinking water: Is it safe?"

- ▶ "You trust them to guard your children, but is your dog a killer?"

- ▶ "You count on it to protect your home, but could your fire extinguisher fail?"

- ▶ "Why are your kids praising terrorists?"

- ▶ "Are your children being taught to cheat?"

- ▶ "You save for years, but is it all for nothing?"

- ▶ "What is your daughter saying behind your back?"

- ▶ "Why is the government making it easy for people to steal your identity?"

Each and every one of these promos ended with a similar statement, "Details at Eleven!" To the viewer these techniques seem like hype. To the TV station, they're an inevitable result of the info-fog. When people are curious, they pay attention. Unfortunately for the news providers, the news is often ordinary. And yet, the commercial dynamics of TV require viewership. As a result, TV misapplies an ages-old storytelling technique: exaggeration. When the details of a story appear ordinary, storytellers fear the listener will lose interest. As a result they creatively embellish what they say. When discussing supermarket sales, advertising expert Luke Sullivan offered this explanation:

> **"When a supermarket wants to increase sales of a given product, they'll put up a promotion sticker in front of it, saying something like 'Everyday Low Price!' The price will stay the same. The product will just be featured more prominently. When they do that, supermarkets find that invariably the sales of the product will go through the roof, the same way they would if the product had actually been put on sale."[26]**

Whether the venue is supermarkets or local news shows, the technique is the same. Of course, there is a critical distinction between the motives of storytellers and of local stations. Storytellers have the enjoyment of their listeners at heart, whereas the TV stations

Nightly News   By Millbower and Yager

Breaking News . . . Details at Eleven.

. . . and that's the way it is.

are focused on sales. Readers should not mistake my observations as praise of the TV industry. The opposite is true. It is my belief that trust between entertainer and audience is a basic responsibility of entertainment, and that the misapplication of entertainment to news does the community a disservice. Nevertheless, infotainment exists, and increases viewership. As a result, TV stations misapply entertainment techniques.

NETWORK NEWS

Infotainment isn't restricted to the local level. Even the network TV nightly newscasts have placed a toe into the entertainment waters.

Of the three network TV nightly newscasts, the *CBS Evening News* is perhaps the most traditional. It begins with anchor Dan Rather seated behind a desk. Most of the presentation is serious, until it is time for a commercial break. One night, to prevent the audience from changing channels, Rather sent the broadcast to commercial with the following teaser: "Prescription drugs . . . are they overpriced? You may turn purple when you hear the next report." The next night, the teaser was, "Genetically altered salmon. What will happen if they ever get to your dinner table?"

ABC's *World News Tonight* has a slightly more upbeat presentation. It begins each broadcast with attention-catching phrases that suggest the stories to follow. On one night, those phrases included "No Warning, "Zero Tolerance," and "Seeking Justice." In addition, the screen graphics display some movement whenever the anchor is on screen.

At NBC, *The Nightly News* begins, like the ABC broadcast, with several short phrases. Samples included "Dangerous Delivery," War of Words," and "Hidden Dangers." In an attempt to make his presence less static, anchor Tom Brokow has moved out from behind a desk, and faces the camera. As on *World News Tonight,* the graphics behind him add subtle movement.

On the morning news circuit, NBC built *The Today Show* into an entertainment powerhouse. The thrust of the show is light on news, with short news interviews and breezy infotainment segments. The result has been a drift away from true journalism. As *The Today Show* host Matt Lauer himself explained: "The audience has made us personalities, and sometimes they demand things of us that don't follow the strict standards of journalism."

It must work. *The Today Show* generated $450 million in annual revenue for 2000.[27] In one month, January 2002, *Today* scored an average rating share of 5.9 million viewers, making it the strongest of all the morning shows. The next most watched show was ABC's *Good Morning America,* with an average of 4.5 million viewers. Of the three networks, CBS trailed, its *Early Show* averaging 2.5 million total viewers. But regardless of individual ratings, when combined, 12.9 million people tuned in to these shows.[28]

CABLE NEWS CHANNELS

Perhaps the best application of infotainment can be found in the presentation of news at the Fox News Channel (FNC). FNC programming displays an irreverent humor, with puns in their titles, video game style graphics, and news anchors who have personality and are not afraid to show it. Viewers are encouraged to call in and are heard on the air.[29]

FNC's signature news show, *The Fox Report,* presents news dressed up as entertainment. It features staccato pacing, hyperactive graphics, and a sharp, stylistic look. It is news tailored to the quickened pace of Generations X and Y. Host Shepard Smith, a veteran of the local news format, raises his voice a few decibels above the soft-spoken tone usually adopted by news anchors. He speaks in staccato bursts, offering phrases such as "A street called Wall" as an introduction to the stock market report, and "The G-Block," as he calls the entertainment news segment.

Smith intentionally focuses on keeping his show lively. He covers more stories in an hour than most news shows, all packaged with catchy buzz phrases and stimulating video clips, and announcing important facts with musical motives. And it works. The Nov. 2001 Nielson figures gave it a rating of 1.4 million viewers, and climbing.[30]

Another example can be found in the use of music on *The Fox Sunday News* (FSN). In a manner similar to advertising techniques, FSN humorously places songs at the end of each segment. For example, when the topic concerned two formerly political allies who had a falling out, the song played was Neil Sedaka's "Breakin' Up Is Hard to Do." In another instance, "Would I Lie to You" by Annie Lennox could be heard after segment showcasing some promises offered by various politicians. During a budgetary debate in which additional available funds were "discovered," FSN played Steve Miller's "Abracadabra."

Fox News Channel's application of show biz techniques has worked. In three short years, FNC has become a major competitor to the Cable News Network (CNN). Neilson Media Research reported that among the demographic between the ages of 25 and 54, Fox's viewership increased by 430 percent in just three years, while CNNs declined by 28 percent. By the first quarter of 2002, FNC had topped the cable news networks in primetime and total day viewership per quarter, with viewership numbers up 81% from 2001.

Meanwhile, in an attempt to stop the erosion to FNC, CNN revamped its stodgier looking Headlines News program, adding splashy graphics, rock music, and a video game style look with multiple stories splashed on the screen. Jamie Kellner and Garth Ancier, the two executives behind the change, explained the update by saying that they believed that younger viewers want their news fast. As a result, reports were shortened and the pace of delivery increased.[31]

Regardless of the success of the CNN makeover, or of future viewership numbers for *The Fox Report,* or the success of any news network in general, I believe that the future of news presentations is clear: it will entertain to inform.

And while news entertains to inform, entertainment informs to entertain. Perhaps the biggest TV programming trend of the late 1990s to early 2000s was "reality" television, shows in which people were filmed interacting in supposedly real-life situations. Two early examples were MTV's *The Real World* and Fox's *Cops.* Both shows sought to capture reality, and in the process entertainmentized it. They were followed by the megahit *Survivor,* and by other copycats including *Big Brother, Blind Date, The Bachelor* and *The Amazing Race.* All of these shows aggressively blurred the line between entertainment and information.

Businesstainment

With the rise of the Internet, brick and mortar storefronts have suddenly found themselves competing against the urge to stay home. When Amazon.com can conveniently deliver a book or CD overnight at a comparable, or lower, price, businesses have to create a reason to get people out of their homes and into their store. Often, businesses do this by creating an in-store experience so memorable that people want to visit them again. More often than not, businesses create that feeling through entertainment. Entertainment provides an emotional hook that is unique to every business. When a business can engage a person at a deeply personal, emotional level, the memory of the experience will stay with the individual, and bring that person back again and again.

DISNEYLAND

Perhaps the first businessperson to recognize the value of an entertainment experience was Walt Disney. The three-dimensional world that Disney created in Disneyland was something entirely new. It not only provided rides, but it also immersed its visitors in a three-dimensional world of sights, sounds, smells, things to touch, and emotion-based triggers. As Walt Disney himself explained: "I don't want the public to see the world they live in while they're in the Park. I want them to feel they're in another world."[32]

Even though Walt Disney passed away in 1965, the tradition continues to this day at the Disney theme parks. Jeff Kurtti of Walt Disney Imagineering offered this observation: "At its heart, the Disney park experience is that of storytelling. As an audience member, you are participating as opposed to sitting in a chair watching it."[33]

Disney's theme park may have been the first to create a full experience for patrons, but it is not the only entity to do so. Other amusement parks quickly adapted to become "theme" parks. Universal Studios, Six Flags, Busch Gardens, and SeaWorld have all become fully enveloping experiences.

RESTAURANTS

Although Disneyland may have gained the most attention, restaurateurs have been entertaining for years. Chefs know that the look of the plate matters as much, and sometimes more, than the taste of the food. From food presentation to entertainment is a small leap, and many restaurants made that leap years ago. Whether the motif is the sea, the Australian outback, Hollywood, rock and roll, or blues, restaurateurs design their buildings like stage sets. Several restaurant chains have even established "show kitchens" by placing the kitchen in plain view. Some restaurants have gone so far as to place the servers in "show" roles.

Skeptics reading this may ask, "But what about those themed restaurants that have had financial troubles?" It is true that themeing cannot flavor ordinary food. It cannot hide overly inflated prices, but when the food is great and the price is reasonable for the value, entertainment themeing is often the critical difference in restaurant success.

Restaurant themeing is not limited to fancy establishments. McDonald's, Burger King, Wendy's, and the other major fast food chains are heavily themed to entertain children. All the major chains sponsor tie-in promotions to Hollywood's latest kid-friendly films. Many of them have playgrounds for the kids. Their children's meals are packaged with toys. Most will host children's birthday parties. All these techniques allow the restaurants to become more than a restaurant; they have become an entertaining experience. In a way, the Broadway style environment represented in the previously discussed McDonald's commercial has come into being.

RETAIL

Retail establishments have also added entertainment elements. Nike stores offer one example. With its trendy look, bold accents, sports photos, and video walls, Nike stores reinforce the brand's "Just do it!" image.

Where Nike's presentation is high tech, Wal-Mart's is low tech, but nevertheless highly themed. The superstore-warehouse look is intentional. Its stage suggests plenty of stock, helpful informality, and low prices.

An excellent retail example can be seen in the Virgin Records Megastores. Rather than just selling CDs and audiotapes, these stores are a music theme park. Virgin Records Megastores are usually multilevel. They offer a huge selection of CDs, a wall of listening stations, separate rooms for different kinds of music, computer software, and children's sections, reading areas, and an upscale coffee shop. It doesn't really matter that the overly loud background music prevents you from sitting and reading. It is enough that the sitting area *looks* impressive. The total experience is what matters, and the sum of the experience is greater than any of the details.

SPORTS

Sports have also been entertainmentized. The National Football League's Superbowl, with its mega-extravaganza half-time show (and pregame show), flashy graphics, and the debut of Hollywood's newest commercials is about much more than football. It is an entertainment.

On a more regular basis, the National Basketball Association (NBA) entertains at every game. Players enter the arena through fog, flashing lights, and pulsating music. The cheerleading squad performs dance steps worthy of a Broadway show. The players also, sometimes unfortunately, have become a show unto themselves.

Edutainment

Another area that has successfully harnessed entertainment is *edutainment.* In edutainment, show biz techniques are melded with education to capture and maintain attention.

SESAME STREET

Perhaps the father of edutainment was *Sesame Street.* It was created in 1969 by Joan Gantz Cooney, Jeff Moss, Jim Henson, and a team of young writers, most of whom did not have children, but who understood entertainment. It was the first TV program to use show biz techniques to capture and maintain attention; and to use song and dance, skits, and rhymes to teach.

Interestingly, *Sesame Street* was patterned after a then popular TV show, *Rowan and Martin's Laugh-In. Laugh-In* was a maniacally fast paced, short segment, series of jokes strung together around a specific subject in recurring segments, all themed to the "hippie" generation. Two ironies come to mind when discussing *Laugh-In.* The first is the fact that it was the only show to have gotten future President Richard Nixon to say, "Sock it to me." The second is that, despite its love-in texture, its material and pacing came straight out of live vaudeville theater. In fact, most of *Laugh-In*'s recurring gags were simply repeats of old comic lines given a hippie twist. In this way, *Sesame Street* owes its concept directly to show business. The connection is so close that a former comedy writer, Michael Loman, is *Sesame Street*'s executive producer.[34]

Originally, *Sesame Street* was aimed at an audience of three- to five-year-olds, with the stated purpose of educating poor children who didn't go to preschool. But two-year-olds sitting at home had a different idea. They took to the show, and are now its primary audience.[35]

In addition to getting younger, *Sesame Street* has discovered that the attention span of its two-year-old audience has shrunk. *Sesame Street,* as a result, changed its basic structure in 2002. For years, *Sesame Street* focused on one street story interspersed throughout the entire program. The restructured version of the show features stories told in 10-minute blocks.[36] Its shorter stories are tailor made for the shorter attention spans of today's children.

This attention to both the entertainment and education needs of its audience has made *Sesame Street* a continued success, both as an entertainment and as a tool for increasing its audiences' reading and learning skills.[37]

SCHOOLHOUSE ROCK

Created by George Yohe and George Newall, *Schoolhouse Rock* relied heavily on entertainment. Both Yohe and Newall were executives at New York ad agency McCaffrey & McCall, and thus were familiar with the use of entertainment techniques. The co-chairman of the agency, David McCall, noticed that his son could sing every Beatles lyric but couldn't remember multiplication tables. He asked Newall, who also played jazz piano, if multiplication tables set to music would help his son learn. Newall agreed to try. He formed a team that created a song about counting: "Three Is a Magic Number." The song worked for McCall's son. Convinced of the value of their idea, they produced a record album. Its sales were lackluster.

Yohe, McCaffrer & McCalls other creative directors then became involved. Yohe supplied some drawings and "Three Is a Magic Number" became a three-minute animated short. The resulting video worked so well that it attracted the attention of an agency client, Michael Eisner, then the head of ABC's children programming. (Later, Eisner would go on to success in Walt Disney's old job as CEO of the Walt Disney Company.) ABC quickly bought the concept and Eisner placed it on the air in three-minute segments, sandwiched between ABC's Saturday morning cartoon segments.

Over a period of 12 years, from 1973 through 1985, 41 segments were produced on a variety of subjects in four categories: Multiplication Rock, Grammar Rock, America Rock, and Science Rock. The end result was a television icon that, at its peak, rivaled *Sesame Street*'s success. Not surprisingly, the ad men had a hit. According to Newall, "More kids saw *Schoolhouse Rock* than ever watched *Sesame Street,* and the big irony is that it was all done by a bunch of ad guys in their spare time."[38]

BLUE'S CLUES

Another show that teaches through entertainment is *Blue's Clues.* The show, about a blue puppy named Blue, helps prepare children for kindergarten and the first grade. It entertains through a highly interactive game show format and animated characters. In fact, the only nonanimated character is the host. All the action takes place in Blue's animated world as the host helps the young viewers solve Blue's clues.

The action begins when Blue leaves a pawprint on three items, each one being a clue to what she wants to do that day. The host will look directly into the camera and ask questions that help the young viewers process the clues. After the puzzles have been solved, the preschool viewers help the host determine what Blue wants.

Perhaps the most unusual fact about *Blue's Clues* is that the same episode airs every day for a week. The repetition allows the preschoolers to figure out the clues, and learn the lessons embedded in the content. *Blue's Clues* made its debut in 1996 on Nickelodeon as part of the Nick Jr. preschool programming block, and has won numerous awards, including the Television Critics Award for Outstanding Children's show in 1998 and 1999, and a 2001 Peabody award.

THE BLUES SCHOOLHOUSE

The combining of entertainment and education is not limited to TV. Many educational providers have discovered the teaching advantages of entertainment techniques. One excellent example comes from the restaurant chain created by Dan Aykroyd, the House of Blues, and its educational program, *The Blues SchoolHouse.* Part of the International House of Blues Foundation, *The Blues SchoolHouse* performs for school age children in House of Blues restaurant locations. In 2001 alone, *The Blues SchoolHouse* was presented to more than 38,500 students and teachers.

The show intertwines the history of American Blues, the history and culture of African-Americans, and the struggles for, and success in, achieving equality. The show ends with the inspirational message that every voice matters; that each and every student has a future; and that no one should let his or her voice go to waste. It is a truly uplifting and entertaining performance that captivates the students lucky enough to attend.[39]

ENTERTAINMENT ARRIVES

The importance of shows such as *Sesame Street, Schoolhouse Rock,* and *The Blues School-House* cannot be overstated. *Sesame Street* and *Schoolhouse Rock* raised the bar, not just for kids, but also for all those former kids who grew up watching them. They proved that edutainment was both possible and preferable. Experiences such as *The Blues School-House* continue that lesson today, proving to kids, who grow up and become the adults of today's workforce, that learning doesn't have to be boring.

The Internet places additional challenges in front of live instruction. As Michael Wolf explained:

> **"The Internet brings value in ways that more traditional entertainment forms cannot easily duplicate. No other media format can provide such a broad array and depth of content on demand. As the Net embraces entertainment, it will be superior in offering us fun on demand, making it more powerfully attractive for audiences who want to control what they see and the doses in which they want to see it."[40]**

If screen-based learning is fun and classroom-based learning is not, the future of classroom-based learning may be bleak. When you consider the amount of entertainment learning channels on TV, and the speed at which information is available on the Internet, you begin to see a future in which on-line instruction becomes the norm and live instruction fights a continuous battle for relevance. I believe that trainers will find their clout diminishing as more and more learning situations transition to computer and Web-based learning. Although trainers cannot compete with the ease and wealth of information available on line, they can compete and succeed in creating one-of-a-kind events that captivate as they teach.

Fortunately, the desire to gather and socialize, begun as stories around the cave fire, remains. This basic fact of human nature is an advantage for live instruction. People want to share pleasurable experiences. It's not an accident that comedies are funnier in the theater than they are on a TV at home; and that when we do see something funny in the privacy of our homes, we feel compelled to tell others what we saw.

Entertainment has always been communal. People want to share it. And exceptional live instruction offers something that e-learning cannot, an emotional, pleasurable, *communal* experience.

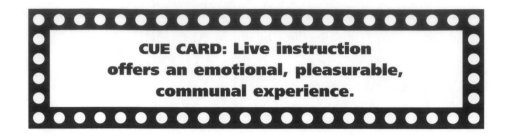

In this context, the trainer's challenge is to make classroom instruction equal in entertainment value to screen-based versions, to lift classroom instruction from expected to exceptional, from required to desired, from painful to pleasurable—in short, to make it fun! For I believe the future of live instruction lies in enjoyment, and the delivery vehicle is entertainment.

[1] *Webster's Dictionary of Quotations* (1992). New York: Smithmark.

[2] Sylwester, Robert (1995). *A Celebration of Neurons: An Educator's Guide to the Human Brain.* Alexandria, VA: ASCD.

[3] Ibid.

[4] U.S. Department of Labor, Bureau of Labor Statistics.

[5] Ibid.

[6] Wolf, Michael J. (1999). *The Entertainment Economy: How Mega-Media Forces Are Transforming Our Lives.* New York: Random House.

[7] Ibid.

[8] Ibid.

[9] Ibid.

[10] Smith, Dave (2001). *The Quotable Walt Disney: It Was All Started by a Mouse.* New York: Hyperion.

[11] Sullivan, Luke (1998). *Hey Whipple, Squeeze This: A Guide to Creating Great Ads.* New York: John Wiley & Sons.

[12] Gladwell, Malcolm (2000). *The Tipping Point: How Little Things Can Make a Big Difference.* Boston: Little, Brown and Company.

[13] Wolf, Michael J. (1999).

[14] Morreall, John, Ph.D. (1997). *Humor Works.* Amherst, MA: HRD Press.

[15] Ibid.

[16] Sullivan, Luke (1998).

[17] Ibid.

[18] Well, M. *USA Today,* May 24, 1999.

[19] Stewart, David W., Farmer, Kenneth M., and Stannard, Charles I. (1990). University of Southern California School of Business, *Journal of Advertising Research,* Aug–Sep, 30(4):39–48.

[20] Boltz, M., Schulkind, M., and Kantra, S. *Memory and Cognition,* 1991; Nov, 19(6):593–606.

[21] Thomas, Tony (1997). *Music for the Movies,* 2nd edit. Los Angeles: Silman-James Press.

[22] Millbower, Lenn (2000). *Training with a Beat: The Teaching Power of Music.* Sterling, VA: Stylus.

[23] Smith, Jeff (1998). *The Sounds of Commerce: Marketing Popular Music Film Music.* New York: Columbia University Press.

[24] Audit Bureau of Circulations, Schaumburg, IL.

25 Robin Chapman, *Orlando Sentinel,* 8/12/01.

26 Gladwell, Malcolm (2000).

27 Hal Boedeker, *Orlando Sentinel,* January 2, 2001.

28 <www.variety.com>.

29 Marshall Sella, *The New York Times* Sunday magazine, June 24, 01.

30 Orlando Sentinel, 12/09/01.

31 Jim Rutenberg, College Times, *The New York Times,* 8/5/01.

32 Smith, Dave (2001). *The Quotable Walt Disney: It Was All Started by a Mouse.* New York: Hyperion.

33 Kurtti, Jeff Quoted by Lanza, Joseph (1994). *Elevator Music: A Surreal History of Muzak, Easy Listening, and Other Moodsong.* New York: Picador USA.

34 *The New York Times,* AP, Feb. 5, 2002.

35 Ibid.

36 Ibid.

37 Gladwell, Malcolm (2000).

38 <www.nethomeschool.com/schoolhouserock/history.htm>

39 For more information about *The Blues SchoolHouse* please contact the International House of Blues Foundation 6255 Sunset Boulevard, 18th Floor, Hollywood, CA 90028, (323) 769–4901.

40 Wolf, Michael J. (1999).

CHAPTER FOUR

LEARNER-TAINMENT

GOOD FUN

Her name was Roach. And boy, did it fit. She masqueraded as a sixth grade teacher, but to him, she was a bug. Her glasses made her eyes real big, black, multifaceted, like a bug. Her speech sounded whiny, like a bug. As she walked up and down the aisles, you could hear her move toward you and away, like a bug circling a light. You could almost see the students recoil, afraid that she was going to strike.

He wasn't a bad student. On the contrary, he was exceptional. He always did his homework. He turned it in on time, sometimes even early.

In reading, he was ahead of the class. He would read all the stories in the book, even if they weren't assigned. It's not that he understood them all. He didn't. But, unlike Roach, they sparked his imagination. Besides, it was better than paying attention to the bug's buzz.

He did well in history, but not the facts kind. It didn't matter to him when Columbus sailed the ocean, or what color the ocean was. He saw the adventure of sailing to the end of the world in his head, and wanted to talk about that. Unfortunately, Roach focused on when, and then scurried away.

One time, he had tried to make history interesting. After visiting an Old West style theme park, he proposed to Roach that the class recreate a Western town of their own. She looked at him like he was a can of Raid. He never offered an idea again. That is, until today.

The world outside the classroom was so much more interesting. Out there, he imagined a whole world as he watched TV, went to the movies, played video games, and surfed the Internet. He did all these things, but what he could not do was sit still while Roach buzzed.

Today was Friday. He looked out the classroom's big windows. It was the first nice spring day, and gorgeous outside. He couldn't wait for 3:30. If only he had a teacher remote control. What a remote control that would be, he thought. One click and she could be muted. Another, and she could be shut off.

He looked at the clock. It ticked slowly.

3:25 . . . 3:26 . . . 3:27 . . . 3:28 . . . 3:28 and a half, 3:29 . . . but something was wrong. She wasn't stopping.

3:29 and a half, 3:30 . . .

Finally, he had had enough. He raised his hand. Roach called on him, and he said, "Miss Roach, don't forget, we leave at 3:30." She gave him her Roach startled look, and responded, "Yes, you are right. It is 3:30. Class is dismissed."

He stood up to leave. "Finally," he shouted to himself.

"All except for you," Roach continued, pointing at him. "You will stay."

"What did I do? It WAS time to leave." He thought. Dejectedly, he sat back down as his classmates ran out of the room.

Once they had all left, Roach explained that he was to be punished for his imprudence. He would have to stay an additional 15 minutes. For each of those 15 minutes, he would have to write on the board, "I will show more respect in class." Once that was done, he was to smack the chalk out of the erasers.

He argued, to no avail. Roach just responded that the longer he argued, the later he would stay. So, he stopped talking, and began writing. He got through the 15 sentences fairly quickly, with little focus on the words.

He then opened a window and began clapping the erasers together. The chalk billowed and rose. They looked like miniature . . . clouds! He was creating clouds! He watched them float and fall. "Now, this is interesting," he thought. He was suddenly having fun. As he played he wondered, "Why is it that you get to have fun when the teacher thinks you're bad? Wouldn't it be great if school could be fun when you're good?"

"Seeing is believing,
but feeling's the truth."—PLUTARCH[1]

In the last chapter, we concluded our examination of the factors distracting today's learners. We discovered that an info-fog exists, and that to be successful, entities must cut through that fog. We also determined that entertainment has enveloped many facets of society. Finally, we learned that these factors place live instruction at risk.

In this chapter, we begin examining an entertainment-based solution. We intend to do this by exploring the ways in which our brains take in information. Ultimately for learning to occur, a trainer must influence thinking, and to influence thinking, a trainer should know how the learners think.

We will provide a general overview of our brain systems, explore the role of emotions in creating memories, examine a learning system focused on engaging those emotions, and discover the amazing connection between entertainment and learning. We will learn how entertainmenet enhances the learning environment, and conclude with the basic tenets of Show Biz Training.

We begin with the source of thought: the brain.

BRAIN BASICS

The human brain is an amazing organ:

- ▶ It weighs about 3 pounds.[2]

- ▶ It occupies 2 percent of our weight.[3]

- ▶ It uses 20 percent of our energy.[4]

- ▶ It has a trillion cells.[5]

- ▶ Its cells are capable of connecting with a hundred thousand other cells.[6]

- ▶ It contains one hundred billion neurons.[7]

- ▶ There are more possible interconnections between these neurons than there are atoms in the universe.[8]

- ▶ All the world's telephone connections would have to be recreated 1,349 times to equal the total number of possible brain connections.[9]

- ▶ It can record a thousand new bits of information every second of our lives.[10]

These facts can amaze, but pale in comparison to another, more alarming fact: *We use less than 10 percent of our brain's capacity! Many of us use just 1 percent or less!*[11] That under-utilization can, in part, be explained in one word: survival.

The Role of Survival

Survival is the baseline concern of our brain. Without survival, learning is irrelevant. Our brain knows this. In fact, it never stops focusing on survival. Even those higher order components of the brain responsible for logic and the arts will refocus in a split second if the brain perceives a threat.

This dynamic cannot be ignored in the classroom. Ideas, and the intellectual application of those ideas, are important, but are of little consequence to a brain searching for potential threats. It is therefore useful to consider the ways in which our brain functions, and how the mere possibility of danger impedes learning.

One note of caution should be added before we proceed. Research into human brain functioning has come a long way in the last century. We do have a general idea of what happens within the brain, but no one knows exactly how it functions. There are no absolutes. To help us understand basic brain processing, we can, however, make educated generalizations. With that qualifier in mind, let's examine what we think we know.

The Brain Scouts

The human brain must scan its surroundings for signs of danger, but cannot physically do so alone. It has no direct connection with the outside world. Instead, the brain gathers information from a number of "scouts," perhaps the most basic of which is our skin.

THE SKIN

In a way, our skin and brain are twins. They both emerged out of our embryonic self. Two weeks after conception, a layer of embryonic tissue begins to develop in two different ways, with skin developing on one side, and the brain on the other.[12] It's an entirely logical growth pattern when you consider that our skin helps our brain connect with the physical world.

THE TASTE BUDS AND SCENT GLANDS

Our taste buds and scent glands are subtle but important information gatherers. They warn us of potential danger in the air that we breathe or in the food that we eat. Odor has, in

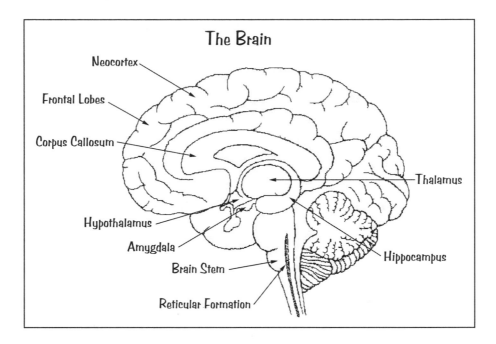

fact, been proven to affect levels of relaxation and agitation, disrupt sleep, improve performance, and help people relax.[13] Our sense of taste makes one of life's most basic requirements, nourishment, such a pleasurable experience that we continually seek it out.

THE EYES AND EARS

Two other information gatherers allow our brain to extend its reach outside of our body: our ears and eyes. Our ears tell us the volume, pitch, and timbre of sound waves that bounce up against our bodies, in the process helping our brain identify the direction and intensity. Our eyes, perhaps the most important of our brain scouts, allow us to picture what the world around us looks like.

Taken all together, that's it: the sum total of the ways in which our brain scouts out the information it needs to help us survive and prosper, five different methods that allow us to make sense of our world. We now move from the brain scouts to the brain itself, starting with the cerebellum.

The Cerebellum

There is an internal partner to the five senses that serves basic but critical functions. The cerebellum, located at the back of the brain, controls our automatic motor systems so that we can focus our attention outward rather than inward.

The Brain Stem

As information is gathered by the external scouts, it travels through the body, to the spinal cord, and up to the brain. The lowermost portion of the brain is the brain stem. This region, perhaps our ancient ancestors' original brain, emerges out of our spinal column. Its functions include controlling our breathing, pulse, and heart rate, and our fight-or-flight instincts.

It also collects information from our skin. Input gathered on our skin makes its way to the spinal column, and then up into the brain stem. The brain stem does not think about the information it receives. Owing to its limited processing power, the brain stem is primarily concerned with ordering this information for processing in the brain's higher regions.

The Limbic System

Wrapped around our brain stem is the limbic system. The phrase "limbic system" is actually a catchall identifier for several small structures, each approximately the size of a grape, that emerge out of our brain stem.

THE THALAMUS AND HYPOTHALAMUS

At the top of our brain stem, the thalamus and hypothalamus function as relay stations. The thalamus focuses on the external environment. It functions as a relay for the information gathered from the senses to the brain. The hypothalamus serves a similar function by monitoring body systems and informing the brain about the internal state of our body.[14]

THE RETICULAR FORMATION

The reticular formation, at the upper end of our brain stem, sorts the incoming sensory information relayed to it by the thalamus and hypothalamus, determining which input deserves the most attention, and which the least.[15]

THE AMYGDALA

Next to the hypothalamus lies the amygdala. With a general level of attention indicated by our reticular formation, the amygdala swings into action. Its job is to process the stimuli's emotional implications. To do this, it evaluates information sent to it in the context of that information's potential for danger. It then begins to initiate what it perceives to be appropriate emotional responses.[16]

THE HIPPOCAMPUS

The hippocampus, behind the amygdala, begins selecting facts and situations that could be important in the future, or are likely to recur, and sends them to other regions of the brain so that they can join related information in long-term memory.[17]

Up to this point, most of the incoming information has been dealt with on an instinctual, organizational, or emotional level. This is an important point that we return to later, but for now, we continue our journey upward into higher brain functions.

The Neocortex

As the information travels into our cerebral cortex thought begins to influence decisions. It is at this level that most instruction functions. Table 4-1 lists some facts about the neocortex.

THE TWO HEMISPHERES

Our neocortex consists of a left and a right hemisphere, attached by connecting tissue, the corpus callosum. The corpus callosum provides a communications bridge between the two halves.[18] The two hemispheres need all the communication help they can get, as they perceive very little in the same manner. They resemble two siblings whose experience is the same, but who rarely agree about what they experienced. When joined together by the corpus callosum, the two hemispheres are able to comprehend simultaneously the details and the context.

NEOCORTEX FACTS

► The word *neocortex* comes from the ancient Latin, meaning *bask.*[1]
► The neocortex is a 1/4-inch thick, wrinkled, skin-like tissue layer.[2]
► The neocortex would be about the size of an office desk when spread out.[3]
► The neocortex occupies five-sixths of the human brain.[4]

---

[1] Ayto, J. (1990). *Dictionary of Word Origins.* New York: Arcade Publishing.

[2] Jensen, Eric. (1998). *Introduction to Brain Compatible Learning.* San Diego: The Brain Store.

[3] Merriam, Sharan B., and Caffarella, Rosemary, S. (1999). *Learning in Adulthood: A Comprehensive Guide.* San Francisco: Jossey-Bass.

[4] Caine, Renate Nummela, and Caine, Geoffrey. (1991). *Making Connections: Teaching and the Human Brain.* Parsippany, NJ: Dale Seymour Publications.

TABLE 4-1

HEMISPHERIC COMPARISON CHART	
THE LEFT HEMISPHERE IS:	**THE RIGHT HEMISPHERE IS:**
Sequential	Metaphorical
Factual	Cerebral
Controlled	Emotional
Rational	Emphatic
Structured	Spontaneous
Theoretical	Experimental
Objective	Subjective
Analytical	Synthesizing
Logical	Intuitive
Detailed	Patterned
Positive emotion	Negative emotion

TABLE 4-2

As shown in Tables 4-2 and 4-3, where the left hemisphere thinks logically; the right thinks holistically. The left is sequential; the right is random. The left analyzes; the right synthesizes. The left comprehends words; the right comprehends metaphors. The left examines what is said; the right discerns how it is said. The left focuses on facts and details; the right focuses on stories and visuals.

This duality allows the brain to size up unknown situations quickly. The right hemisphere surveys the big picture and looks for possible hints of trouble. Meanwhile, the left hemisphere analyzes the potential threats, and if no threat is present, looks for the positive aspects of the situation. As Robert Sylwester describes it:

> **"The right hemisphere processes the negatives aspects of emotion that lead to withdrawal behaviors (e.g., fear, disgust), while the left hemisphere processes the positive aspects that lead to approaching behaviors (e.g., laughter and joy). Strong feelings tend to be negative, probably because**

it's more important for the brain to communicate that a problem exists than to say that everything is okay."[19]

Survival vs. Pleasure   By Millbower and Yager

Ignore him. Let's have some fun.

Interestingly enough, research has determined that when the incoming information doesn't fit any recognizable pattern, our brain tags the information as a potential threat. Immediately, the brain is on alert. If the right hemisphere perceives the information as negative, it directs the release of cortisol. If the left hemisphere determines the information as positive, adrenaline is released. Both of these brain chemicals fix memories into our brain, allowing us to remember the events for years afterwards.[20]

Frontal Lobes

Within the neocortex are the frontal lobes. They are larger than the capacity needed for day-to-day activity.[21] In other words, we all walk around with extra firepower available to us. This extra firepower comes to the fore when survival seems threatened. During situations where the limbic system and brain stem send emotional snap judgments to our neocortex, the frontal lobes evaluate, and in some cases overrule the emotional responses.[22]

In many ways, the brain is complicated. But taken as a whole, it functions quite logically. Imagine the brain as a prison-yard searchlight, using the five senses to scan the landscape continually for danger. When it sees danger, it stops searching and focuses tightly on the perceived threat. If the threat turns out to be unimportant, the brain continues its search. All this survival energy is unconscious. It exists below or level of awareness, but it dictates much of our behavior.

CUE CARD: The search for danger dictates our behavior.

MOVIES IN THE MIND

BRAIN STRUCTURE	FUNCTION	MOVIE RESPONSE
Cerebellum	Controls the automatic motor system.	Allows you to eat your popcorn unconsciously.
Brain Stem	Conduit for incoming information.	Absorbs the movie's audio vibrations, and the vibrations you feel when the person behind you kicks the back of your seat.
Reticular formation	Integrates the amount and type of incoming information into general levels of attention.	Suggests that the movie deserves more attention than the popcorn, but the seat kicker is a potential threat.
Hypothalamus (limbic system)	Monitors internal regulatory systems, informs our brain of internal systems status.	Reminds you of the restroom visit you should make.
Thalamus (limbic system)	Relay center for incoming sensory information, informs our brain about what's happening outside our body.	Tells you that the popcorn bag is empty, but the seat kicking continues.
Amygdala (limbic system)	Processes emotion, filters and interprets incoming sensory information in the context of our survival and emotional needs, helps initiate appropriate responses.	Feels the emotional content of the film, and builds anger towards the chair kicker.
Hippocampus (limbic system)	Classifies and stores selected memories in appropriate memory networks.	Sorts and stores the movie character names and story details.
Left hemisphere (neocortex)	Analyzes, processes information sequentially, processes the positive impacts of emotion.	Comprehends the sequential details of the story and decides you should visit the restroom and buy more popcorn on the way back to your seat.

Right hemisphere (neocortex)	Syntheses, processes information conceptually, processes the negative aspects of emotion.	Evaluates the story for conceptual validity and, as you return to your seat, causes you to lash out at in anger at the seat kicker.
Corpus callosum	Allows the two hemispheres to communicate and collaborate.	Helps the hemispheres match the details to the concept as you enjoy your popcorn without distraction.

TABLE 4-3

SUGGESTOPEDIA

A learning theory that engages this unconscious region of the brain is Dr. Giorgi Lozanov's Suggestopedia. Working as psychotherapist 1950s Bulgaria, Lozanov studied the mediation, concentration, and self-discipline exercises that are staples of yoga. He noticed the psychophysiological changes in pulse and brain waves that occurred with each yoga posture, the relationship between the Savasana posture and the state of relaxation, and the effects of breathing exercises and mental concentration. From his studies, he concluded that yogis were able to tap into reserves beyond those utilized in most learning environments. Lozanov then designed a holistic learning method to activate those brain reserves.

In explaining Suggestopedia, Lozanov stated: "One of the most important tasks of Suggestopedy has been to free and to explain to all students that human capabilities are much greater than expected, and to provide liberating-stimulating methods to bring these locked-up human resources into play."[23]

An overview of Lozanov's theory can be stated in three major points:

► Adults have memory reserves developed during childhood but forgotten in adulthood. An atmosphere of playfulness taps into those reserves.

► Adults bring personal learning barriers into the classroom with them. Facilitators should create an aura of joyfulness, and then use that aura to suggest positive learning outcomes.

► Adults react to information on many levels simultaneously, both consciously and paraconsciously. All the signals in a classroom should be in concert with the learning goal.

An Atmosphere of Playfulness

Lozanov focused on the "*paraconscious*," those human brain functions normally beyond conscious control. He believed that adults have forgotten learning capabilities they had developed during childhood, but then abandoned in a push toward adultness. He called these capacities *"hidden reserves."* He believed that, although dormant, these hidden reserves can be tapped into when the right conditions are present. Suggestopedia, as Lozanov called his method, was designed to tap those reserves. Lozanov believed that once those reserves were accessed, the learner's memory would be stimulated, and memory retention would increase.

Lozanov recommended creating an atmosphere of playfulness through the use of the arts. A typical Suggestopedic class would include information presented with Baroque music accompaniment, colorful artwork on display, rhymes and songs, play acting, and other emotive devices. The use of these techniques was specifically designed to awaken the right cerebral hemisphere. As Lozanov himself explained it: "Life's experience and one's intellectual abilities are not reduced but rather supplemented by the plastic qualities of the earlier age periods, since these are liberated to a considerable extent."[24]

In this way, Lozanov believed he could increase the amount of brainpower applied to learning.

An Aura of Joyfulness

Lozanov believed that adult suspicions about the classroom, documented in Chapter 1, "The Distracted Learner," block learning. He viewed a joyful attitude on the part of the instructor; one in which the instructor positively suggested relaxed and tension-free learning as the key to transcending inhibitions.

It is important to note the use of the word *suggestion*. Lozanov defined suggestion as "a constant communicative factor which chiefly through paraconscious mental activity can create conditions for tapping the functional reserve capacities."[25]

Lozanov felt that dictates would be doomed to failure, and that positive, subtle, repeated suggestion, or *"focused positive attention,"* would create an atmosphere in which learners would believe in themselves and embrace the learning.

Lozanov also hypothesized that suggestion is more easily accepted if the learner can be placed in a deeply relaxed condition, like the conditions created by yoga. He would use muscle relaxation techniques, deep breathing exercises, Baroque background music, and almost hypnotic recitations of learning material to reach the reserve capabilities.

Signals in Concert

Lozanov believed that all the elements of the learning environment must be in sync with the message of the instruction. In Lozanov's words, the classroom environment is an "enormous signaling stream of diverse stimuli which, unconsciously or semiconsciously, are emitted from or perceived by the personality."[26] He believed that any items out of sync, be they drab walls, workbooks with misspellings, a trainer who continually checks the clock, or even a momentary hesitation on the part of the trainer may go unnoticed consciously, but will speak volumes about the instruction on a subsconcious level. That subsconcious message will affect moods, relationships, decisions, and even the importance the instructor places on the instruction itself. To guard against contradictory signals, Lozanov placed great value on orchestrating every element of the environment, so that, regardless of the level, the instruction is congruent with itself.[27]

What a Suggestopedic Class Looks Like

Suggestopedic classrooms have a distinct look. A Suggestopedic learning design would begin in a way in which the learning is imperceptible. It would include games, singing, and dancing. If accompanied by a textbook, the text would look and read like a stage play. Positive emotions and energy would be exhibited by the trainer and passed on to the learners. The class would seem more like purposeful play than hard learning.

Although it would appear at first glance that the pace of learning would be slow due to the seemingly pointless playing, the truth is that, as the learners draw on more of their brain fire power, the speed of learning accelerates beyond what would be possible in a traditional facts-and-dates learning environment. This truth has propelled the theory into some prominence in the business world, gaining wide popularity under the general umbrella title of *Accelerated Learning*. There are many books on the subject, whole corporate training programs built around Accelerated Learning, and organizations, such as The International Alliance for Learning, devoted to the use of Suggestopedia.

LEARNERTAINMENT

> "The mind is like a sheet of white paper in this,
> that the impressions it receives the oftenest, and retains the
> longest, are the black ones." —JULIUS C. HARE AND AGUSTUS W. HARE[28]

We now apply what we have learned about brain functioning and Suggestopedia as we examine four steps in the learning process that form the basis for Learnertainment. The first of those four steps follows.

The Learnertainment Chain

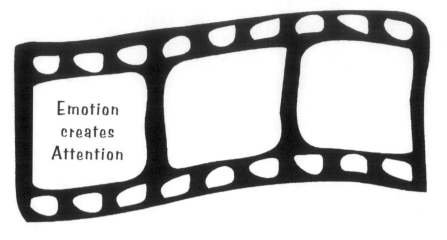

Emotion
creates
Attention

Emotion Creates Attention

The word emotion comes from the Latin *exmovere,* meaning "to move out of," and "to agitate." Aristotle believed that people are persuaded not just by logic, but also through emotion.[29] Plato agreed when he said, "All learning has an emotional base."[30] Carl Jung added, "There can be no transforming of darkness into light and of apathy into movement without emotion."[31] They were correct in many ways. As we shall discover, emotions start a chain of events that lead to persuasion.

For centuries, folklore stated that emotion was a creature of the heart. As science gained ascendancy over folklore, it was argued that emotions were a brain function. More recent research reveals that both folklore and science had it right. We have discovered that emotion is in fact generated not just in our brain, but also in our immune and endocrine systems. Scientists have also discovered that emotions affect our whole body, including our heart, lungs, stomach, and skin.[32] If you think back through your own life experience, you instinctively know this to be true. We have all felt the goosebumps of fear, the sweat of nervousness, and the rapid breathing that comes from excitement. A "gut reaction" is just that, an emotional signal from the gut.

The wisdom of gut reactions makes even more sense when you consider that the heart starts beating in a human fetus before the brain is formed,[33] and that, as the brain develops, it begins with the brain stem. From the brain stem, the emotional limbic system emerges. Next, the thinking brain grows out of the emotional regions.[34] Perhaps as a result, more neural connections go from the limbic system to the cortex than the other way around.[35] Certainly as a result, emotional reactions occur before we think. We feel first, and think later.[36]

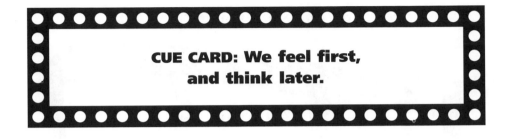

CUE CARD: We feel first,
and think later.

As researchers Doc Childre, Howard Martin, and Donna Beech explained in their book, *The HeartMath Solution:* "Emotions are constantly regulating what we experience as 'reality.' The decision about what sensory information travels to our brain and what gets filtered out depends on what signals the receptors (for emotion) are receiving."[37]

The body's up-front focus on feelings is essential to our survival. In situations where life or death stands in the balance, quick responses are critical. Emotion serves the purpose of identifying general threat levels. The emotional meaning in any situation captures our attention and helps us make snap fight-or-flight decisions. Our brains are designed to flee, or think the worst, at the first sign of danger.

This response is automatic. Although we may be able rationalize our emotions, we can barely control them. They often control us. Sylwester explained it as follows: "Our attentional system separates foreground from background, and focuses on the foreground. We don't consciously control the decision about what's important, the system will revert to survival needs—and we'll end up trampling the beautiful flowers at our feet in a mad dash toward survival."[38]

Even when we overpower emotions with logic, the feelings that created the emotion remain, perhaps forever.[39]

The next step in our cycle explores the ways in which the brain makes meaning out of the attention it has focused.

Attention Creates Meaning

We have learned that the brain shifts into a heightened level of attention once danger is suspected. This heightened level is difficult, if not impossible, to maintain for a long period of time. To protect itself from overload, and to free up its capacity for the next potential threat, the brain searches for the meaning of the stimuli.

The brain explores our memories, searching for something to compare the present stimuli to. The brain activates neurons that search through its networks for similar events. Once a comparison is found, the brain concocts a mental concept or model to explain the stimuli that confronts it. Through a comparative mental concept, the brain determines

The Learnertainment Chain

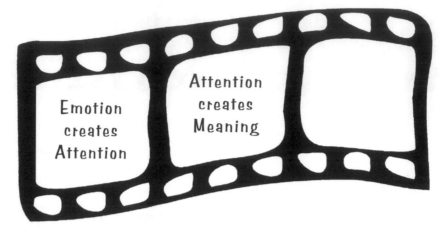

the appropriate response. This is not to suggest that we have made an intellectual decision. Rather, we have captured the general concept of what is happening, and respond accordingly.[40]

While this process is occurring, the stimulus that captured our attention is held in short-term memory. Short-term memory is that portion of our memory devoted to the things we need to remember in the moment, but may not be significant in the long term. Our short-term memory can store items for around 30 seconds. This memory is ever changing. As new bits of information come in, the new information replaces the old.[41] When the brain determines that the current information is, or may be, important to us in the future, the information is forwarded into long-term memory, as we explain in the next step of the Learnertainment Chain.

Meaning Creates Memory

The memories we carry in our brains are of two types: "doing" or "knowing" memories. Doing memory is the type of memory that allows your car to find its own way to work in the morning. Obviously, the car doesn't drive itself, but you have little conscious awareness of having controlled the movement of your vehicle. You did it without awareness. Doing memory comes about by repeating something so often that the brain can repeat the procedure without our focusing attention on it.

Knowing memory is more complicated. Knowing memories are those memories in which we are conscious of thinking about a subject. There are two kinds of knowing memory: short-term and long-term. Learning, if successful, resides in long-term memory.

Unlike short-term memory, long-term memory has an almost unlimited capacity. Long-term memories develop when the brain determines that the experience has emotional meaning and might occur again.[42]

The Learnertainment Chain

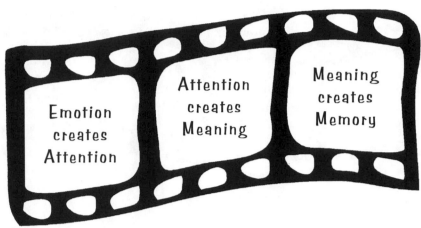

Emotion creates Attention

Attention creates Meaning

Meaning creates Memory

We have discovered that emotion creates attention, attention creates meaning, and meaning creates memory. We have almost completed the loop, but must first consider methods for generating the emotion that creates attention. Entertainment is one such source.

Entertainment Creates Emotion

"What we learn with pleasure
we never forget."—LOUIS MERCIER[43]

Have you ever cried at the movies? Ever been scared by the bad guys? Ever felt moved by the hero's tenacity? Ever cheered the triumphal ending? Entertainment creates that kind of emotion. And entertainment is everywhere in our modern world, except in most of our classrooms.

In Chapters 1 through 3, we learned that people are faced with a glut of information and choice, resulting in shortened attention spans. We also discovered that advertisers, news, and businesses all use comedy, props, magic, and music to capture attention and maintain interest. Finally, we determined that learning methods have not kept pace with societal change, despite some entertainment inroads into educational venues.

We also studied the words of advertising executive Bill Bernach: "The truth isn't the truth until people believe you, and they can't believe you if they don't know what you are saying, and they can't know what you're saying if they don't listen to you, and they won't listen to you if you're not interesting, and you won't be interesting unless you say things imaginatively, originally, freshly."[44]

The Learnertainment Chain

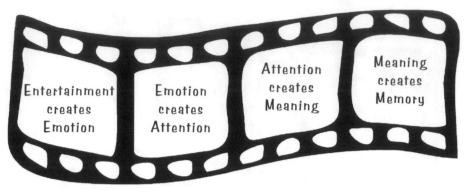

If we reread the Bill Bernach quote, and place it in the context of a learning environment, we can see that the underlying point applies to learning. If the learners don't pay attention to you, they can't hear what you say, and they won't pay attention to you if you're not interesting, and you won't be interesting unless you present your information in an original fashion. This need to engage people imaginatively, originally, and freshly raises an important question: How do we teach learners to ignore the cell phones, stop humming the jingles, and step away from the info-fog so that they can focus on our instruction? I believe the answer is by capturing their attention and refocusing their energies through the pleasant emotionally based content that results when you combine learning and entertainment into *Learnertainment.*

LEARNERTAINMENT WORKS

Learnertainment aids learning because:

► Novelty cuts through the info-fog.

► People expect to be entertained.

► Entertainment engages the brain.

► Entertainment overpowers negative emotion.

Novelty Cuts Through the Info-Fog

Novelty cuts through the info-fog because it attracts attention. In their book *Making Connections,* learning scholars Renate Nummela Caine and Geoffrey Caine make the point that people are stimulated by novelty.[45] And brain scholar Sylwester reported:

"Learning is not primarily dependent on a reward. In fact, rats—as well as humans—will consistently seek new experiences and behaviors with no perceivable reward of impetus. Experimental rats respond positively to simple novelty. Studies confirm that the mere pursuit of information can be valuable by itself and that humans are just as happy to seek novelty."[46]

From the entertainment field, but with the same sentiment, magician Sam Sharpe stated: "Variety, or anything that increases interest, helps to shorten the idea of time; whereas monotony induces boredom and makes time drag."[47] Comedic writer Thomas Hood added: "There are three things which the public will always clamor for, sooner or later: namely, Novelty, novelty, novelty."[48]

CUE CARD: People are stimulated by novelty.

All of these statements have in common the viewpoint that people seek out the unusual. Messages that are different from the norm have a greater chance of being noticed. If a message is ordinary, but somehow becomes noticed, it will be regarded as mediocre, and treated accordingly. Michael J. Wolf elaborated on this point in *The Entertainment Economy:* "If my product seems as if it does the job and offers fun, an escape, absorbing information, you are going to choose it over another plain-vanilla one. The alternative product may do the job but if it doesn't engage the emotions, it loses."[49]

Think of your classroom as a product. Is it the plain vanilla variety, or does it entice your learners? If your teaching style is boring, it may be successful, but if it is filled with novel, engaging learning connected stimuli, it will capture and maintain attention. As Malcolm Gladwell, in *The Tipping Point,* explained it, "By tinkering with the presentation of information, we can significantly improve its stickiness."[50]

People Expect to Be Entertained

We have become a service, rather than an industrial, society. One of the results of our transformation from an industrial to a service model is a change in people's expectations.

In past generations, assembly-line style orderliness and a "Yes Sir!" willingness to follow commands were valued. Today, people instead focus on their individuals needs, with little adherence to the dictates of others. They expect to be catered to, and will spend more to patronize organizations that provide an enjoyable experience.

Wolf explained "Fun, usually in the form of entertainment content (or, at the very least, content that is entertaining), is an overriding cultural value among modern consumers. They expect it. They treat it as an entitlement, and they feel shortchanged when they don't get it."[51]

To provide that fun, many organizations have "entertainmentized" their products. The result is a culture in which the lines between entertainment and non-entertainment are evaporating. As master showman Walt Disney once said about edutainment: "We have long held that the normal gap between what is generally regarded as 'entertainment' and what is defined 'educational' represents an old and untenable viewpoint."[52]

Entertainment is becoming the norm. Shakespeare was correct. The world IS a stage.

Entertainment Engages the Brain

Leonardo DaVinci believed that to learn a subject completely, a person had to perceive the subject from at least three different perspectives.[53] Learnertainment relies heavily on multiple perspectives. Great entertainments routinely establish one perspective, and then, once the audience has fully embraced it, reveal that perspective to be false. The surprises of comedy, magic, and drama are all achieved in this manner. Using these entertainment techniques, learners can explore the multiple perspectives of any subject.

Beyond multiple perspectives, Learnertainment engages the brain on multiple levels. Psychologist Carl Rogers once wrote the following: "Significant learning combines the logical and the intuitive, the intellect and the feelings, the concept and the experience, the idea and the meaning. When we learn in that way, we are whole."[54]

Trainers already have facts and figures at their disposal to be processed by the logical, analytical portions of the brain. As with Suggestopedia, Learnertainment appeals to other regions, the emotive portions of the brain. When several regions of the brain are simultaneously engaged, more neurons fire, more brainpower is at work, and greater illumination of the subject at hand can be achieved. As a result learners receive not a one-dimensional view of the subject, but rather experience multilayered insights.

Learnertainment also engages the brain through physical movement. Carla Hannaford, in her book *Smart Moves,* demonstrated that physical activity leads to the firing of more neurons, which in turn leads to more available brain power for application to the subject at hand.[55] From laughter, to applause, to toe tapping, to audience participation, much of entertainment is based on physical movement. This physical movement wakes the brain up, making it more amenable to learning.

CUE CARD: Entertainment appeals to the emotive portions of the brain.

Entertainment Engages Emotion

Emotion is a critical component of many memories.[56] In his pioneering work *Emotional Intelligence,* Daniel Goleman explained: "We have two very different ways of knowing—the rational and the emotional—which are, for the most part, intertwined and 'exquisitely coordinated; feelings are essential to thought, thought to feelings.'"[57]

Entertainment focuses on the emotional. Master magician Sam Sharpe captured the point when he said, "What is done with feeling; that is to say, artistically, becomes enjoyable and therefore eagerly acceptable."[58] It is impossible to be entertained without feeling emotion. And, by engaging learners emotionally, entertainment speaks to both emotions and thought.

CUE CARD: Entertainment speaks to both emotions and thought.

Entertainment Overpowers Negative Emotion

Negative emotion rarely sleeps, especially in the classroom. The brain's crisis prevention focus often blocks learning. After all, a classroom can be an uncomfortable, almost foreign, environment. The very act of learning, to some adults, implies a lack of completeness. Learners suspicious of facilitator motives, or fearful of their own learning disabilities, can become so wrapped up in their emotions that their mood prevents them from learning. Given that emotion cannot be stopped, smart trainers find ways to harmonize with and harness that emotional energy.

Studies have demonstrated that "the right hemisphere processes the negatives aspects of emotion that lead to withdrawal behaviors (e.g., fear, disgust), while the left hemisphere processes the positive aspects that lead to approaching behaviors (e.g., laughter and joy)."[59]

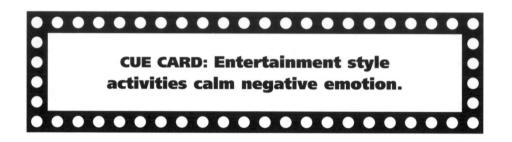

**CUE CARD: Entertainment style
activities calm negative emotion.**

Survival vs. Pleasure II   By Millbower and Yager

He's fine until he senses trouble.

Learnertainment is geared toward relaxing the fears that the limbic system urgently relays to the right hemisphere. In effect, entertainment style activities *baby-sit the right hemisphere,* keeping it busy with things it likes: cartoons, music, games, activities, visuals. These kind of activities provide the pessimistic right hemisphere with a positive context for the subject being taught. Once the right hemisphere is playfully engaged, learning can commence without the blocking negative emotion brings forth.

Learnertainment further reinforces this dynamic by creating positive emotion for the left hemisphere. It engages learners in an experience so enjoyable that *attention is riveted on the positive aspects of learning.* Simultaneously, Learnertainment allows a trainer to compete effectively with the quickened pace of life and overcome the info-fog that confronts all learners.

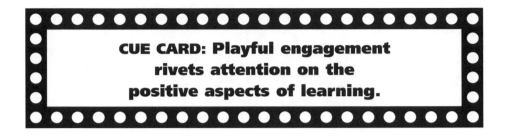

LEARNERTAINMENT PRINCIPLES

We have come to the conclusion of Act One. We have discovered the need for, and the reasons behind, Learnertainment. It is now time to introduce the basic principles of Learnertainment. They are:

Principle 1: Make it fun—create an atmosphere of playfulness.

Principle 2: Layer meaning—present your message on several levels.

Principle 3: Cue the audio—add the auditory signal to the visual.

Principle 4: Evoke emotion—engage your learners emotionally.

Principle 5: Direct attention—suggest the outcomes you expect.

Principle 6: Stage the environment—orchestrate every detail of the environment.

Principle 7: Use mnemonics—provide visual learning cues.

Principle 8: Stage the performer—orchestrate every detail of your performer.

Beginning in the next chapter, and throughout the remainder of this book, we will explore the techniques that bring these principles to life. We will learn the how to apply Learnertainment through a series of skills collectively called Show Biz Training.

---

[1] *Webster's Dictionary of Quotations* (1992). New York: Smithmark.

[2] Jensen, Eric (1998). *Introduction to Brain Compatible Learning.* San Diego: The Brain Store.

[3] Ibid.

[4] Ibid.

[5] Ornstein, Robert, and Thompson, Richard (1984). *The Amazing Brain.* Boston: Hougton-Mifflin.

[6] Ibid.

[7] Ibid.

[8] Ornstein, Robert, and Thompson, Richard (1984).

[9] Jensen, Eric (1998).

[10] Lawlor, Michael, and Handley, Peter (1996). *The Creative Trainer: Holistic Facilitation Skills for Accelerated Learning.* London: McGraw-Hill.

[11] Ibid.

[12] Sylwester, Robert (1995). *A Celebration of Neurons: An Educator's Guide to the Human Brain.* Alexandria, VA: ASCD.

[13] Howard, Pierce J. (1994). *The Owner's Manual for the Brain: Every Day Applications from Mind–Brain Research.* Austin, TX: Leornian Press.

[14] Sylwester, Robert (1995).

[15] Ibid.

[16] Ibid.

[17] Ibid.

[18] Ibid.

[19] Ibid.

[20] McGaugh, James L., et al. (1990). Involvement of the amygdaloid complex in neuromodulatory influences on memory storage, *Neuroscience and Biobehavioral Reviews,* 14(4):425–31. Quoted by Parkin, Margaret (2001). *Tales for Trainers.* Sterling, VA: Stylus.

[21] Sylwester, Robert (1995).

[22] Ibid.

[23] Lozanov, Giorgi (1978). *Suggestology and Outlines of Suggestopedia.* New York: Gordon & Breach.

[24] Ibid.

[25] Ibid.

[26] Ibid.

[27] Ibid.

[28] *Webster's Dictionary of Quotations* (1992).

[29] Aristotle. *Rhetoric.* New York: Modern Library.

[30] *Webster's Dictionary of Quotations* (1992).

[31] Ibid.

[32] Sylwester, Robert (1995).

[33] Rose, Colin, and Nicholl, Michael L. (1997). *Accelerated Learning for the 21st Century.* New York: Delacorte Press.

[34] Childre, Doc, and Martin, Howard, with Beech, Donna (1999). *The HeartMath Solution.* San Francisco: HarperCollins.

[35] Sylwester, Robert (1995).

[36] Childre, Doc, and Martin, Howard, with Beech, Donna (1999).

[37] Pert, Candace B. (1997). *Molecules of Emotion: Why You Feel the Way You Feel.* New York: Scribner.

[38] Sylwester, Robert (1995).

[39] Ibid.

[40] Ibid.

[41] Merriam, Sharan B., and Caffarella, Rosemary S. (1999). *Learning in Adulthood: A Comprehensive Guide.* San Francisco: Jossey-Bass.

[42] Sylwester, Robert (1995).

[43] Phillips, Bob (1993). *Phillips' Book of Great Thoughts and Funny Sayings.* Wheaton, IL: Tyndale House.

[44] Sullivan, Luke (1998). *Hey Whipple, Squeeze This: A Guide to Creating Great Ads.* New York: John Wiley & Sons.

[45] Caine, Renate Nummela, and Caine, Geoffrey (1991). *Making Connections: Teaching and the Human Brain.* Parsippany, NJ: Dale Seymour.

[46] Richard Restak, M.D. (2001). *The Secret Life of the Brain.* New York: Dana Press in partnership with Joseph Henry Press.

[47] Sharpe, S. H. (1988). *Conjurers' Psychological Secrets.* New York: Hades Publications.

[48] *Webster's Dictionary of Quotations* (1992).

[49] Wolf, Michael J. (1999). *The Entertainment Economy: How Mega-Media Forces Are Transforming Our Lives.* New York: Random House.

50 Gladwell, Malcolm (2000). *The Tipping Point: How Little Things Can Make a Big Difference.* Boston: Little, Brown and Company.

51 Wolf, Michael J. (1999).

52 Smith, Dave (2001). *The Quotable Walt Disney: It Was All Started by a Mouse.* New York: Hyperion.

53 Michalko, Michael (1998). *Cracking Creativity: The Secrets of Creative Genius.* Berkeley, CA: Ten Speed Press.

54 Rogers, Carl (1983). *Freedom to Learn.* New York: Macmillian.

55 Hannaford, Carla (1995). *Smart Moves: Why Learning Is not All in Your Head.* Arlington, VA: Great Ocean.

56 Rosenfeld, I. (1988). *The Invention of Memory.* New York: Basic Books.

57 Goleman, Daniel (1995). *Emotional Intelligence: Why It Can Matter More than IQ.* New York: Bantam Books.

58 Sharpe, Sam H. (1988). *Conjurers' Psychological Secrets.* New York: Hades.

59 Sylwester, Robert (1995).

ACT TWO

LESSONS FROM ENTERTAINMENT

CHAPTER FIVE

BERTHA AND BO

This is a true story. I saw it happen.

The year was 1967 and the location was the New York State Fair. It was a big performance for us Rhythm-Lite kids, and to us, the stage was huge. It was a nice outdoor amphitheater, with a downward slope of grass and orange construction fencing separating the audience from the performers.

We were on the same bill with New York State Governor Nelson Rockefeller, Victor Borge, and an elephant act named Bertha and Bo. The plan was for Rockefeller to proclaim the 1967 New York State Fair officially open. We Rhythm-Lites would then perform. Next, the elephant act would do its thing. The entertainment would conclude with pianist-funnyman Victor Borge.

In typical politician fashion, Rockefeller did not arrive at show time. We all waited backstage for what seemed to this 17-year-old to be hours. During that time, we got to meet and talk to Victor Borge. We had little else to do, so we played cards and shared our show biz dreams with him. He was absolutely delightful toward us would-be stars. There was no hint of the pretentiousness that some stars display.

Rockefeller finally arrived and gave his proclamation. Our performance went next. Then it was time for the elephant act, Bertha and Bo. We had been so taken in with Borge, that we hurriedly packed our props and costumes, and slipped in front of the orange construction fencing, and the audience, at the bottom of the stage slope.

Bertha and her trainer, Bo, were already performing. Bo directed the huge elephant through her routine: lifting legs, kneeling, bowing toward the audience, and various other circus style tricks. It was very ordinary. But then, something went wrong.

Bo placed a bell on a stool and indicated that the elephant should grasp the bell with her trunk and ring it. There must have been some prior difficulties with this routine, because the elephant was not interested in the bell. Bo prodded Bertha, but got no response. He physically placed her trunk on the bell. Bertha swung her trunk back at the now startled trainer.

Bo, seeing his own performance career jeopardized, started poking Bertha with his prod. This got a violent headshake in response. The trainer, desperate now, swung his prod, and whacked Bertha on the rump. Bertha reacted by facing the audience, lifting her front legs into the air, stretching to an intimidating height of 20 feet. As she pawed the air, she let loose with a piercing bellow. The sound frightened the audience and especially us would-be stars sitting at the bottom of the slope. We suddenly realized that with one quick gallop, Bertha's feet would crush us.

Desperate now, the trainer started beating Bertha. His blows were so hard that they repulsed the audience. Bo had lost the crowd, but Bertha had not. For Bertha turned out to be the smartest being in the amphitheater. She looked one way, then another, and perhaps realizing the dire consequences of a run, chose a different strategy. She let loose a sustained avalanche of brown and yellow substance that coated the stage.

The mood changed immediately. With that action, Bertha had won. The act was over. Bertha triumphantly marched off stage, with the trainer slumping embarrassingly behind.

This unexpected set of circumstances caused another performance delay as the poor technicians cleaned the mess up. Somehow, the audience didn't notice. Their mood had been fouled by the situation. They were anxious and nervous. Various audience members whispered, giggled nervously, and pondered quietly as the technicians worked. After much mopping and squeegying, the stage was clean enough for Borge's grand piano.

Once the piano was in place, the show was ready to resume, but the audience wasn't. Paradoxically, they needed to laugh now, but the combination of trampling danger, animal cruelty, and the mess on the stage had brought forth a flood of negative emotion. They had become fearful, tense, and reflective. If Borge didn't handle the situation properly, he would never reach this audience.

Into this swirl of emotion, Victor Borge entered stage right. He walked up to the mike stand and said . . . nothing. He let the tension mount. The audience suddenly had another situation and emotion to ponder: the performer was not performing. Borge waited a minute, then two. He put his thumb in his mouth. He began sucking on it. This left the audience puzzled. Had the man reverted to childhood?

After a minute of thumb sucking, and at precisely the moment of maximum tension, Borge pulled his thumb out of his mouth and held it in the air. He waited another minute, before finally looking at the audience. It was at this point, four minutes into his act, that Borge said his first words, "The wind's blowing this way."

The house was immediately his. After the laughter subsided, he added, "Let's move the piano down wind." This got another laugh, and added a funny visual as the technicians scurried to move the piano. Borge, tiptoeing, and looking carefully at the stage floor as if he was afraid of stepping on something, gingerly approached the piano. This caused a third laugh.

Borge's sat down to play, and of course serenaded the audience with the "Baby Elephant Walk." That got laugh number four.

But the best was yet to come. One of Borge's standard funny bits was to play wrong notes intentionally. This time, as he hit his first wrong notes, he stopped playing, reached into his jacket pocket, and pulled out the elephant's bell! Somehow, in the confusion following Bertha's exit, Borge had gotten hold of the prop. Now, he rang that bell as loudly as he could. He then plopped it down on his piano, and muttered, "Stubborn elephant. Stupid trainer. Smart piano player."

It was a masterful touch. He could have ended his performance right then. The audience was his. Borge had no way of knowing that the situation would occur, but knew that he would suffer if he didn't handle it properly. It seems that he and Bertha had become a comedy team, with her setting up the joke, and him delivering the punch line. Instead of Bertha and Bo, the act should have been called Bertha and Borge.

> "Laughter is no enemy
> to learning." —WALT DISNEY[1]

The Show Biz Training techniques in this chapter are based on the following Learner-tainment Principles:

Principle 1: Make it fun—create an atmosphere of playfulness.
Principle 2: Layer meaning—present your message on several levels.

Other Learnertainment Principles applicable to this chapter are:

Principle 4: Evoke emotion—engage your learners emotionally.
Principle 7: Use mnemonics—provide visual learning cues.

LEARNING AND FUN

In his book, *Creative Training Techniques*, training guru Bob Pike stated, "People learn in direct proportion to how much fun they are having."[2] Colin Rose and Michael Nicholl, in *Accelerated Learning for the 21st Century*, agreed, "Play is an important part of the learning experience. When we enjoy learning, we learn better."[3] So did William Reinsmith in *Archetypal Forms in Teaching*, "The more learning is like play, the more absorbing it will be."[4] In this chapter, we will discover how an atmosphere of fun impacts health and emotions, and makes learning irresistible.

We will also explore the ways in which comedy adds depth to learning. In *Cracking Creativity*, Michael Michalko discussed the differences in thought processes between geniuses and people of average intelligence. He reported that "Genius often comes from finding a new perspective that no one else has taken."[5] For example, Albert Einstein was once asked what the greatest difficulty he encountered was when creating his theory of relativity. He replied, "Figuring out how to think about the problem."[6] Another genius, Leonardo da Vinci, believed that the key to true learning was to view any subject from as many different angles as possible.[7] Comedy is unique in this regard. As we explore the ways comedy interacts with subject matter, we will discover that comedy is predicated on viewing a situation from multiple vantage points.

THE COMEDY BEGINS

The audience waits. The air is thick with expectation. Finally, the performer steps on stage. A round of applause welcomes her. She acknowledges the applause and begins her act. She makes a statement, and then another, consistent with the first. She makes a third statement. This one, however, is different. It is at odds with the first two. It rearranges the meaning of the first two statements. In response, something miraculous happens. One person makes a sound of surprise. He sucks in his breath, holds it for a second, and lets it out. A repeating sound results. The people near him repeat his action, as if catching a fever. They make similar sounds, and a ripple effect begins. In a few seconds, the performer must stop and wait, for the whole audience has suddenly come down with convulsions. The laughter has begun.

Unlike this comedian's experience, no one knows what caused the very first laugh. Some scientists believe that human laughter evolved out of the panting behavior of our ancient primate ancestors.[8] We cannot prove that point, but we do know the origin of the word "comedy." It comes from the Greek word "*kõmos*," which meant revelry. This word was combined with the word for "singer," "*õido's*." When placed together, the two words produced "*kõmõido's*," meaning a singer of revels.[9] In other words, it was a description of the storytellers of old. Another hint of laughter's ancient roots comes from this statement in the Koran: "Blessed is he who makes his companions laugh."[10]

The ability to laugh exists within each of us at the beginning of our lives. Scientists believe that babies begin chuckling very early in life, perhaps within a month of birth. At four months old, even though they cannot speak, most babies can laugh. No one has accurately counted how often a person laughs, but it is believed that four-month-old babies laugh about once per hour and four-year-olds once every four minutes.[11] In general, children laugh on an average of 400 times a day.[12]

Laughter seems to be an automatic response to an unexpected, but not unpleasant, occurrence. Genuine laughs occur without our conscious input. Our brain simply decides it is time to laugh. In one sense, this automatic response is similar to the way your car seems to drive itself to work. Obviously, brainpower is required, but not at a conscious level. On those rare occasions where we consciously force a laugh, our laughter sounds, and is, fake.

What appears to happen when we laugh is that our brain has followed a path of logic. One idea leads to another, and then to another, as our brain organizes incoming information in our short-term memory. Then suddenly, in great surprise, our brain realizes that we have been tricked: that there is more than one interpretation for the information. The result is a reflexive intake of breath, followed by a release air, and a laugh. This reflex is universal, regardless of culture, race, or gender. It simply exists.

We seek out this reflex. We want this experience so much that we pay others money to make us laugh. Many of the most successful American feature films have been comedies. In 2002, for instance, four comedic films were among the top ten grossing American films. The four, *My Big Fat Greek Wedding, Austin Powers in Goldmember, Men in Black II,* and

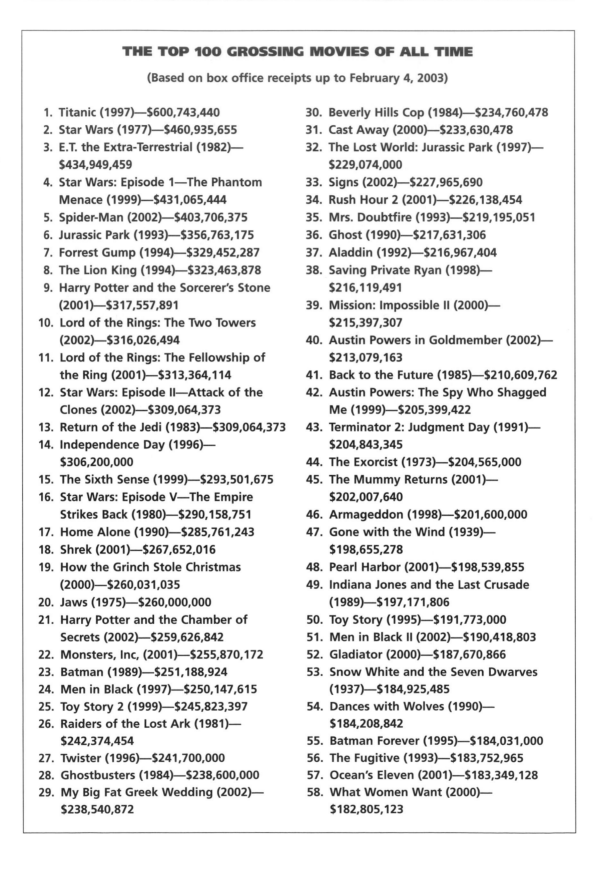

THE TOP 100 GROSSING MOVIES OF ALL TIME

(Based on box office receipts up to February 4, 2003)

1. Titanic (1997)—$600,743,440
2. Star Wars (1977)—$460,935,655
3. E.T. the Extra-Terrestrial (1982)—$434,949,459
4. Star Wars: Episode 1—The Phantom Menace (1999)—$431,065,444
5. Spider-Man (2002)—$403,706,375
6. Jurassic Park (1993)—$356,763,175
7. Forrest Gump (1994)—$329,452,287
8. The Lion King (1994)—$323,463,878
9. Harry Potter and the Sorcerer's Stone (2001)—$317,557,891
10. Lord of the Rings: The Two Towers (2002)—$316,026,494
11. Lord of the Rings: The Fellowship of the Ring (2001)—$313,364,114
12. Star Wars: Episode II—Attack of the Clones (2002)—$309,064,373
13. Return of the Jedi (1983)—$309,064,373
14. Independence Day (1996)—$306,200,000
15. The Sixth Sense (1999)—$293,501,675
16. Star Wars: Episode V—The Empire Strikes Back (1980)—$290,158,751
17. Home Alone (1990)—$285,761,243
18. Shrek (2001)—$267,652,016
19. How the Grinch Stole Christmas (2000)—$260,031,035
20. Jaws (1975)—$260,000,000
21. Harry Potter and the Chamber of Secrets (2002)—$259,626,842
22. Monsters, Inc, (2001)—$255,870,172
23. Batman (1989)—$251,188,924
24. Men in Black (1997)—$250,147,615
25. Toy Story 2 (1999)—$245,823,397
26. Raiders of the Lost Ark (1981)—$242,374,454
27. Twister (1996)—$241,700,000
28. Ghostbusters (1984)—$238,600,000
29. My Big Fat Greek Wedding (2002)—$238,540,872

30. Beverly Hills Cop (1984)—$234,760,478
31. Cast Away (2000)—$233,630,478
32. The Lost World: Jurassic Park (1997)—$229,074,000
33. Signs (2002)—$227,965,690
34. Rush Hour 2 (2001)—$226,138,454
35. Mrs. Doubtfire (1993)—$219,195,051
36. Ghost (1990)—$217,631,306
37. Aladdin (1992)—$216,967,404
38. Saving Private Ryan (1998)—$216,119,491
39. Mission: Impossible II (2000)—$215,397,307
40. Austin Powers in Goldmember (2002)—$213,079,163
41. Back to the Future (1985)—$210,609,762
42. Austin Powers: The Spy Who Shagged Me (1999)—$205,399,422
43. Terminator 2: Judgment Day (1991)—$204,843,345
44. The Exorcist (1973)—$204,565,000
45. The Mummy Returns (2001)—$202,007,640
46. Armageddon (1998)—$201,600,000
47. Gone with the Wind (1939)—$198,655,278
48. Pearl Harbor (2001)—$198,539,855
49. Indiana Jones and the Last Crusade (1989)—$197,171,806
50. Toy Story (1995)—$191,773,000
51. Men in Black II (2002)—$190,418,803
52. Gladiator (2000)—$187,670,866
53. Snow White and the Seven Dwarves (1937)—$184,925,485
54. Dances with Wolves (1990)—$184,208,842
55. Batman Forever (1995)—$184,031,000
56. The Fugitive (1993)—$183,752,965
57. Ocean's Eleven (2001)—$183,349,128
58. What Women Want (2000)—$182,805,123

59. The Perfect Storm (2000)—$182,618,434	80. Three Men and a Baby (1987)—$167,780,960
60. Liar Liar (1997)—$181,395,000	81. Meet the Parents (2000)—$166,225,040
61. Grease (1978)—$181,360,000	82. Robin Hood: Prince of Thieves (1991)—$165,493,908
62. Jurassic Park III (2001)—$181,166,115	83. Hannibal (2001)—$165,091,464
63. Mission: Impossible (1996)—$180,965,237	84. Big Daddy (1999)—$163,479,795
64. Planet of the Apes (2001)—$180,011,740	85. The Sound of Music (1965)—$163,214,286
65. Indiana Jones and the Temple of Doom (1984)—$179,870,271	86. Batman Returns (1992)—$162,831,698
66. Pretty Woman (1990)—$178,406,268	87. A Bug's Life (1998)—$162,792,677
67. Tootsie (1982)—$177,200,000	88. The Waterboy (1998)—$161,487,252
68. Top Gun (1986)—$176,781,728	89. The Sting (1973)—$159,600,000
69. There's Something About Mary (1998)—$176,483,808	90. Die Another Day (2002)—$159,488,587
70. Ice Age (2002)—$176,387,405	91. The Firm (1993)—$158,348,367
71. Crocodile Dundee (1986)—$174,634,806	92. X-Men (2000)—$157,175,311
72. Home Alone 2 (1992)—$173,600,000	93. Scary Movie (2000)—$156,997,084
73. Air Force One (1997)—$172,888,056	94. Fatal Attraction (1987)—$156,645,693
74. Rain Man (1988)—$172,825,435	95. What Lies Beneath (2000)—$155,370,362
75. Apollo 13 (1995)—$172,100,000	96. The Mummy (1999)—$155,247,825
76. The Matrix (1999)—$171,383,253	97. Who Framed Roger Rabbit (1988)—$154,112,492
77. Beauty and the Beast (1991)—$171,301,428	98. Beverly Hills Cop II (1987)—$153,665,036
78. Tarzan (1999)—$171,085,177	99. Jerry Maguire (1996)—$153,620,822
79. A Beautiful Mind (2001)—$170,708,996	100. Scooby Doo (2002)—$153,288,182

Source: Exhibitor Relations Co., Inc.

TABLE 5-1

Ice Age grossed a combined $807,903,000. If you examine Table 5-1, a list of the top 100 grossing films of all time, you discover that 30 of those films were comedies, and that virtually every film in the top 100 contained some comedic elements.

Comedy success extends beyond movies. Situation comedies (sitcoms) permeate television. In the first week of April 2002, the major broadcast networks featured a combined prime-time total of 54 sitcoms, or 27 hours of comedy. In other words, sitcoms made up one third of the prime-time television schedule—the largest amount of any genre.

In May 2002, *TV Guide* published what it considered to be the Top 50 TV shows of all time. The listing is instructive. Of the top 50, 21 were comedies, and an additional 9 had large comedic elements. In other words, 30 of the top 50 TV shows of all time were comedic.

Comedy is so desired that the comedians who make us laugh are celebrities. From Tim Allen, through the Marx Brothers, Milton Bearle, Jack Benny, George Carlin, Rodney

Dangerfield, Red Foxx, Bob Hope, Jay Leno, Eddie Murphy, Chris Rock, Adam Sandler, and Robin Williams, comedians hold special places in our lives. We admire them for their wit. They become our companions. They help us determine how to see the world.

The Benefits of Comedy

Our admiration of comedians should not be a surprise. Laughter is one of the great joys of humanity. It is a feature of all communal gatherings. It is present in stories. It permeates advertising, entertainment, infotainment, and edutainment. It is also, as we discovered in Chapter 1, "The Distracted Learner," missing from many learning plans. It is not, however, missing from the learning environment.

Regardless of an instructor's comedic intent, comedy hangs about the classroom waiting for a moment to surface. If it is not coordinated and supplied as a vehicle for instruction, it will find its own entry. Learners will always seek comedy out, and for good reasons. Comedy offers a number of tangible benefits. Comedy:

1. Improves health.
2. Releases tension.
3. Transcends negative emotion.
4. Deflects conflict.
5. Builds rapport.
6. Attracts attention.
7. Illuminates content.
8. Aids memorization.

Comedy Improves Health

Scientists have discovered that laughter has an effect on health similar to moderate exercise. During a laugh, our heart pumps harder, blood circulation increases, and our blood pressure rises. Meanwhile, our lungs take in six times more oxygen than normal. Simultaneously, our abdomen, chest, shoulders, and face muscles contract. After the laughter stops, amazingly, our muscle tension, heart rate, and blood pressure drops to levels *lower* than those before we started laughing. Laughter has also been found to enhance our immune system, release internal painkillers, and reduce inflammation. Finally, and perhaps most importantly for learning, laughter triggers the release of catecholamine in the brain, heightening alertness.[13]

CUE CARD: Laughter
heightens alertness.

Comedy Releases Tension

One reason people laugh, especially in the learning environment, is to release the tension they feel. People will often laugh even if the statement that preceded the laugh is not funny. Laughter at not-very-funny remarks is a mechanism for relieving tension, and we all use it. In fact, most laughter does not occur as a result of hearing a joke.[14]

Tension, or stress, is both a physical and a mental state. It affects our endocrine system as we feel our stomach grow queasy, our circulatory system as our heart begins pounding, and our muscles as we tense up; our respiratory system works harder as we breathe more quickly. During stress, our brain functioning also changes. Our dominant hemisphere shuts down. We behave in ways unlike our usual selves. We are incapable of functioning at our best.[15]

Comedy has an amazing affect on stress. As we discovered in Chapter 4, "Learner-tainment," stress occurs when our brain perceives a survival challenge. The source of most comedic material is the tragedies and absurdities of life. Once a challenging subject is presented in a comedic fashion, the tension that builds around that subject dissipates and people begin to focus on real issues, instead of survival-based emotions.[16] As positive emotions increase, our body system normalizes itself, and then relaxes. Suddenly, what a moment ago was perceived as a threat now becomes a source of joy. This in turn enhances immune system functioning, regulates blood pressure, increases order and balance in the nervous system, and produces smooth, harmonious heart rhythms.[17]

Comedy Transcends Negative Emotion

As Steve Allen said in his book with Jane Wollman, *How to Be Funny:* "Since comedy is in some way about tragedy, one of its functions is to alleviate the pain we would constantly be suffering were we to concentrate on the tragedy that characterizes life on this planet. Humor is a social lubricant that helps us get over some of the bad spots. It is a humanizing agent."[18]

Most instructors have experienced situations in which participants refused to learn because of negative emotions. Comedy transcends those emotions. As we look for the humorous aspects of any situation, we redefine that situation. Humor presents those negatives in such a humorous, enjoyable, nonthreatening manner that people are able to transcend their negativity.

Comedy Deflects Conflict

In *The Singing Entertainer,* Jon Davidson and Cort Cassady stated: "Humor is one of the most attractive and disarming tools a performer can use. Laughter breaks down barriers—it makes people feel less inhibited. Once the audience is laughing, they are more accessible. If you can reach an audience with humor, you can win them."[19]

Although Davidson's area of expertise is vocal performance, his advice is applicable to the training environment. As people laugh together, conflict dissipates. When we laugh, we communicate playful intent. It is therefore difficult, if not impossible, to laugh AND argue simultaneously. For at moment laughter occurs, there is no "they," only "we."

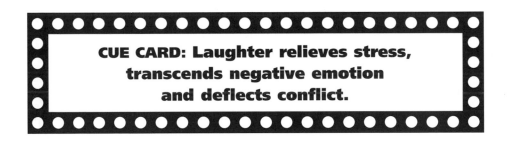

CUE CARD: Laughter relieves stress,
transcends negative emotion
and deflects conflict.

Comedy Builds Rapport

Laughter, perhaps because of its roots around the cave fire, is a social activity. Certainly Hollywood knows this truth. For most of its history, the entertainment industry has dealt in group gatherings where laughter becomes infectious. Movie comedies, for instance, seem less funny when watched in the privacy of our homes. With the advent of TV, live studio audiences substituted for the group. Sitcoms were another matter. Without communal laughter, they felt cold and aloof. Hollywood responded by creating virtual people, the laugh tracks, so that people sitting alone at home can join in.

Humor builds rapport by establishing relationships between people. Think about what you do when you first meet someone. Chances are you smile, strive to be pleasant, and make a joke if one comes to you. Many romantic relationships have begun because of the simple statement, "(S)He makes me laugh." Laughter is communal, and its major function is to establish relationships between people.[20]

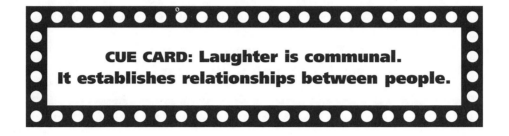

The bonding glue that laughter provides is a major classroom resource.[21] As Regina Barreca wrote in *They Used to Call Me Snow White:* "If you can make people laugh with you, you have won them over, however briefly, to your side. You have created an atmosphere of consensus, a moment of agreement when everyone is in sync."[22]

Comedy draws instructors and learners closer together. When people laugh at the absurdities of life together, they become partners in humanity. Suddenly, they have something in common; they have discovered a way to understand, and to relate to each other more fully.

In *The Laughing Classroom,* educators Diane Loomans and Karen Kolberg explained: "Humor can act as a social lubricant or a social retardant in the educational setting. It can educate or denigrate, heal or harm, embrace or deface."[23] Fellow educator Gilbert Highet, in *The Art of Teaching* concurred when he said: "The real purpose of humor in teaching is to link the pupils and the teacher, and to link them through enjoyment. When a class and its teachers all laugh together, they cease for a time to be separated by individuality, authority, and age. They become a unit, feeling pleasure and enjoying the shared experience."[24]

Comedy Attracts Attention

Our attention is quickly drawn by laughter. If we are near a gathering of laughing people, we instinctively turn toward the laughter. We wonder what we missed. Often, we join the group, and the laughter, *before* we know what the humor is about. In fact, experts have stated that we focus our attention on people who make us laugh.[25] As we discovered in Chapter 1, a major difficulty facilitators face is the info-fog that surrounds learners. Comedy is a major resource for cutting the fog. It gains and maintains attention. As Highet explained: "One of the most important qualities of a good teacher is humor. It keeps the pupils alive and attentive because they are never quite sure what is coming next."[26] And when people pay attention, they are more likely to absorb your message.

CUE CARD: Laughter gains
and maintains attention.

Comedy Engages Both Hemispheres

In Chapter 4, we learned that the brain's right cerebral hemisphere tends toward negative emotions. Comedy suppresses these negative emotions by presenting holistic views of the subject. In this way, the right hemisphere is engaged.

Comedy also engages the left hemisphere by forcing logical processing. A joke presents details that seem to lead toward a specific conclusion. The joke then takes what we logically expect, and turns that expectation on its head. Suddenly, the listener discovers that the details have a completely different, also logical, interpretation. This realization causes the left hemisphere to process the information logically. In this way, both hemispheres are brought to bear on the subject.

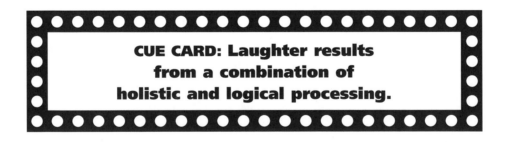

CUE CARD: Laughter results
from a combination of
holistic and logical processing.

Comedy Illuminates Content

Comedy illuminates a subject in ways impossible through lecture alone, by taking a naturally occurring situation and pointing out the absurdities to be found in that situation. It adds an extra dimension to learning environments, illuminating the subject matter in new, unexpected ways, that challenge participants to focus on details. In *A Smile in the Mind*, graphic design experts Beryl McAlhone and David Stewart offer this analogy:

"When wit is involved, the designer never travels 100% of the way [toward the audience] . . . The audience may need to travel only 5% or as much as 40% toward the designer in order to unlock the puzzle and get the idea . . . it asks the reader to take part in the communication of the idea. It is as if the designer throws a ball which then has to be caught. So the recipient is alert, with an active mind and a brain in gear."[27]

Comedy requires processing; it asks the participant to take part in the communication. People, on hearing a joke, process the joke in their mind and then retain the underlying information.

In addition, a joke requires the examination of a subject from multiple perspectives. Geniuses often demonstrate this same multiple-perspective ability. In *Cracking Creativity,* creativity expert Michael Michalko explained: "Geniuses think productively, not reproductively. When confronted with a problem, they ask themselves how many different ways they can look [sic] the problem, how they can rethink it, and how many different ways they can solve it, instead of asking how they have been taught to solve it."[28] He also explained: "Einstein was once asked what the difference was between him and the average person. He said that if you asked the average person to find a needle in a haystack, the person would stop when he or she found the needle. He, on the other hand, would tear through the entire haystack looking for all possible needles."[29]

The act of examining a subject from multiple angles greatly enhances the comprehension of that subject.

CUE CARD: Comedy forces learners to examine a subject from multiple angles.

Comedy Aids Memorization

Learning psychologist Jack Mezirow, in the article "Contemporary Paradigms of Learning," described learning as: ". . . a process of using a prior interpretation to construe a new or revised interpretation of the meaning of one's experience in order to guide future action."[30] Brain theorist Michael Gazzaniga, in *Nature's Mind,* described learning as: ". . . a search through our brain's existing library of operating basic networks for the combinations of those that best allow us to respond to the immediate challenge."[31]

Great comedy twists the common meaning of experiences to create new insights. To comprehend a joke, participants must focus on the details. The result is a higher absorption of information. In addition, when people see a joke they reconstruct it in their minds, causing them to repeat the material.[32]

As funnyman and learning expert John Cleese explains: "Make sure that all humor arises out of the teaching points . . . if they remember the joke, they've remembered the training point."[33]

CREATING COMEDY

"Some of the greatest comedians of all time never ad-libbed a line in their lives."—STEVE ALLEN[34]

But I'm Not Funny!

At this juncture, you may be thinking, "But I'm not funny!" It's entirely rational to think that. When you watch a performer as gifted as Robin Williams, it is easy to become intimidated. But the truth is, everyone is funny. You're funny too! This doesn't mean you will be the next Robin Williams. Performers like Williams spent years honing their craft. Fortunately, learners don't expect Robin Williams. What they expect is a boring classroom. What they want is an escape from that boredom.

Learners are so desperate for humor, and the learning environment so devoid of it, that a mildly amusing presentation is often enough. You certainly have the capacity to be mildly amusing. The remainder of this chapter provides you with tools and insights to help you tap into your natural comedic abilities.

Comedians are often no funnier than you or I. When comedians are off stage, many of them are actually reflective. They must be so. For their comedic material is based on deep insights about the world around them. Deep insight is difficult, if not impossible, without reflection. In *How to Be Funny,* writer Jane Wollman recorded comedian Steve Allen's observations:

"The popular conception of a humorist or comedian is of someone who writes, does or says funny things. But a funny person is also someone to whom funny things happen. The comedian's experiences are probably no more amusing than other's; he or she simply has a certain sensitivity

to the environment and circumstances and so perceives humor that a more serious person might miss."[35]

All the best performers have this ability. In 2002, the A&E Television Network selected whom they considered to be the greatest comedians of all times. Their choices were Steve Allen, Lucille Ball, Jack Benny, Milton Berle, Carol Burnett, Sid Caesar, Johnny Carson, Bill Cosby, Jackie Gleason, Bob Hope, Ernie Kovacs, Steve Martin, Groucho Marx, Richard Pryor, and Robin Williams.

Every one of these comics was (is) a great performer. Most of them were (are) not ad-libbers. Virtually all of them did their best work by following a routine. For example, Groucho Marx's classic *You Bet your Life* game show was entirely scripted.[36] So were most of Johnny Carson's *The Tonight Show* conversations. Ditto with Bob Hope's monologues.

It's not that comedians don't improvise. They do. But their improvisation relies upon a carefully built-up store of memorized material. Comedians draw from, and expand on, that material during a performance. To the audience, it looks spontaneous. For the performer, superb craftsmanship and a great memory are at work. The words of Steve Allen are illustrative:

> **"Comics with this ability [to ad-lib] are extremely rare. There may be fewer than fifty professional comedians on the planet that are skilled at doing it. [Most] comedians are indeed working without a script, but there is the crucial distinction that what they are doing is *recalling* jokes that already exist, which they apply to the situation of the moment. This is no small feat either, since one has to think rapidly and also have a remarkable memory—a memory card file through which the comic's brain can riffle at lightning speed. But again, as impressive as this feat is, it is more a matter of craftsmanship and professionalism than art."**[37]

We now turn our attention to this craftsmanship as we explore some joke telling formulas the comedians use to create their art. In the process, we will view several templates and worksheets that may aid you in creating jokes tailored to your learning environment.

Joke Structure

> "It's not wise to violate the rules until
> you know how to observe them." —T. S. ELLIOT[38]

Most comedy is built around a basic structure involving three steps:

1. *Introduction.* First, the subject is introduced in a way that builds curiosity.
2. *Detail.* Next, additional detail is added. The details build curiosity and tension without giving away the surprise. As a general rule, the longer the tension can be sustained, the greater the laugh will be in the surprise ending that follows.
3. *Surprise.* Finally, a surprise ending occurs. This ending releases the tension built during the joke, fits the *Introduction* and the *Detail,* but is not the expected conclusion.

For example, here's a joke for the magicians of the world:

My Dad, the Magician
On the first day of school, the teacher went around the room, asking each child about his or her family.
"What's your father's occupation?" asked the teacher to one boy.
"He's a magician, Ma'am," said the boy.
"How interesting." replied the teacher. "What trick does he do?"
"He saws people in half."
"Interesting! Who else is in your family?"
"One half brother and two half sisters."

Now, let's look at how the three steps work in this joke.

On the first day of school, the teacher went around the room, asking each child about his or her their family.

1. *Introduction.* First, the subject is introduced. We can immediately picture the teacher quizzing each class member. Interestingly, the age of the boy, his name, and the class size are left out. Those details would not add value to the joke, and thus are omitted.

"What's your father's occupation?" asked the teacher to one boy.
"He's a magician, Ma'am," said the boy.
"How interesting." replied the teacher. "What trick does he do?"
"He saws people in half."
"Interesting! Who else is in your family?"

2. *Detail.* Next, additional detail is added. We learn that the father is the magi-cian, and that his trick is sawing people in half. We begin to wonder who else is in the family, and what skills they might hold.

"One half brother and two half sisters."

3. *Surprise.* Much to our surprise, we discover that the subject of the joke is not the family members, but rather the dual meaning of the word "half" and that the word applies to this situation in more than one way, and that the second appli-cation implies magic tricks gone awry.

Table 5-2 provides a template for writing jokes. Use it to create some of your own.

With this basic structure in mind, we will now explore different categories of comedy, beginning with Comedic Words.

Comedic Words

Instructors know that words are powerful tools. So do comedians. Much of comedy is based on placing the right word in the right context at precisely the right moment. Below are four different word formulas comedians use:

- ▶ Silly Sounds
- ▶ Double Talk
- ▶ 'Punnish'ment
- ▶ Saying the Opposite
- ▶ Twist
- ▶ Multiple Twist

SILLY SOUNDS

In comedy, all words are not equal. Some are more powerful because they sound silly. See if you can select the comedic words from the listing in Table 5-3.

Comedic words provide an immediate comedic edge. Some words, such as *grape*, are not funny. Other words, suc;h as *papaya,* are. The word *carrot* does not inspire laughs. *Kumquat* does. Three points set the funny words apart:

JOKE CREATION TEMPLATE

Part 1: How To Write a Joke

1. Identify the subject you wish to joke about (class introductions).
2. List every idea you can think of that relates to that subject (family, family members, brothers and sisters, half brothers and sisters/occupations, magician sawing a woman in half).
3. Group related ideas (half brothers and sisters/sawing a woman in half)
4. Identify two ideas that fit together but have alternative meanings (half brothers and sisters could be siblings or part of a magician's sawing-in-half trick).
5. Write an *Introduction* (student introductions during the first day of class).
6. Select one of the ideas to be your *Surprise* (half brothers and sisters).
7. Add *Detail* that obscures the other idea (father's occupation is as a magician, his favorite trick is sawing a woman in half).
8. Set up the surprise (any brothers and sisters?).
9. Try your joke out on people, and keep tweaking it until it gets a favorable response.

Part 2: Structure Template:

1. *Introduction.*
   Introduce the subject.

   _____

2. *Detail.*
   Provide additional detail.
   ▶ *Detail 1.*

   _____

   ▶ *Detail 2.*

   _____

   ▶ *Detail 3.*

   _____

3. *Surprise.*
   Conclude with a surprise ending.

   _____

1. Funny words have more than one syllable.
2. Funny words include hard consonants.
3. Funny words have syllables that create an unusual rhythm.

The cartoon Witches' Brew, on page 109, provides on example. Where the words *Turkish crown* can be mildly amusing, *circus clown* has a decidedly funny ring to it.

Part 3: Structure Analysis:

1. *Introduction.*
   Is the Introduction brief?

   _____

   Is it easily comprehensible?

   _____

   Is the subject introduced in a way that builds curiosity?

   _____

2. *Detail.*
   Do the details build curiosity?

   _____

   Do they add tension?

   _____

   Is the tension sustained as long as possible?

   _____

   Do the details effectively hide the surprise?

   _____

4. *Surprise.*
   Does the ending release the tension?

   _____

   Does it fit the *Introduction*?

   _____

   Does it fit the *Detail*?

   _____

   Is the ending different from the expected conclusion?

   _____

TABLE 5-2

DOUBLE TALK

In a *Double Talk* situation, a word or phrase is used in its common context, only to be turned completely around and given a different meaning by the follow up statement. For illumination purposes, we will examine some real comedic lines. But out of respect for

WORDS I CONSIDER FUNNY

Below is a table listing a series of paired words. Circle the word in each pair that you think is the funnier of the two.

Absolutely	Indubitably
Banana	Apple
Celery	Cucumber
Collie	Aardvark
Cornbread	Cupcake
Horse Feathers	Cat Fur
Kazoo	Flute
Nebraska	Minnesota
Sarsaparilla	Soda water
Sausage	Kielbasa
Sorghum	Rutabaga
Succotash	Spinach

What are some other words you consider funny? List them below.

▶ _____   ▶ _____

▶ _____   ▶ _____

▶ _____   ▶ _____

▶ _____   ▶ _____

What are some possible uses for the words you consider funny?

_____

_____

_____

_____

_____

_____

ANSWER KEY: INDUBITABLY, BANANA, CUCUMBER, AARDVARK, CUPCAKE, HORSE FEATHERS, KAZOO, MINNESOTA, SARSAPARILLA, KIELBASA, RUTABAGA, SUCCOTASH

TABLE 5-3

currently working comedians, we will limit the jokes we examine to some past greats. See if you can spot the dual meaning in each of these classic lines:

> **"It's hard to lose my mother-in-law. In fact, it's almost impossible."**
> **—W. C. Fields**
>
> **"Marriage is a wonderful institution . . . but who wants to live in an institution?"—Groucho Marx**
>
> **"I just got back from a pleasure trip. I took my mother-in-law to the airport."—Henny Youngman**

Witches Brew   by Millbower and Yager

I said, "Turkish crown," not CIRCUS CLOWN!!!

Copyright © 2002 Stylus Publishing, LLC. Reprinted by permission from Cartoons for Trainers, Stylus Publishing, Sterling, VA.

Although these jokes are short on detail, they fit the basic introduction, surprise format. As in the "My Dad, the Magician" joke, the surprise occurs when the listener realizes that a key word has dual meanings, and that the one that is more obscure, less obvious, is the true meaning.

Table 5-4 lists several words with dual meanings. Try to identify the dual meanings.

'PUNNISH'MENT

A pun occurs when two words sound similar, but have different meanings, and when one word is substituted for another in a sentence. The result is an unexpected meaning that adds dimension to the statement. Here are some examples:

> **"Ice water? Get some onions—that'll make your eyes water!"—Groucho Marx**
>
> **"Say what you want about long dresses, but they cover a multitude of shins."—Mae West**
>
> **"He who hesitates is last."—Mae West**

Puns are good for moans and groans. They do not require great delivery skills, and yet they demonstrate wit. They also function well as morals to stories. Here is one possible example themed to customer service and Intranet technology.

DUAL MEANINGS

Below is a list of words or phrases. Determine an alternate meaning for each one.

Word/phrase: Sentence
  Common meaning: A group of words that make up a complete thought

  Alternate meaning: _A length of time spent in confinement_

Word/phrase: Institution
  Common meaning: An entity that has become a long-standing tradition

  Alternate meaning: _____

Word/phrase: Tea Bag
  Common meaning: A paper bag holding tea leaves

  Alternate meaning: _____

Word/phrase: Outgoing Mail
  Common meaning: Packages and letters to be mailed

  Alternate meaning: _____

Word/phrase: Fish Tank
  Common meaning: A box of glass designed to hold water and fish

  Alternate meaning: _____

Word/phrase: Civil Servant
  Common meaning: A governmental employee

  Alternate meaning: _____

Word/phrase: Stage Coach
  Common meaning: A mode of horse-drawn transportation

  Alternate meaning: _____

Word/phrase: Autopilot
  Common meaning: A mechanical feature that allows a plane to fly itself

  Alternate meaning: _____

ANSWER KEY: SENTENCE—A PRISON TERM; INSTITUTION—AN INSANE ASYLUM; TEA BAG—A SACK FULL OF "T'S"; OUTGOING MAIL—FRIENDLY MAIL; FISH TANK—A MILITARY VEHICLE FOR FISH; CIVIL SERVANT—A NICE BUTLER; STAGE COACH—AN ACTING TEACHER; AUTOPILOT—A CAR DRIVER

TABLE 5-4

The Naming of a Continent
Once upon a time, a global organization faced a tremendous challenge. This organization was contracted by computer manufacturers to provide customer telephone-based answer services. With independent branches in more than 20 countries, the organization was large,

but in danger of losing its contracts. Customers of all the branches except one, the Australian branch, complained that their questions were not being answered quickly. Desperate to fix the problem, the CEO sent a fact-finding mission to Australia. The result was a realization that the Australian branch had continually upgraded its Intranet [local area network (LAN)] technology, where the other branches had not. The company responded by upgrading its LAN at all the branches. Within three months, customer complaints had dropped by 30 percent. The contract was saved and the company discovered the value of frequent technology upgrades. And from that day forward, the company paid special attention to its Australian branch. It became their LAN down under.

This story has several potential applications. It could be used in communications, leadership, computer, and customer service classes. The writing of the story took a half-hour. I simply took a pun that matched the point I wanted to make, and concocted a story that would lead up to the pun. It is fairly easy to do, and requires only a ready collection of puns to choose from. Table 5-5 provides an opportunity to try your hand at creating such a story.

SAYING THE OPPOSITE

In this situation a comedian makes a statement, and then, speaking literally, says the exact opposite. See if you can spot the literal opposites:

> **"I could dance with you till the cows come home, on second thought I'll dance with the cows till you come home."—Groucho Marx**

> **"It's not the men in my life that counts—it's the life in my men."—Mae West**

> **"It is better to be looked over than overlooked."—Mae West**

Like *Double Talk* and *'Punnish'ment*, *Saying the Opposite* works because the lines surprise. Only in this case, the surprise comes from the contrast between the two statements. In Table 5-6, some phrases are listed. See what opposites you can come up with.

TWIST

Where *Say the Opposite* works by contrasting two statements, a *Twist*, achieves its humor through an unexpected twist on a prior reasonable statement. Some examples include:

> **"I have had a perfectly wonderful evening, but this wasn't it."—Groucho Marx**

'PUNNISH'MENT ANALYZER

Part One: How To Write a Pun:

1. Identify the subject of your pun (Communication).
2. List every idea you can think of that relates to that subject (electronic communication, Internet, intranet, LAN).
3. Select ideas from the list that could have alternate meanings, or are similar to other words. (What could "LAN" mean? What if the problem was related to Australia? Could it then be the "LAN" down under?).
4. Write the *Surprise* (the LAN down under).
5. Write an *Introduction* (a company was having customer service problems).
6. Add *Detail* that sets up the *Surprise* without giving it away (traveled to Australia where computer communications had been upgraded, the Australian branches intranet became the model).
7. Try your pun out on people, and keep tweaking it until it gets a groan.

Part 2: Pun 2: Pun template:

1. *Introduction.*
   Introduce the subject.

   _____

2. *Detail.*
   Provide additional detail.
   ▶ *Detail 1.*

   _____

   ▶ *Detail 2.*

   _____

   ▶ *Detail 3.*

   _____

3. *Surprise.*
   Select a surprise ending.

   _____

"When I'm good I'm very, very good. But when I'm bad, I'm better."—Mae West

"There was a girl knocking on my hotel room door all night! Finally, I let her out."—Henny Youngman

In these examples, the first statement seems innocuous enough. The second statement completely detours the meaning in a whole new direction.

Part 3: Pun analysis:
1. *Introduction.*
   Is the Introduction brief?

   _____

   Is it easily comprehensible?

   _____

   Is the subject introduced in a way that builds curiosity?

   _____

2. *Detail.*
   Do the details build curiosity?

   _____

   Do they add tension?

   _____

   Is the tension sustained as long as possible?

   _____

   Do the details effectively hide the surprise?

   _____

4. *Surprise.*
   Does the pun release the tension?

   _____

   Does it fit the *Introduction?*

   _____

   Does it fit the *Detail?*

   _____

   Is the ending different from the expected conclusion?

   _____

TABLE 5-5

In Table 5-7, several statements are listed. How would you twist them?

MULTIPLE TWIST

A *Multiple Twist* is similar to a regular *Twist,* but either delays its twist until the third statement, or twists twice. The first statement is altogether reasonable. The second is a little less so. The third completely veers into absurdity. Here are some examples from *Multiple Twist* expert Groucho Marx:

SAYING THE OPPOSITE

Below is a series of statements. Add a second statement that *Says the Opposite.*

He gets up with the chickens.

The chickens get down with him.

The early bird catches the worm.

_____

He who hesitates is lost.

_____

It is better to give than to receive.

_____

Only the strong survive.

_____

I have always believed in destiny.

_____

Hard work is always rewarded.

_____

She may be right.

_____

TABLE 5-6

> "He may look like an idiot and talk like an idiot but don't let that fool you. He really is an idiot."—Groucho Marx

> "I suggest we give him 12 years in Leavenworth, or 11 years in twelve-worth. I tell you what, I take 5 and 10 in Woolworth.—Groucho Marx

> "Look, if you don't like my parties, you can leave in a huff. If that's too soon, leave in a minute and a huff. If you can't find that, you can leave in a taxi."—Groucho Marx

Both the regular and the *Multiple Twist* are especially useful to facilitators who display a list. Simply twist the last item on the list, and read it off as if it were a serious point. For instance, a musical list of three could be:

TWIST

Below is the same series of statements used in Table 5-6, *Saying The Opposite*. Using those statements again, add a second statement that *Twists* the meaning.

He gets up with the chickens.

    Twist: <u>He sleeps in the hen house!</u>

The early bird catches the worm.

    Twist: _____

He who hesitates is lost.

    Twist: _____

It is better to give than to receive.

    Twist: _____

Only the strong survive.

    Twist: _____

I have always believed in destiny.

    Twist: _____

Hard work is always rewarded.

    Twist: _____

She may be right.

    Twist: _____

TABLE 5-7

> **Those famous classical musicians Beethoven, Mozart, Madonna, or Bach, Beethoven, Backstreet Boys.**

One example from my music in training presentations, based on my book *Training with a Beat,* is a situation in which I use the *Multiple Twist* formula. I begin by discussing classic pieces of music. With the words, "Here's a classic by . . ." I introduce two samples of classical music. My third example is then introduced as a classic by "Berry." Only in this instance, the classic I refer to is Chuck Berry's 'Johnny Be Goode.' This is the first non-classical reference in the presentation, and as such, the *Twist* is a complete surprise. It always evokes strong laughter.

In Table 5-8, several *Multiple Twist* statements are incomplete. How would you complete them?

MULTIPLE TWIST

Below is the same series of statements used in Table 5-7, Saying the Opposite. Using those statements again, add a second statement that twists the meaning.

Example: He gets up with the chickens.

    Twist: _He sleeps in the hen house._

    Multiple twist: _Yesterday he laid four eggs!_

The early bird catches the worm.

    Twist: _____

    Multiple twist: _____

He who hesitates is lost.

    Twist: _____

    Multiple twist: _____

It is better to give than to receive.

    Twist: _____

    Multiple twist: _____

Only the strong survive.

    Twist: _____

    Multiple twist: _____

I have always believed in destiny.

    Twist: _____

    Multiple twist: _____

Hard work is always rewarded.

    Twist: _____

    Multiple twist: _____

She may be right.

    Twist: _____

    Multiple twist: _____

TABLE 5-8

We have now completed our look at Comedic Words. Our next joke telling formula is Comedic Declarations.

Comedic Declarations

In contrast to Comedic Words, Comedic Declarations make comments that are at their core true, but have been overextenuated for effect. Here are three such formulas:

► Blunt Truth

► Exaggerated Truth

► Outrageous Retort

BLUNT TRUTH

Sometimes, the truth is all the comedy people need. *Blunt Truth* works best in situations in which no one expects to hear the truth. This format follows the basic structure of a joke, but ends with a bit of disarming honesty, spoken plainly, bluntly, and in an unexpected manner. Here are some examples:

> **"I generally avoid temptation . . . unless I can't resist it."—Mae West**

> **"A child of five could understand this . . . Fetch me a child of five."—Groucho Marx**

> **"From the moment I picked your book up until I laid it down I was convulsed with laughter . . . Someday I intend reading it."—Groucho Marx**

Table 5-9 lists several incomplete statements. Try to complete the statements with *Blunt Truths*.

EXAGGERATED TRUTH

An *Exaggerated Truth*, like a *Blunt Truth*, deals in fact, but stretches the truth to its comic limits. Some examples include the following:

> **"All the men in my family were bearded, and most of the women."—W. C. Fields**

BLUNT TRUTHS

Below is a series of uncompleted statements. Complete the statements in a manner that makes them *Blunt Truths.*

This was great.

It's almost as much fun as visiting the dentist.

I really enjoyed this class.

_____

You are the smartest person I have ever met.

_____

Only someone of your intellect could say that.

_____

That gave me goosebumps.

_____

The wonderful thing about relatives is their dependability.

_____

My mother-in-law is a delightful person.

_____

You car looks clean.

_____

TABLE 5-9

"I once spent a year in Philadelphia, I think it was on a Sunday."—W. C. Fields

"My hotel room is so small, the mice are hunchbacked."—Henny Youngman

During his heyday on the *Tonight Show,* Johnny Carson was famous for jokes that began with, "Yesterday was so hot . . ." The audience would respond with, "How hot was it?' Carson would take the opening to offer an exaggeration such as "Yul Brenner (a famous baldie) was frying eggs on his forehead." Table 5-10 provides a format for creating your own Exaggerated Truths.

EXAGGERATED TRUTHS

Below is a series of uncompleted statements. Complete the statements in a manner that makes them *Exaggerated Truths.*

The test was so hard that . . .

. . . even the teacher flunked.

Yesterday's class went so long that . . .

_____

Today we will have so much fun that . . .

_____

There was so much cheese on the pizza that . . .

_____

Our car is so old that . . .

_____

TABLE 5-10

OUTRAGEOUS RETORT

An *Outrageous Retort* is a completely absurd reply to a direct statement or question. The key to making an Outrageous Retort work is in the surprise the retort brings out.

(When asked: "How do you like children?") W. C. Fields: "Fried!"

(When asked by a Hangman: "Have you any last wish?") W. C. Fields, "Yes, I'd like to see Paris before I die . . . Philadelphia will do."

"Outside of a dog, a book is man's best friend. Inside of a dog, it's too dark to read."—Groucho Marx

An Outrageous Retort works because it is so unexpected and absurd in contrast to the introductory statement.

Table 5-11 lists several statements. Try to create some Outrageous Retorts.

OUTRAGEOUS RETORTS

Below is a series of statements. Reply to the statements in a way that makes them *Outrageous Retorts.*

Are you an only child?

I sure hope so.
_____

What makes you successful?

_____

How did you learn so much?

_____

What makes you so special?

_____

How is your day going?

_____

If you could do anything, what would you do?

_____

Why should I believe you?

_____

What's you favorite food?

_____

TABLE 5-11

Comedic Items

Just as some words are funny and others are not, some items have an inherent comedic potential. See if you can select the comedic items from the listing in Table 5-12.

For centuries, comedians have used props to create laughter. Ancient storytellers wore masks to identify themselves with the powers and properties of animals and gods. The waving of magical staffs added to the effect by enhancing their height. Ancient Greek actors wore masks to convey emotions to the audience, eventually inspiring the tradition of a costumed party.[39] Jesters wore multipointed hats and held scepters. Vaudevillians sprayed each other with seltzer bottles and danced with straw hats and canes. Groucho Marx wore funny glasses and gestured leeringly with his cigar. Jack Benny showcased his

COMEDIC ITEMS

Below is a table listing a series of paired items. Circle the item in each pair that you think is the funnier of the two.

Banana	Peach
Broccoli	Spinach
Clarinet	Kazoo
Harpsichord	Accordion
Lemon meringue pie	Apple pie
Oversized clothes	Undersized clothes
Pie tin	Rolling pin
Seltzer bottle	Champagne bottle
String beans	Cucumber
Tuxedo tie	Polka-dot tie
Volkswagen beetle	Lincoln town car
Watermelon	Strawberry

What are some other items you consider funny? List them below.

▶ _____   ▶ _____

▶ _____   ▶ _____

▶ _____   ▶ _____

▶ _____   ▶ _____

What are some possible uses for the words you consider funny?

_____

_____

_____

_____

_____

ANSWER KEY: BANANA, BROCCOLI, KAZOO, ACCORDION, LEMON MERINGUE PIE, OVERSIZED CLOTHES, ROLLING PIN, SELTZER BOTTLE, CUCUMBER, POLKA-DOT TIE, VOLKSWAGEN BEETLE, WATERMELON

TABLE 5-12

violin but not his wallet. And Gallagher displayed prop after prop, with his "Sledge-o-matic," actually two pie tins and a sledgehammer, smashing watermelons.

It is difficult to say what makes one object funny and the next not. Some of the lure of individual objects is in the way the object is handled. Jack Benny's violin wouldn't have been funny if it didn't play into Benny's pomposity. On the other hand, smashing watermelons is absurdly funny on its own.

Some comedic items include bananas, broccoli stalks, cream pies, glasses with an attached nose and mustache, plastic fish, hand buzzers, noise makers, plungers, potatoes, and hats. Hats can practically be considered a whole subdivision of comedic items. The simple act of putting a hat on transforms the person wearing it to anything the hat suggests.

For detailed information on Comedic Items, please see the props section in Chapter 7, "Lessons from Magic."

Comedic Situations

Not all jokes are verbal. Some involve situations. *Comedic Situations* are extremely helpful to noncomedians. When situations are properly set up, they are funny without the need to tell jokes. The comedy emerges organically from the material. In essence, the situation does the work for you. This is perhaps the biggest secret to television comedy. A properly set up situation can play out over several years. It is no accident that TV comedies are called sitcoms. Four sitcom formulas are of interest to us here. They are:

▶ Double Use

▶ Fish Out of Water

▶ Opposites Attract

▶ Practical Jokes

DOUBLE USE

In a *Double Use,* as in *Double Talk,* one item or a context is used for a purpose completely different from its original intent. In the movie *Mrs. Doubtfire* Robin Williams scored a huge laugh with a *Double Use.* Mrs. Doubtfire is based on the premise that the only way a divorced husband can see his children is by masquerading as a female housekeeper for his ex-wife. In one scene, the ex-wife's boyfriend is about to discover Williams' true identity because Williams' face isn't made up. To prevent discovery, William's character pushes a pie into his face. The pie serves as some sort of bizarre facial treatment, and preserves Doubtfire's secret. Beyond that, it's funny. The use of the pie is unexpected, and as a bonus, the pie also happens to be a time-honored, pie-fight-based, funny item.

Another example comes from the classic TV sitcom, *The Beverly Hillbillies.* It is filled with Double Use humor. The Hillbillies' "fancy eating table" (pool table) and "pot passers" (cue sticks) are two such examples.

From a learner's perspective (Figure 5-10), Role-play Extravaganza offers a visual example, in this case, recasting a role-play activity into a full-blown Hollywood production. For additional information, examine Table 5-13, which lists several items and some potential misuses for those items. See if you can match them.

Role-play Extravaganza   By Millbower and Yager

Quiet on the set!

This is the last time I'll volunteer!

MISMATCHED ITEMS

Below is a series of items. Connect them in a manner that makes them *Mismatched Items.*

Banana	Drumsticks
Blanket	Bulging eyeballs
Bread basket	Sword
Fork	Woman applying makeup
Marshmallows	Spaghetti
Pencils	Comb
Shoelaces	Hat
Wet Paint sign	Tent

ANSWER KEY: BANANA—SWORD; BLANKET—TENT; BREAD BASKET—HAT; FORK—COMB; MARSHMALLOWS—BULGING EYEBALLS; PENCILS—DRUMSTICKS; SHOELACES—SPAGHETTI; WET PAINT SIGN—WOMAN APPLYING MAKEUP

TABLE 5-13

FISH OUT OF WATER

A *Fish Out of Water* takes something from its usual habitat and places it where it doesn't belong. Although *The Beverly Hillbillies* relied on *Double Use* comedy, the show was based on the *Fish Out of Water* premise that the unsophisticated hillbillies were plucked down in the middle of upper crust Beverly Hills. The resulting misunderstandings created the comedy. In one example, upper-crust banker Drysdale advised the Hillbillies to invest in stock, so they bought some cattle and pigs.

Biker Sharing   **By Millbower and Yager**

Share your feelings with your neighbor.

Copyright © 2002 Stylus Publishing, LLC. Reprinted by permission from Cartoons for Trainers, Stylus Publishing, Sterling, VA.

Some examples of this formula include Hawkeye Pierce, the peace-loving doctor, serving in a *M.A.S.H.* combat hospital, Frasier Crane, the pompous psychiatrist, hanging out in a bar in *Cheers,* and Samantha, the witch, trying to fit into American suburban society in *Bewitched.*

In the adjacent cartoon, Biker Sharing, a rough and tough biker is placed in a sensitive classroom discussion environment. Although his discussion partner doesn't see the humor, it is a classic fish out of water situation. Another resource is provided in Table 5-14, which lists some potential habitats. See if you can mismatch people with those habitats.

OPPOSITES ATTRACT

In *Opposites Attract,* two incompatible people or items are placed together. The tension that results creates humor. This is a well-used structure of many comedies. Examples include Felix the neatnick and Oscar the slob living together in *The Odd Couple,* Martin Crane living with his son Frasier in the sitcom *Frasier,* and Sam Malone, the ladies man bartender, becoming involved with Diane Chambers, the pretentious intellectual, in *Cheers.*

Figure 5-12, Cave Conflict, presents an example of two mismatched individuals, a Neanderthal and a human. In addition, several different types of people are listed in Table 5-15. See if you can identify their direct opposites.

PRACTICAL JOKES

Please turn to page 521, and Table 14-1 for a full description of the appropriate classroom applications of practical jokes.

FISH OUT OF WATER

Below is a listing of people and environments. Mismatch the people and environments in a manner that places the people in the most ridiculous *Fish Out of Water* situations.

Beat cop	Convent
Blind man	Hardhat job
Cowboy	War battle
Hooker	China shop
Lounge singer	Harvard Law School
Peace activist	Country farm
Pretentious professor	Society party
Urban teen	Urban ghetto

ANSWER KEY: BEAT COP—HARVARD LAW SCHOOL; BLIND MAN—CHINA SHOP; COWBOY—URBAN GHETTO; HOOKER—SOCIETY PARTY; LOUNGE SINGER—CONVENT; PEACE ACTIVIST—WAR BATTLE; PRETENTIOUS PROFESSOR—HARDHAT JOB; URBAN TEEN—COUNTRY FARM

TABLE 5-14

LENN'S TEN

Below, I have listed 10 of my favorite instructor-friendly situation comedy bits of business. These activities are of the type that comedians and actors use to hone their improvisational skills. The ten, in alphabetical order, are:

- ► Ask the Expert
- ► Finger Rating
- ► Face Off
- ► Gibberish Interpreter
- ► Good News, Bad News
- ► I'd like to help, but . . .
- ► Read the Instructions
- ► Self-Alliteration

Cave Conflict   By Millbower and Yager

© 2002, Stylus Publishing, LLC.

Can't you two just get along?!

Copyright © 2002 Stylus Publishing, LLC. Reprinted by permission from Cartoons for Trainers, Stylus Publishing, Sterling, VA.

OPPOSITES ATTRACT

Below is a list of different people. Mismatch them so that they are in *Opposites Attract* situations.

Bachelor	Hooker
Businesswoman	High school dropout
College professor	Classical guitarist
Cowboy	Neatnik
Hard rocker	Construction worker
Nun	Baby
Peace activist	Army sergeant
Slob	City girl

ANSWER KEY: BACHELOR—BABY; BUSINESSWOMAN—CONSTRUCTION WORKER; COLLEGE PROFESSOR—HIGH SCHOOL DROPOUT; COWBOY—CITY GIRL; HARD ROCKER—CLASSICAL GUITARIST; NUN—HOOKER; PEACE ACTIVIST—ARMY SERGEANT; SLOB—NEATNIK

TABLE 5-15

► Theme Park

► What's Different?

Ask the Expert

The Action: Learners, one at a time, are brought to the front of the room and introduced as experts on a ridiculous subject. The learner is required to give a two-minute impromptu talk on the subject, and take questions about the subject from the other learners.

Suggested Use: Speech, communications, crisis management (thinking on your feet).

Parameters: Any subject will do, but the more ridiculous the expertise, the better the results. For instance, I have themed this activity to an automotive convention, and introduced learners as "New Car Smell" inventors, alien abduction record holders, and professional map folders.

Finger Rating

The Action: Learners rate a just concluded activity by standing, holding the number of fingers in the air that represents their rating, and finding another participant with the same rating, or an opposite rating, depending on the learning need. The new pair then discusses their observations.

Suggested Use: Interactive evaluations and discussions.

Parameters: Before the activity, provide instruction regarding appropriate finger usage. During the activity, play appropriate music.

Face Off

The Action: Learners pair off and face each other. The learners turn away from each other briefly. On the instructor's signal, they turn back around, and make funny faces at each other. The task repeats three times.

Suggested Use: Introductions, reenergizing activity.

Parameters: May be used in other contexts by directing the type of faces learners should make: angry faces for customer complaints or conflict resolution.

Gibberish Interpreter

The Action: One learner speaks gibberish, while the other translates what was said.

Suggested Use: To increase nonverbal communication skills.

Parameters: Can be used for paired introductions.

Good News, Bad News

The Action: Learners are asked to complete the paragraph, "I have some good news and some bad news."

Suggested Use: To dispel negative emotion.

Parameters: Emphasize the good news statements and treat the bad news statements as jokes.

I'd Like to Help, but . . .

The Action: Learners offer excuses for not doing something.

Suggested Use: To build a team spirit of cooperation.

Parameters: After all the excuses have been aired, gain consensus that the learners will help each other, and not offer excuses for avoiding teamwork.

Read the Instructions

The Action: A trainee, functioning as a assistant, reads a bulleted list of instructions that the trainer then follows. When the trainer reaches the third bullet, he or she reads, "I don't like this." The trainer pauses, startled, and says, "Nevertheless, we have to get through the instructions. Read the third point." The trainee repeats, "I don't like this." The trainer, realizing that something is wrong with the instructions, looks at them, and then responds, "Well, never mind that point. Read the next one." The trainee responds with the next line, "I still don't like this." The trainer then snatches the instructions away, and replaces them with a nondoctored set.

Suggested Use: In any situation where point-by-point instructions must be followed.

Parameters: The trainee must be able to read.

Self-Alliteration

The Action: Learners alliterate their own names, as a way of telling others something about themselves. Some examples might be "Daring Denise," "Lovable Larry," or "Rebecca the Rebel."

Suggested Use: Introductions.

Parameters: The same principle can be used with any word. By applying the technique to a classroom subject, the instructor can determine learner attitudes. For instance, feedback on a test could range from "Thought-Provoking Test" to "Terrible Test."

Theme Park

The Action: Learners are asked the following question: "If my organization were a theme park, it would be . . ."

Suggested Use: To open lines of communication regarding workplace issues.

Parameters: The thrust of the question is important, not the term "theme park." The sentence can be tailored to the specific training need.

What's Different?

The Action: Similar to *Face Off,* learners pair off and face each other. Next, they turn away from each other and rearrange an article of clothing. Both learners are tasked with spotting the changed item when they face each other again. The task repeats three times.

Suggested Use: Introductory activity, nonverbal communication, observation/listening.

Parameters: Limit the articles of clothing that can be rearranged.

FINDING THE COMIC YOU

"Little as I knew about movies, I knew that
nothing transcended personality." —CHARLIE CHAPLIN[40]

Now that we know some basic joke telling formulas, and some easy-to-use activities, we should turn our attention to finding the comic within you. For the truth is that comedy doesn't work unless it is genuine. And, it cannot seem genuine unless it naturally fits the person delivering it. As agent extraordinaire Bob Vincent explained in *Show Business Is Two Words:* "There must be basic honesty in the delivery of humorous material. Comedy is a very difficult, and a very delicate part of the entertaining arts, and there's nothing worse than a forced comic or a forced performer."[41] The key points are:

- ► Be Yourself.

- ► Look Funny.

- ► Develop a Sense of Timing.

- ► Find Funny.

Be Yourself

Look for the humor naturally present in your personality. For instance, when a person first meets me, my personality comes across as dry and self-controlled. I know this perception and use it to my advantage. When on a stage, I dress in conservative suits. I don't try to smile. I portray myself as semistuffy. But then things start to go awry in my performance. Sometimes it's a case of something unintended happening, where other times, it's a simple case of presenting very funny material with the straight face of an academician. The jarring contrast between my persona and the wackiness of what occurs makes the situation funny.

Look Funny

Studies demonstrate that people who smile are more likely to be hired and trusted in the workplace.[42] Smiling is a good start. Because of my persona, as I indicated before, I rarely smile. Pomposity looks funny without smiling. Whether you use a smile or not, you should strive to build a reputation as someone who is funny. Once you have that reputation, it is easier to make people laugh. They will expect funny out of you.

There are several ways to establish such a reputation. Eccentricity helps. So does looking funny. Outlandish ties, frizzy hair, and comedic items help. Hats, for instance, are great tools for tickling your funny bones. I have, readily available, a hard hat for taking flack, an Australian outback hat for walking about, a fisherman's cap for talking to people over cubicle walls (like the character Wilson in *Home Improvement*), and a Mountie hat when I need to find someone. The truth is that I rarely wear these hats, but they establish an attitude of offbeat eccentricity.

Perhaps my favorite hat, in combination with a prop, has helped give me a reputation as both an intellectual and a comic. I have, always near at hand and always on display, a prince's crown and a rubber skull. Invariably, when people first visit me, they will ask about the significance of the two items. I will reply, as dryly as possible, that the items are my emergency *Hamlet* kit. Often, the statement itself, an example of an *Outrageous Retort,* is odd enough to get a laugh of surprise. Other times, I must *Twist* the answer to get a reaction. In those cases, I put the crown on my head, and say, "To be or not to be." I then explain that you never know when you will feel the need to rant about the madness that surrounds you. The items and the application I have assigned them are just eccentric enough that my reputation for an offbeat outlook is enhanced. It makes funny easier.

Develop a Sense of Timing

As we have seen, the greater the tension leading up to a joke's surprise ending, the bigger the potential laugh. One of the worst mistakes novice performers make is stepping on their own punchlines. It is critical to wait so that the audience can catch up with you. When you present a surprise ending, your audience must figure out the meaning of the joke, and that takes time. If you do not give them time to process the joke's meaning, they won't laugh.

Once your participants have figured out the meaning of the joke, they still need time for the laughter to take hold physically. If you give them enough time to process the meaning, but not enough time to laugh, you will stifle the laugh. Worse yet, you will discourage future laughs. The audience will determine that the act of laughing prevents them from hearing what you are saying, and they will not laugh. In effect, you will have trained them not to laugh. The only solution is to stop and wait for the participants to catch up with you.

In music, the true art often comes not from the notes, but from the pauses *between* the notes. Just as you can't appreciate beauty without ugly, you can't appreciate the music without silence. The same dynamic holds true for comedy. Silence makes the joke funnier. Say what you want to say, and stop. Wait. After they have reacted, then continue.

Find Funny

Next, we want to turn our attention to ways of finding funny material, including the following:

► Look for Absurdity.

► Watch Comedy.

- ▶ Read Comedy.

- ▶ Collect Comedy.

- ▶ Try It Out.

LOOK FOR ABSURDITY

Finding funny is not difficult. The world is full of absurdity. One needs only to look for it. After all, what great comedians do is comment on the situations we all share. The difference between comedians and average people is that most people are too busy reacting to the info-fog to focus on the absurdities of life. Comedians instead focus on everyday details, and look for the absurdities inherent in those details. George Carlin, with his routines about carrying personal items on vacation, words you can't say on television, and different meanings for the same words, made a career of such observations.

WATCH COMEDY

We all watch comedy. But to find funny, you should stop watching comedians as an audience member, and begin watching them clinically. Try to identify the joke telling formulas they use. Watch for timing. Look at the ways in which their personas enhance their comedic presence. Most of all dissect the mechanics. The closer you look, the more you will appreciate the craftsmanship these performers demonstrate. You will find that you appreciate their work on a much deeper level.

READ COMEDY

The daily newspaper features a ready source of comic strips. The closer you read them, the more you will notice that the same gags recur time after time. As you read, you will begin to get a feel for how comedy is created.

COLLECT COMEDY

Start a file. If you find a comic strip you think is funny, clip it out and save it. Seek out jokes on the Internet. Join a daily joke list. Get a subscription to *Reader's Digest* or other magazines that feature comedy. Whatever source you use, the key is to have ready examples available to look through for comedic inspiration. When you have a funny observation, put it in the file too. Pay special attention to anything that makes you laugh. If you think it is funny, it probably is.

TRY IT OUT

When you come up with something you think is funny, try it out. Slip it into conversation. Share it with your family. Test it out in a classroom. If it gets a laugh, keep it. But don't stop there. Expand the joke. Try twisting it. See how much mileage you can get out of the basic insight behind the joke. As long as you still get a laugh, keep expanding it. When the laughs stop coming, you will know you have gone too far. Simply revert to the prior version. Then, look for another nugget of humor. Most of all keep working it. For although comedy looks natural when done correctly, it is hard work.

When Should I Use Comedy?

So, when should you use comedy? I don't know. There is no formula that answers that question. The audience, the subject matter, the class length, the venue, and your personality are all variables that must be considered. Look for comedic placements that support and enhance the learning, and use it there. If you have seriously evaluated what you are saying, and why those words make your instruction more meaningful, then you will make the correct choices.

If on the other hand, you sense your classroom has turned into a comedy club, then you are overdoing it. A little earlier, we discussed the concept that silence is necessary for music to be appreciated. The same idea holds true for the placement of humor. Humor is not a substitute for good instruction. Imagine instruction as a cake. Comedy is not the "cake." It is the "icing." If you use too much of it, you lose the flavor of the cake.

Comedic Pratfalls

"Comedy is a serious business. A serious business with only one purpose—to make people laugh."—W. C. FIELDS

As we said, comedy is hard work. Avoiding comedic pratfalls is even harder. Comedy requires a level of trust between the audience and the performer. Especially in the classroom, the rapport that comedy can build is too valuable to be carelessly gambled away. Here is a general list of don'ts that should help you avoid comedic pratfalls:

▶ Never announce in advance that you are going to tell a joke.

▶ Comments such as, "You'll really like this one" guarantee a nonfunny result.

► Don't explain a joke, either before or after the telling.

► If the joke falls flat, move on. Don't dwell on it.

► Humor is not a way of exerting power. Don't flaunt yourself.

► Never make jokes at another person's expense, especially if he or she is present.

► Be sensitive to your audience's sensitivities.

► Comedy should be good natured, not mean spirited.

► Don't overdo the jokes. Comedy is not a substitute for solid content.

This list may seem like common sense, and it is. In fact comedy is, in its worldview, its delivery, its attitude, and its application, common sense. For that reason, its use should not be feared. It is a part of the natural rhythm of life, and a helpful learning tool. The trainer who uses humor as an instructional tool will soon discover that trainees respond. If you use comedy effectively, your learners will enjoy your classroom; they will admire you for your wit; and, most importantly, they will retain your message.

[1] Smith, Dave (2001). *The Quotable Walt Disney: It Was All Started by a Mouse.* New York: Hyperion.

[2] Pike, Bob (1989). *Creative Training Techniques: Tips, Tactics, and How-to's for Delivering Effective Training.* Minneapolis: Lakewood.

[3] Rose, Colin, and Nicholl, Michael L. (1997). *Accelerated Learning for the 21st Century.* New York: Delacorte Press.

[4] Reinsmith, William (1992). *Archetypal Forms in Teaching: A Continuum.* Westport, CT: Greenwood Press.

[5] Michalko, Michael (1998). *Cracking Creativity: The Secrets of Creative Genius.* Berkeley, CA: Ten Speed Press.

[6] *Webster's Dictionary of Quotations* (1992). New York: Smithmark.

[7] Ibid.

[8] Provine, Robert, Ph.D. Special Report to MSNBC. May 27, 1999. <www.msnbc.com.>

[9] Ayto, John (1990). *Dictionary of Word Origins.* New York: Arcade.

[10] *The Koran* (500)

[11] Allen, Steve, with Wollman, Jane (1998). *How to Be Funny: Discovering the Comic You.* Amherst, MA: Prometheus Books.

[12] Feinsilber, Mike and Mead, William B. (1987). *American Averages: Amazing Facts of Everyday Life.* Garden City, NY: Dolphin Books.

[13] Morreall, John, Ph.D. (1997). *Humor Works.* Amherst, MA: HRDV Press. Childre, Doc, and Martin, Howard, with Beech, Donna (1999). *The HeartMath Solution.* San Francisco: HarperCollins.

[14] Provine, Robert, Ph.D. (1999).

[15] Vermeulen, André (May 22, 2000). ASTD International Conference. Session M508.

[16] Morreall, John, Ph.D. (1997).

[17] Childre, Doc, and Martin, Howard, with Beech, Donna (1999).

[18] Allen, Steve, with Wollman, Jane (1998).

[19] Davidson, John and Casady, Cort (1979). *The Singing Entertainer: A Contemporary Study of the Art and Business of Being a Professional.* Los Angeles, CA: Alfred Publishing.

[20] Provine, Robert, Ph.D. (1999).

[21] Ibid.

[22] Regina, Barreca (1991). *They Used to Call Me Snow White . . . But I Drifted: Women's Strategic Use of Humor.* New York: Viking.

[23] Loomans, Diane, and Kolberg, Karen (1993). *The Laughing Classroom: Everyone's Guide to Teaching with Humor and Play.* Tiburon, CA: H. J. Kramer.

[24] Highet, Gilbert (1977) *The Art of Teaching.* New York: Random House.

[25] Morreall, John, Ph.D. (1997).

[26] Highet, Gilbert (1977).

[27] McAlhone, Beryl, and Stewart, David (1996). *A Smile in the Mind: Witty Thinking in Graphic Design.* London: Phaidon Press.

[28] Michalko, Michael (1998). *Cracking Creativity: The Secrets of Creative Genius.* Berkeley, CA: Ten Speed Press.

[29] Ibid.

[30] Mezirow, Jack (1996). Contemporary paradigms of learning. *Adult Education Quarterly,* 46(3):158–172 quoted by Merriam, Sharan B., and Caffarella, Rosemary S. (1999). *Learning in Adulthood: A Comprehensive Guide.* San Francisco: Jossey-Bass.

[31] Gazzaniga, Michael (1992). *Nature's Mind: The Biological Roots of Thinking, Emotions, Sexuality, Language, and Intelligence.* New York: Basic Books.

[32] Sullivan, Luke (1998). *Hey Whipple, Squeeze This: A Guide to Creating Great Ads.* New York: John Wiley & Sons.

[33] Cleese, John quoted by Rose, Colin. and Nicholl, Michael L. (1997).

[34] Allen, Steve, with Wollman, Jane (1998).

[35] Ibid.

[36] Ibid.

[37] Ibid.

[38] Sullivan, Luke (1998).

[39] *The 1995 Grolier Multimedia Encyclopedia.* (1995). vr. 7.0.2. Grolier Electronic Publishing.

[40] Johnson, Bruce "Charlie" (1988). *Comedy Techniques for Entertainers: Charlie's Comedy Creation Course.* La Crosse, WI: Visual Magic Publications.

[41] Vincent, Bob (1979). *"Show-Business" Is Two Words.* Studio City, CA: Main Track Publications.

[42] Morreall, John, Ph.D. (1997).

CHAPTER SIX

LESSONS FROM MUSIC

ONE MORE TIME

My mom was a greaser. Or rather, she thought she was. Somehow, she never outgrew the fifties. She wore ponytails and angora sweaters right up until her death in 1995.

Another thing I remember is that movie: American Graffiti. She couldn't get enough of it. She said it reminded her of her high school days. Anyhow, we had the first videotape player in our neighborhood and a copy of American Graffiti as soon as it came on the market.

She made me watch it over and over. "Watch this!" she'd demand, "Maybe you'll learn something." Every Friday night, it was "One, two, three o'clock, four o'clock rock . . ." How I hated that thing.

Perhaps the worst time was the night my friends slept over. We were watching Solid Gold with Dionne Warwick, and the Bee Gees were being interviewed. "Staying Alive" was the number one song in the country, and we all had a crush on Maurice. Anyhow, Mom made us shut off the Bee Gees and watch that stupid American Graffiti again. To emphasize the point, she even moved the couch closer to the TV, "So that you can see it better," she said. I was mortified. After that, I watched Solid Gold at my friend's house.

But then the world changed. I went to college. Got a job. Got married. Had a daughter. Got divorced. And moved into Mom's old house. That's why I was cleaning out the attic today. While going through the various boxes and junk, I stumbled on a trunk of Mom's. In it were her old angora sweaters, some of her school assignments, her high school yearbook, dated 1961, and one other item.

And, I got to thinking. My daughter never got to know her grandmother. We had moved too far away. I took the item, went downstairs, moved the couch closer to the TV, and called my daughter.

"What are we doing Mom?" she asked as I motioned toward the couch.

"Come, sit here baby. I want you to meet your grandmother." I said, as I started American Graffiti one more time.

> "Music, when soft voices die, vibrates in the memory." —PERCY BYSSHE SHELLEY[1]

The Show Biz Training techniques in this chapter are based on the following Learnertainment Principles:

Principle 3: Cue the audio—add the auditory signal to the visual.
Principle 4: Evoke emotion—engage your learners emotionally.

Other Learnertainment Principles applicable to this chapter are:

Principle 2: Layer meaning—present your message on several levels.
Principle 6: Stage the environment—orchestrate every detail of the environment.

TRAINING WITH A BEAT

In my 2000 work, *Training with a Beat,* I fully explored the application of music in the learning environment. At that time, I listed 12 *Training with a Beat* applications:

- ► Music establishes a positive learning environment.

- ► Music minimizes negative conditions surrounding a subject.

- ▶ Music creates a metaphor for the task to be learned.

- ▶ Music provides background sound.

- ▶ Music assists with repeated tasks.

- ▶ Music aids memorization.

- ▶ Music transports learners to different times and locales.

- ▶ Music enhances reviews.

- ▶ Music frames games and activities.

- ▶ Music changes energy levels.

- ▶ Music fosters creativity.

- ▶ Music provides closure.

In this chapter, we will explore the techniques show business professionals use to enhance their entertainment with music. We will then search for interrelationships to the *Training with a Beat* applications.

MUSIC AND ENTERTAINMENT

Music comes from the Greek word, *mousiko's,* meaning "of the muses," in honor of the Greek goddesses who inspired all artists.[2] As the history of the word implies, music is an ancient art. Robert Sylwester, in *A Celebration of Neurons,* stated what many scholars believe:

> **"It's possible that music was a precursor of language—a primal ability to recognize and respond to rhythms and tonal variations that eventually led to greater complexities of language. When we humans went on to develop language, we may have kept music around because we liked the positive emotional overtones that it added to our life and discourse."[3]**

John Blacking, in *A Common Sense View of all Music,* concurred: "There is evidence that early human species were able to dance and sing several hundred thousand years before *homo sapiens* emerged with the capacity for speech as we now know it."[4]

The first cave fire stories were likely musical in nature. We will never know this for sure, but we can say assuredly that music was present in early entertainments. Ancient cave drawings tell us so. Often, they depict people dancing, and dancing implies some sort of music. In addition, remnants of musical instruments that date back 30,000 years have been discovered,[5] and artifacts found in ancient caves include bone flutes and percussion instruments.[6]

It is easy to imagine that early humans who could vocalize would have become known for their singing. The reverberating acoustics of the caves would probably have encouraged songs around the fire. In fact, archeologists have discovered that caves with the most primitive wall paintings tend to have the best acoustics.[7]

We may be able to discover adequate proof in the oral tradition. For example, Australian Aborigines make a life's study of music, including oral records of the society's customs, history, and social order."[8] Professional musicians (griots) act as historians in many African societies.[9] The African Tiv tribe, for instance, uses music to teach and define cultural norms within its society,[10] and Mande bards recount the histories of kingly lineage and offer counsel to contemporary rulers through music.[11]

As entertainment became an organized activity, its music usage became codified. Cave shamans gave way to jongleurs, troubadours, and minstrels. In time, solo instrumentalists became trios and quartets, and eventually whole symphony orchestras. As music developed into its own art form, entertainment forms that used music came to the fore. Opera became an established art form. Opera in turn led directly to the vaudeville and the dance hall stages. From there, it was a short leap to Broadway, and to film. All along, music grew in importance, until it reached its current stature as a driving force in the success of entertainment.

In a perfect world, we could discuss the application of music to entertainment in the context of live performance. However, I cannot bring an orchestra into each of your homes. And even if I could, the addition of 40 people plus instruments to your household would be disruptive. Instead of trying to discuss live without being live, we will focus on the application of music in motion pictures. For, although a film performance is not live, the musical applications are the same and have relevance to the learning environment.

HOLLYWOOD BEFORE MUSIC

Believe it or not, films didn't always have music. In the beginning of the motion picture industry, the films were silent, and the silence was not welcomed.

Moving pictures, usually a few minutes long, were first shown as a segment on a bill between live performances. From the first moment people saw the films, there was something wrong. It was too quiet. There was sound, but it was distracting noise. Every cough and shuffle of feet could be heard. So could the slightest whisper. The projectors rattled and clanged annoyingly. In that era before air conditioning, all the windows and doors stayed open, allowing street sounds to intrude on the entertainment. It was not a pleasant experience.

But that wasn't the worst of it. When a door closed on a screen, no sound accompanied it. Explosions were silent. And the people talked without sound. Worse yet, the people on the screen were pale white vapors; little more than reflected ghosts. Contemporary audiences described films unfavorably as "noiseless fleeting shadows," "cold and bare," "ghostly shadows," "lifeless and colorless," "unearthly," and "flat."[12]

Silent Scream   **By Millbower and Yager**

Go ahead, scream. No one can hear you. This is a silent film.

It was a ghastly experience. Fortunately, because these films were displayed in live theater halls, the exhibitors had a quick solution available to them. Much to the chagrin of their on-break musicians, they told them to play something during the film. Instinctively the theater owners knew that music would simultaneously neutralize both distracting sounds and silence. Music became such an internal part of the film experience that it was played continuously. If the picture moved, the musicians played. In fact, screening a film in silence was considered to be "an unforgivable offense" worthy of "severest censure."[13]

This "quick, play something" approach meant that the music performed had little relationship to the film being shown. It took several years for the film makers to realize what their live entertainment colleagues already knew. Music was more than a masking tool. The kind of music played was important too. In musician historian Charles Berg's words, "musical accompaniment could and should relate to the moving images."[14]

Unfortunately for the film makers, there was no effective control over the musical accompaniment, until, in 1926, the Bell Telephone Laboratories created a sound-on-disc recording system. One year later, The Warner Brothers studio released the first American "talkie," *The Jazz Singer,* with Al Jolson.

As a result of *The Jazz Singer,* by 1928, one short year later, the whole silent film industry was wiped out. Silent film stars, directors, musicians, and nontalkie theater locations went out of business. The public clearly preferred sound to silence, and wanted music as an integral part of that sound. As musicologist George Burt explained in *The Art of Film Music:* "When placed together to achieve a common goal, a great deal more is expressed than would be possible by means of either medium alone."[15]

Years later, radio faced a similar crisis. Television supplanted radio as the entertainment option of choice. In sharp contrast to the experience of silent film, radio did not die. It adapted, and exists to this day. It seems that the visual signal needed an auditory component, but the auditory signal did not need the visual image. In other words, people would accept the audio without the visual, but not the visual without the audio.

CUE CARD: People will accept audio without video, but not video without audio.

The classroom implication I take from this is the importance of the auditory signal. Learners who listen to a book on audiotape, will invariably supply their own mental images. Learners who watch a nonverbal video will invariably start talking to fill the silence.

In many classrooms, great effort is spent on supplying materials, easel pads, posters, and other visual aids. But, other than the instructor's voice, little emphasis is placed on the auditory cues and textures that accompany those images. The end result is similar to driving a car with only four of its six cylinders working. The car can drive, but the gas mileage is significantly reduced. So it is with instruction. The audio signal is too often neglected, and the learning potential significantly reduced.

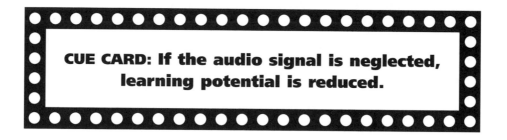

CUE CARD: If the audio signal is neglected, learning potential is reduced.

MUSIC AT THE MOVIES

A large part of a film's success depends on the simultaneous use of both the visual and the auditory signals. Where film directors capture the look of the film, film composers, working with the director, capture the sound of the film. In this way, the film communicates with the audience through both signals.

Orson Welles, the creator of the great film, *Citizen Kane,* was a true film pioneer in this dual communication. Welles approached film making with a novel attitude. He believed that every effort should be made to heighten the drama, and that music should emphasize the dramatic rather than the factual content.[16] It was a revolutionary approach.

Welles probably never met Bulgarian psychologist Giorgi Lozanov, but he would have agreed with Lozanov's comments in *Suggestology and Outlines of Suggestopedia:* "The language of music, rhyme and rhythm reach not only the ear, but the mind of man as well, via a much shorter path than logical facts and arguments."[17]

Other scholars agreed. Composer Arthur Schopenhauser once wrote that "Music was the incarnation of innermost reality, the immediate expression of universal feelings and impulses in concrete, definite form."[18] Sound psychologist John Ortiz, in *The Tao of Music*, added that "Music freezes images into recollections and releases recollections into images."[19]

These observations are backed by practical experience in a completely different field. Oliver Sacks, made famous in the Hollywood movie *Awakenings* and Robin Williams' portrayal of him, first came to professional attention when, in 1966, at the Beth Abraham Hospital in the Bronx, he began exploring the connection between music and individuals with severe neural illnesses. He was able, through music, to reach the most hopeless of individuals. As Sacks explained:

> **"After a stroke, patients may suffer from aphasia, the inability to use or comprehend words. But the ability to sing words is rarely affected, even if an aphasic cannot speak them. Some of my patients are unable to carry out a complex chain of actions: to dress, for example. Here, music can work as a mnemonic—a series of promptings in the form of a verse of song, as in the childhood rhyme, 'One, two, buckle my shoe.'"[20]**

Playwright Tennessee Williams agreed, "In memory everything seems to happen to music."[21]

Music has become such an integral part of film that approximately one third of every film has music accompaniment. In fact, successful films without music are rare. In general, the application of music in films has a basic structure, and Show Biz Training techniques follow that structure. Next, we examine those applications, and then explore applications to the learning environment.

THE STRUCTURE OF FILM MUSIC

As we begin this film music exploration, an important point must be made. Because live theaters playing silent films used their house musicians to provide film accompaniment, film music owes a great debt to the musical traditions of those early house musicians.

Live theatrical music was largely based on melodrama music, and melodrama music was an exaggeration of Wagnerian opera. Thus, film music structure is based on the structure of opera. As musicologist Roy Prendergast explained in *Film Music:* "If we equate the dialogue in a film to the 'sung words' of opera, we can see there is little difference between opera and film."[22]

Therefore, much of the information contained in this chapter is based on the musical norms developed in Wagnerian opera.

The Overture

Traditional live stage productions begin with something called an overture. The purpose of an overture is to set the mood, pace, and style of the presentation to follow. A traditional overture mixes all the musical themes to be featured. Generally, an overture begins brightly, with a fanfare or other attention-getting device that announces its presence. In the next few minutes, the overture transitions through the other major musical themes. The quietest point of the overture, the love ballad, is placed in the center. From the ballad, the overture builds to a rousing conclusion that leaves no doubt that the story is about to begin.

In epic films, this traditional overture format is followed. *Ben Hur* (1959), *The Ten Commandments* (1956), and *West Side Story* (1961) are but three examples. Often, the opening film credits are presented at this point.

Other films adapt their overtures to the emotive style of the film. An example is the John Williams overture for the film *Jaws* (1975). *Jaws* begins with murky movement through the water. With different music, the scene could have just as easily been featured in a Disney film. But instead, we hear a hint of an ominous lower register rumble. The camera picks up speed as it moves through the water, and the music increases in volume and in its threatening tone. Although this overture does not feature a medley of musical themes, it serves the function of an overture. It set the mood, pace, and style of the film to follow. The listener knows that this film will be no day at the beach.

Another classic film, *Star Wars* (1977) uses the overture to throw the viewer immediately into the action. A fanfare announces the beginning. Next, the background story for the film is scrolled on the screen, and the film's main musical theme is introduced. The effect is grand, magnificent, and sweeping. This overture tells the listener that an epic tale has begun, and sets the film up for success.

The James Bond series offers a final example. The Bond overture comes after a prologue. This prologue provides a vignette in which the never-defeated Bond conquers seemingly impossible odds. After the prologue, the overture begins. In this particular overture style, a pop song especially recorded for the film and performed by a well known recording artist is introduced behind the credits. The song will recur throughout the film, and in that manner, fits the classic definition of an overture.

Overtures in the Learning Environment

The same dynamic can work in a learning environment, when two of my *Training with a Beat* applications are applied:

▶ Music establishes a positive learning environment.

▶ Music minimizes negative conditions surrounding a subject.[23]

Many learners tense immediately on entering a classroom. For those people, personal experience suggests that learning is a chore, and learning cannot occur unless the learners face a number of challenges:

▶ The distractions of the info-fog.

▶ Admitting knowledge gaps in front of strangers.

▶ Negative memories of school experiences.

▶ Fear that maturity has dulled learning skills.

▶ Fear that inexperience will make learning difficult.

▶ Employee suspicion about management motives behind the learning.

As learners enter most classrooms, a sign welcomes them. The visual signal is present. But more often than not, the auditory signal is missing. The mood, pace, and style of the class are not projected auditorially, and an opportunity to engage distracted learners is lost. In *Training with a Beat* I explained: "Your learners should experience a positive, accepting climate the moment they enter your classroom. The learning environment you establish should be an irresistible invitation to learn. Music familiar to the learners, or appropriate to the learning environment, can establish this climate."[24] In *Emotion and Meaning*, Leonard Meyer concurred: "Music activates tendencies, inhibits them, and provides meaningful and relevant resolutions."[25] Music reaches past the thinking brain, into the emotions of your learners, disarming anti-learning defenses.

A fast, upbeat overture, directly related to the learning subject at hand, and familiar to the learners, can ease these tensions by, in essence, babysitting the panicky right cerebral hemisphere. It will help trainees open up to the learning in spite of their personal

---

OVERTURE PLACEMENT ANALYZER

Use this matrix to determine the effectiveness of the overture music you select.

Step 1: Select the overture music.
Begin brightly, with a fanfare or other attention getting device.

   Selection 1: _____

Transition through the other major musical themes.

   Follow-up selections: _____

The quietest point is placed in the center.

   Midpoint selection: _____

Build to a rousing conclusion.

   Concluding selections: _____

Step 2: Evaluate the music for effectiveness.

Does the music:	Yes	No
▶ Immediately capture attention?	_____	_____
▶ Set the mood of the training?	_____	_____
▶ Match the style of the presentation to follow?	_____	_____
▶ Establish a positive learning environment?	_____	_____
▶ Sound familiar to the learners?	_____	_____
▶ Directly relate to the subject at hand?	_____	_____
▶ End with a fast, upbeat pace?	_____	_____
Total Score (7 maximum)	_____	_____

The higher the Yes column score, the more effective the overture will be.

TABLE 6-1

challenges.[26] As in the movies, an effective overture will tell your learners that they are entering a different world. The Overture Placement Analyzer (Table 6-1) is one resource for identifying overture music.

Defining Time and Place

Every film occurs in a specific time and place. Where in a book an author can state the time, and discuss the location at length, films cannot. Often, a film must convey its time and place without directly saying so. The visual signal provides some information, and the audio provides the rest. At the first available opportunity, films use music to establish this context. In *Jaws,* it's no accident that the beach scenes have a top 40 radio station playing in the background. The music is from the 1970s, and the "radio station" soundtrack provides an excellent indicator of a lazy summer day at an American beach.

Perhaps the best film ever made, *Casablanca* (1942), takes place in Nazi-occupied Morocco. At that point in history Morocco was a French possession. With the fall of France to the Nazis, Germany began dictating the governance of all French possessions, including Casablanca.

Consider the difficulty director Mike Curtiz and composer Max Steiner encountered in establishing time and place. The location is an Arabic country, but governed by the French, who are in turn being dictated to by the Germans. If this isn't complicated enough, most of the major action takes place in an American cafe. Simultaneously, the music had to represent Arabic culture, French nationalism, German militarism, and American pop culture. A successful mix was achieved by placing Arabic strains, intermixed with echoes of the French national anthem, in the overture. As the film transitions to the American location, Rick's Cafe, the music turns to American jazz, and the song "Knock on Wood."

In one of *Casablanca's* best musical moments, a group of Nazis begin singing a Nazi anthem at Rick's Cafe. This is more than the French loyalists can stand, so the band and the patrons counter by singing the French national anthem. For the film, it is a defining musical moment. The hearts of the occupied French citizens are clear, as is the oafishness of the Nazi occupiers. The very fact that Rick allows the French national anthem to be played by his band also clearly identifies his sympathies.

All this activity takes place with minimal dialog. The actors do not discuss their feelings and motivations. No one explains the action. It just occurs, and in the process, clearly establishes the time and place. As Arthur Schopnenhauer explained in *The World as Will and Representation:* "When music suitable to any scene, action, event, or environment is played, it seems to disclose to us its most secret meaning, and appears to be the most accurate and distinct commentary on it."[27]

Defining Time and Place in the Learning Environment

Music can help establish time or place in the learning environment.[28] For instance:

▶ Nationalistic music can build diversity awareness of a specific culture, region, or country to be studied.

▶ Period music can place a history lesson in context.

▶ Show music can introduce or conclude a role-play exercise.

▶ Renaissance music can foreshadow a Shakespeare reading.

▶ Classical music can establish an aura of elegance for wine tasting seminars.

▶ Contemporary nightclub music can introduce bartender and responsible vendor programs.

▶ Celebratory music can provide closure to any activity, segment, or class.

The possibilities are limited only by the imagination of the trainer. Table 6-2 may provide a helpful overview of different musical styles.

Defining Characters

One of the primary musical applications that silent film musicians, and later film composers, borrowed from Wagnerian opera was the use of leitmotifs. A leitmotif is a musical theme associated with a specific person, place, object, or idea in a film.[29]

The leitmotif assigned to one of these entities is usually previewed during the overture, and fully introduced with the first appearance or mention of the entity. In a way, the leitmotif is the auditory equivalent to the visual identification of the entity. From the

MUSICAL STYLES OVERVIEW

This listing provides an overview of the major musical styles of Western music. It should not be used to limit your options. Select the music appropriate to your needs regardless of its origin.

TYPE OF MUSIC	HISTORICAL TIMEFRAME	MAJOR COMPOSERS	COMPOSITION STYLE	LEARNING USEFULNESS
Medieval	Pre-1450	Gregorian Chant	Voice-based music, simple instrumentation	Voices render it useless for reflection and small group discussions
Renaissance	1450–1600	Desprez, Dowland, von Bingen	Simplistic vocals, light instrumentation	Light instrumental selections helpful for quiet reflection
Baroque	1600–1750	Bach, Vivaldi, Mozart	Objective, steady, passionate	The best source of learning music with steady tones, high structure, and emotive qualities

Classical	1750–1820	Mozart, Beethoven	Complex, insightful, emotional	Varies depending on the individual composition; variations in volume may make it difficult to use effectively.
Early Romantic	1820–1860	Beethoven, Brahms, Wagner	Sweeping melodies, dynamic contrasts	Highly melodic music, changing dynamics can make this music difficult to use.
Late Romantic	1860–1900	Brahms, Bruckner, Tchaikovsky	Bigger, bolder sounds	Widely varying dynamics, choose selections carefully.
Impressionistic	1880–1918	Debussy	Designed to capture moods	Ideal for brainstorming
Twentieth century	1900–2000	Bartok, Ives, Ravel, Stravinsky	Chaotic, atonal, dissonant	Atonal nature renders it useless for learning
Movie Soundtracks	1927–present	Bernstein, Rogers & Hammerstein, Sondheim	Varies, dictated by the movie	Specific songs for specific situations helpful when properly placed, nonvocal selections ideal to recreate specific moods
Pop	1920–present	Various	Top 40, Country, and Easy Listening, and Rhythm and Blues	Use recognized, but not current songs as focal points for discussion or activity, to increase energy levels, to create better moods.
Rap	1985–present	Various	Chants, can be emotionally angry	Rhyming aids retention; use to recite a string of facts or statistics.
Jazz	1880–present	Miller, Benson, Strickland	Small combo to big band	Use light, up-tempo selections during breaks
New Age	1981	Enya, Winston, Yanni	Reflective, floating, dreamlike	Slower selections ideal for brain-storming, discussion, reflection

TABLE 6-2

point of introduction forward, each time the entity appears in the film, the musical theme repeats.

Leitmotifs must meet several criteria:

- ▶ They must match the entity's characteristics.

- ▶ They must remind the listener of the emotion the entity brings forth.

- ▶ They must be recognizable to the audience.

- ▶ They must be adaptable, so that the film composer can use them in a variety of settings.[30]

We will explore the use of leitmotifs through an examination of their applications in a number of highly successful films. All the films we will examine owe their success in large measure to the effectiveness of their film scores, and the way they utilized leitmotifs for their hero, heroine, and villain.

THE JAMES BOND SERIES

Perhaps the most successful film series in movie history is the James Bond films. As of this writing, a total of 20 official Bond films have been produced. Incredibly, the most recent film in the series, *Die Another Day* (2002), was one of the largest moneymakers of the series, with more than $300 million in ticket sales worldwide. Like the Energizer bunny, these films keep going, and going.

The James Bond theme music, written by Monty Norman and orchestrated by John Barry, is leitmotif based. Repeated in film after film, the music has given the films a seamlessness, as if they are chapters of a book, rather than individual films. They have also become ingrained in the pop culture. Musicologist Jeff Smith, in writing about the series in his work, *The Sounds of Commerce,* states that over half the world's population has seen a Bond film, and it is likely that virtually all of them can identify the "James Bond Theme."[31]

The basic film formula, with some variation, consists of five leitmotifs:

- ▶ The hero's theme.
- ▶ The hero swings into action.
- ▶ The scene changes.

▶ The heroine's theme.

▶ The villain's theme.

The Hero's Theme

The hero's theme consists of a repeating low brass four-chord progression. It has an almost catlike predatory quality, as if Bond is about to pounce. This theme is utilized whenever the film makers want to remind the audience that Bond is no ordinary man, and that he is about to solve the predicament he finds himself in.

The Hero Swings into Action

Often, the hero's theme is followed immediately by another that indicates Bond has swung into action. This "hero swings into action" theme features an electric guitar plucking a twangy melody played over the hero theme. Here is where Bond triumphs over adversity.

The Scene Changes

Once the hero has beaten the odds, the scene change leitmotif can be heard. It features a quickly repeating series of four notes, with each set of four being pitched differently than the set that proceeds it. The motif ends with a small fanfare, and a new scene.

The Heroine's Theme

As noted before, each film contained a specially written ballad, sung by known artists, including Rita Cooledge ("An All Time High"), Sheena Easton ("For Your Eyes Only"), Paul McCartney and Wings ("Live and Let Die"), and Carly Simon ("Nobody Does It Better"). Although played in its entirety as an overture, the song then becomes a leitmotif that repeats throughout the film, most often when the heroine is on screen. The song isn't always a love ballad, but it is used in all the softer moments of the film. Many of these songs have, because of their movie tie in, become hits in their own right. In some of the films, the ballad was not directed at the heroine, but rather at the villain. In those cases, special love interest music, soft and flowery, was created.

The Villain's Theme

As the heroine is different for each film, so is the villain, and the villains too got their share of theme songs. "Goldfinger" (Shirley Bassey), "Thunderball" (Tom Jones), and

"Tomorrow Never Dies" (Sheryl Crow), are three examples. In the films where the villain didn't rate his or her own song, there nevertheless was a leitmotif assigned to him or her. These too changed film to film.

THE *STAR WARS* SERIES

Like the Bond films, the *Star Wars* films have relied on leitmotifs, and have experienced a high degree of success. *Star Wars* featured leitmotifs for each of the major characters.

The epic/hero leitmotif used for both Luke and Han Solo is commonly referred to as "The Star Wars Theme." It features trumpet fanfares, an uplifting marchlike pace, and a slightly mellower middle section. This theme is introduced in the overture, and serves as a call to action whenever heroism is required.

A second, more sinister march theme serves as a militaristic theme for the empire. These two major leitmotifs are supported by a number of smaller ones. Princess Leia has her own sweet, soft, theme, Obi-Wan's leitmotif is mystical and majestic; and Darth Vader's is a low brass rumble written to imply menace.[32]

VILLAINOUS PSYCHO JAWS

Perhaps the best villain motifs ever written are John William's frightening lower register cello and bass rumble for *Jaws,* and Bernard Herrmann's slashing violins in Alfred Hitchcock's *Psycho* (1960). Both themes are so vivid and powerful that they are quoted in virtually every horror film.

We have already discussed how the *Jaws* theme is introduced in the overture. What we did not mention is that, during the entire overture, we never see the shark. Director Steven Spielberg had no shark to film. "Bruce," as the film crew dubbed the mechanical shark used during production, wouldn't work for most of the film shoot. Spielberg's only option, fortunately for all of us, was to rely on the auditory signal to portray Bruce. Bruce doesn't show up until almost an hour of the film has passed, and yet, the auditory signal was so powerful, that "ddaaahhh ddaaahhh, dah dah, dah dah, dah, dah" still means underwater terror to people 25 years later!

In *The Art of Film Music,* George Burt once commented: "When we see pictures and hear music at the same time we invariably make a connection, if only on an unconscious level."[33]

Spielberg and Williams, knowing the truth of this statement, used Bruce's leitmotif to play with the audience. Occasionally, Bruce's leitmotif sounded, and the audience tensed, expecting the shark's arrival. Several of these instances turned out to be sharkless audience teases. On other occasions, Bruce showed up without being announced. One such example is the scene in which the Roy Scheider character panned chum, a mixture of fish blood and guts, into the water, and the shark popped up behind him. Because no leit-motif was present, this appearance caught the audience completely by surprise. It was powerful film making, with the auditory signal as a full partner to the visual.

Psycho is another example of a leitmotif stealing the scene. In *Psycho,* Janet Leigh is knifed to death while taking a shower. The movie was filmed in black and white to make it as stark as possible. In addition, film director Hitchcock edited the killing scene so that each image was itself a slash, lasting less than a second. Hitchcock's intent was to not place music in the scene. In keeping with the stark look he had created, he wanted the audio to be as cold as possible. In a famous "I told you so" moment, composer Herrmann insisted that the scene required music. Hitchcock disagreed, paid Herrmann for his work, and told the composer that the score was done.

After several viewings, Hitchcock was forced to admit his error. The scene just didn't work. The lack of an auditory signal doomed it. Hitchcock recalled Herrmann, and Herrmann wrote the slashing sounds that have become the film's lasting implant on the minds of filmgoers.[34]

Leitmotifs in the Learning Environment

All the films we have discussed are rightly famous. Their leitmotifs added an extra di-mension that made them whole. When integrated in this manner, leitmotifs cannot be separated from the images that accompanied them. Simply hearing the music again evokes the feeling of the filmed moment. The two pieces, the auditory and the visual, are so interwoven that they have become one, and speak with greater clarity than either could alone.

Obviously, you don't have characters in your learning environment—that is, in the Hollywood sense. But you do have themes. Properly selected music can enhance and val-idate your theme. From "Short People" for diversity, to "Respect" for sexual harassment, to "Time After Time" for time management, to "Burning Down the House" for change, the pop music world is awash in musical selections that can provide leitmotifs for your learning environment.

Leitmotifs, in the form of sound effects, can be used to add an auditory element to the classroom. A siren to announce fire extinguisher training, a gong that signifies the end of a segment, a triangle to announce lunch, or a referee's whistle to end a game are all useful motifs given the right situation. Table 6–3 can help you select the correct leitmotifs.

Game show style activities are another effective use for leitmotifs. In *Training with a Beat,* I explored this topic: "Any learning activity can be tied to appropriate musical themes. For example, game shows allow instructors to test material in a non-threatening

LEITMOTIF PLACEMENT ANALYZER

Use this matrix to determine the effectiveness of the leitmotifs you select.

Step 1: Select leitmotifs.

1. List the major themes of your learning environment.

   Theme 1: _____

   Theme 2: _____

   Theme 3: _____

   Theme 4: _____

   Theme 5: _____

2. What songs (or sound effects) relate to those themes?

   Theme 1: _____

   Theme 2: _____

   Theme 3: _____

   Theme 4: _____

   Theme 5: _____

3. Where can you place those songs (or sound effects) in the context of your instruction?

   Theme 1: _____

   Theme 2: _____

   Theme 3: _____

   Theme 4: _____

   Theme 5: _____

Step 2: Evaluate the music for effectiveness.

Do the letimotifs you selected: Yes   No

▶ Align with the class content?   _____   _____
▶ Communicate information about their assigned situation? _____   _____
▶ Help the learners connect to the assigned situation?   _____   _____
▶ Make an emotional connection with your learners?   _____   _____

The higher the Yes column score, the more effective the leitmotif will be.

TABLE 6-3

manner. Themed music frames such activities, making them less test like and more enjoyable."[35]

Game show music can be used while:

▶ Introducing the game show—High energy music that hypes the activity and relates to the subject matter is appropriate.

▶ Displaying the prizes—Light, up-tempo music without vocals that stays in the background.

▶ Seeking and introducing game show players—High-energy music that creates a sense of movement and excitement as people come to the front of the room.

▶ Asking questions—Atmospheric nonvocal music that heightens tension without attracting too much attention.

▶ Timing answers—Short, timed, nonvocal pieces of music that stop playing when it is time for the players to answer the question.

▶ Conducting lightning rounds—Very short musical segments that keep the energy level focused and forward-moving; tick tock clock sounds work well in this context.

▶ Thanking the players—High energy music, usually the same as the Seeking and Introducing Players music, that creates a sense of movement as people return to their seats.

▶ Concluding the activity—High energy music that concludes the activity on a positive note, and relates to the subject matter is appropriate; usually the same theme that opened the activity.

Table 6-4, the Game Show Music Placement Analyzer is provided as a resource to aid you in selecting appropriate game show music.

Creating an Atmosphere

As we have learned in prior chapters, people absorb information simultaneously on multiple levels. Learning is more effective when you orchestrate your environment so that all the layers of meaning speak in concert. Film makers pay special attention to this very principle. Music is often present in the background of films. It serves to create an atmosphere in which the film occurs. In *Music for the Movies,* Tony Thomas explained: "Film music is essentially dramatic music, not descriptive music. Music functions to point the

GAME SHOW MUSIC PLACEMENT ANALYZER

Use this matrix to aid you in selecting appropriate game show music.

Introducing the game show

Selection: _____

Does the music	Yes	No
▶ Exhibit high energy?	_____	_____
▶ Hype the activity?	_____	_____
▶ Relate to the subject matter?	_____	_____

Displaying the prizes

Selection: _____

Does the music

▶ Display a light up-tempo feel?	_____	_____
▶ Have no vocals?	_____	_____
▶ Stay in the background?	_____	_____

Seeking and introducing game show players

Selection: _____

Does the music

▶ Display high energy?	_____	_____
▶ Create a sense of movement?	_____	_____
▶ Create a sense of excitement?	_____	_____

Asking questions

Selection: _____

Does the music

▶ Have no vocals?	_____	_____
▶ Heighten tension?	_____	_____
▶ Stay in the background?	_____	_____

Timing answers

Selection: _____

Does the music

▶ Play in short segments?	_____	_____
▶ Length match the timed length required?	_____	_____
▶ Have no vocals?	_____	_____

Conducting lightning rounds

Selection: _____

Does the music	Yes	No
▶ Play in short musical segments?	____	____
▶ Keep the energy level focused?	____	____
▶ Keep the momentum moving forward?	____	____

Thanking the players

Selection: _____

Does the music

	Yes	No
▶ Display high energy?	____	____
▶ Repeat the players' introductory music?	____	____
▶ Create a sense of movement?	____	____

Concluding the activity

Selection: _____

Does the music

	Yes	No
▶ Display high energy?	____	____
▶ Relate to the subject matter?	____	____
▶ Conclude on a positive note?	____	____
Total score (24 maximum)	====	====

The higher the Yes column score, the more effective the overture will be.

TABLE 6-4

dramatic atmosphere of the film and add one more emotional plane to an attack which is already being made on the visual sense."[36]

George Burt explained the application of music to atmosphere as follows: "The music interacts with the intrinsic meaning of the sequence, as distinct from a surface-level meaning; it is addressed to what is implicit within the drama, not to what is explicit (such as the visual action), that is, to what you cannot see but need to think about."[37]

Roy Prendergast, speaking in *Film Music*, added, "The ability of music to make a psychological point in film is a subtle one, perhaps it's most valuable contribution."[38] And Composer David Raksin explained that music's function is to "help realize the meaning of a film."[39]

As these comments indicate, the atmosphere of a film is highly dependent on its music, and the true art of a film composer is to capture the atmosphere for each film he or she works on. Composer Ernest Gold explains that he "tries to find musical atmosphere that belongs to that film alone."[40]

Successful films capture that atmosphere. The *Jaws* theme created an atmosphere of underwater terror. The *Star Wars* theme established the feeling of grand adventure. Francis Ford Coppola's *The Godfather* (1972) and its two sequels makes extensive use of Italian ballads that build a feeling irony and poignancy.

Psycho provides an excellent example of sophisticated film composing techniques. The film's two main characters were fatally flawed psychopaths. The beautiful girl turned out to be a thief, while the nice looking boy was revealed as a murderer. As we mentioned before, Hitchcock filmed the movie in black and white, giving it an empty and stark feel. Composer Herrmann matched the visual mood with a score that had the orchestral texture of strings, but lacked the fullness of a complete orchestra. When placed together, the visual and auditory signals gave the entire film an atmosphere of hollowness that added to the film's eerie mystique.

Creating an Atmosphere in the Learning Environment

Perhaps the most important atmospheric element to any learning environment is a feeling of playfulness suggested by the Learnertainment principle: *Make it fun—create an atmosphere of playfulness.* Music has the ability to create warmth where none exists. Music changes the energy level of a room, depending on the instructor's need:

► Fast music featuring high rhythmic activity and short, quick notes suggest "happiness."

► Slow pieces of music featuring low rhythmic activity indicate "sadness."

► High rhythmic activity implies "excitement."

► Low rhythmic activity suggests "calmness."[41]

With this information, you can establish the atmosphere you want when you want it:

► Fast, major key music can encourage better moods after a period of intense concentration.

► Slow, minor key music can calm your learners down after a heated discussion.

► Fast, major key music with high rhythmic activity and short, quick notes can create a happy atmosphere after a depressing, worrisome discussion.

▶ High rhythmic music can boost excitement levels when learners are bored.

▶ Minor key music with low rhythmic activity can calm aggressive tendencies.[42]

Use the Atmospheric Music Analyzer provided in Table 6–5 as an aid in selecting atmospheric music.

Providing Background Filler

Some film music serves the mundane function of tying the disparate elements of a film together. A true silent film was a jarring experience because of its lack of warmth, and the sense of disjointedness that quick camera shots bring. Music often masks this silence. As Aaron Copeland described it: "This is really the kind of music one isn't supposed to hear, the sort that helps to fill the empty spots between pauses in a conversation. Music can help build a sense of continuity in a film. Music can tie together a visual medium that is, by its very nature, continually in danger of falling apart."[43]

For films, this application of music is functional. There is no motivation except to prevent the film from mentally unraveling. Incidental music serves that function, and film makers were forced by their audience to use music for this purpose. For functional music predated film.

Functional music got its start after the advent of silent film, but before the talkies, when one man, Brigadier General George Owen Squier, had a vision that music could help people be more effective in daily life. In 1922, he created a whole new genre of music, commonly called "elevator music."

Oddly enough, the term "elevator music" is correct. In the late 1880s, elevators were a new phenomenon. To many people, the thought of getting into a platform that would raise them several floors was a nerve-wracking idea. People were even afraid of motion sickness! To overcome popular reluctance, elevator operators were hired. Eventually, the economic cost of elevator operators proved too expensive, and they were replaced with Squire's brain child, Muzak.

Muzak was created to fill silence with an auditory signal that could reduce stress, combat fatigue, and enhance sales. It worked so well that an estimated 90 million people listen to Muzak each day.[44] And, from a musicology standpoint, it is no wonder. Music is well suited to these applications. Among the studies are the findings that background music:

▶ Creates better moods, happier thoughts, and greater relaxation.[45]

▶ Reduces on-the-job accidents.[46]

ATMOSPHERIC MUSIC ANALYZER

Use this matrix as an aid in selecting appropriate atmospheric music.

To enhance feelings of happiness:
► Fast music with high rhythmic activity; short, quick notes

Selection 1: _____

Selection 2: _____

Selection 3: _____

To encourage sadness:
► Slow music with low rhythmic activity

Selection 1: _____

Selection 2: _____

Selection 3: _____

To build excitement:
► High rhythmic activity

Selection 1: _____

Selection 2: _____

Selection 3: _____

To create a feeling of calm:
► Slow, minor key music; low rhythmic activity

Selection 1: _____

Selection 2: _____

Selection 3: _____

To encourage better moods:
► Fast, major key music

Selection 1: _____

Selection 2: _____

Selection 3: _____

To overcome boredom:
► High rhythmic music

Selection 1: _____

Selection 2: _____

Selection 3: _____

TABLE 6-5

▶ Provides an illusion of distended time.[47]

▶ Boosts worker production.[48]

▶ Increases alertness in reaction time.[49]

▶ Creates dedicated and concentrated moods.[50]

▶ Creates a sense of privacy for small group discussion, making conversations more satisfying.[51]

▶ Makes people more likely to say what they feel.[52]

▶ Helps people reach a greater depth of self-exploration.[53]

▶ Increases performance on nonverbal tasks.[54]

▶ Increases retention of vocabulary and grammar.[55]

▶ Promotes more affective interaction between people.[56]

▶ Reduces stress levels.[57]

▶ Helps alleviate wait-related stress.[58]

One of the reasons for Muzak's success has to do with its pacing. Its selections match the hour of the day, with peppy melodies and hyper rhythms in the morning, light pop at lunch time, mellow selections in the mid-afternoon, classic pop at dinner time, and higher energy selections in the evening.

In addition, all of Muzak's programming is arranged into quarter-hour blocks. The music is designed to match the energy cycles of employees. At the beginning of a programming block, the music starts softly. From that point forward, it builds until, at 15 minutes, it reaches its peak in volume. It then starts over again, repeating this cycle every 15 minutes. Muzak's researchers say that this "Stimulus Progression" effectively counters worker fatigue. They have validated that the Stimulus Progression is credited with:

▶ Increased office output

▶ Reduced stress

▶ Enhanced concentration

▶ Improved employee morale[59]

You may be thinking, "I don't like the music." Muzak's research suggests likability isn't necessarily relevant. Joseph Lanza, in *Elevator Music*, quotes one of the principle researchers, Richard Cardinell, as saying: "In some cases, it is possible to achieve a direct production increase by playing a program which completely ignores employee preferences and concentrates on the function aspects only."[60]

Creating Background Filler in the Learning Environment

Obviously, you do not want background music playing throughout your class. Movies don't feature continuous background music either. Instead, look for those occasions where background music can enhance the environment. Possibilities include:

► When many people are talking at once

► During small group discussions

► In solo reflection periods

► During creative visioning exercises

► While practicing repetitive tasks

► During breaks

► To enhance reviews

WHEN MANY PEOPLE ARE TALKING AT ONCE

When large groups are tasked with talking simultaneously, the noise can be deafening. Music can take the edge off of the sound. In a crowded room, music acts much like lemon to a plate of fish. Lemon, when sprinkled on the fish, cuts the odor. Music, when played softly in the background of a discussion period, serves as a masking agent, and cuts the noise.

DURING SMALL GROUP DISCUSSIONS

During small group discussions, learners who are sitting near, and in some cases, next to each other are placed in different groups. To help your learners focus on their own group, rather than listening to another group's conversation, play music. Music adds a layer of sound that prevents learners from focusing on other groups.

IN SOLO REFLECTION PERIODS

When learners are asked to reflect on a subject, any sound can disrupt their thoughts. Much as theaters used house bands to cover up crowd noise during the projection of silent films, light, slow, reflective music serves as a buffer between individual coughs and whispers. An additional bonus is the fact that slow, reflective music helps learners think.

DURING CREATIVE VISIONING EXERCISES

In *Music and the Mind,* musicologist Anthony Storr commented: "Music plays a special role in aiding the scanning and sorting process which goes on when we are day-dreaming."[61]

Music has been proven to enhance creativity.[62] For example, it was reported that classical music intensifies the ability of people, regardless of their visualizing ability, to be creative. Music used during brainstorming exercises helps your learners develop and link material in connecting applications.[63] Music can give your learners musical anchors to attach their brainstorms too.[64]

Table 6-6 may help you select appropriate background filler.

WHILE PRACTICING REPETITIVE TASKS

Repetitive tasks are made easier by music. If you exercise, you may already know this to be true. Our bodies have a rhythm. Our heart beats, we breathe in and out, and our blood

---

BACKGROUND MUSIC ANALYZER

Use this matrix as an aid in selecting appropriate background filler.

Part 1: The need for music

Are your learners:	Yes	No
▶ Involved in a group discussion?	_____	_____
▶ Involved in a paired discussion?	_____	_____
▶ Reflecting on a subject?	_____	_____
▶ Working privately, on solo activities?	_____	_____
▶ Practicing creative visioning?	_____	_____

If you answered "Yes" to any of these questions, background music would be effective.

Part 2: Selecting appropriate music

Is the music you would like to use:	Yes	No
▶ Slow	_____	_____
▶ Reflective	_____	_____
▶ Melodic	_____	_____
▶ Nonvocal	_____	_____
▶ Instrumentally light	_____	_____

If you answered "Yes" to all of these questions, you chose an effective selection.

TABLE 6-6

pulses, all in time. Some amazing feats have been accomplished by tying tasks to music. African slaves, for instance, used work chants to survive the backbreaking work of picking cotton. The workmen who built the transcontinental railroad sang as they drove spikes into the rails. The soldiers who fought for freedom sang as they marched hundreds of miles.

If your trainees are required to learn repetitive tasks, background music can help. Music helps learners:

- ▶ Repeat monotonous tasks with a higher level of interest[65]

- ▶ Alleviate anxiety[66]

- ▶ Work longer[67]

- ▶ Elongate their attention span[68]

- ▶ Improve task concentration[69]

- ▶ Increase task speed[70]

- ▶ Build consistency[71]

Simply select a piece of music that pulses at a speed complementary to the task at hand. Table 6–7 is an aid you can use.

REPETITIVE TASK MUSIC ANALYZER

When selecting music for repetitive tasks, answer the following questions:

	Yes	No
▶ Is the music steady in its rhythm?	_____	_____
▶ Can you walk to the rhythm of the music?	_____	_____
▶ Can you perform the repetitive task to the music?	_____	_____
▶ If the music has lyrics, will the learners be able to sing them?	_____	_____
▶ Can the lyrics be rewritten to correspond with the repetitive task?	_____	_____
▶ Do you have the ability to speed up the music as task skills increase?	_____	_____
▶ If the music is sped up, does it still sound acceptable?	_____	_____

If you answered "Yes" to all the questions, the music is appropriate for repetitive tasks.

TABLE 6-7

DURING BREAKS

The lack of sound on breaks can undercut the comfortable atmosphere you may have built. Select and play music appropriate to the instruction that just occurred. If your learners are all keyed up and you feel the need to calm them down, play some slower reflective music. If the segment just ended required intense concentration, play up-tempo music that will help your learners unwind. As the break reaches its halfway point, switch music. Play selections more appropriate to the segment you will soon begin. One minute before the break ends, turn the music up to indicate that the learners should return, and then turn it off when you are ready to start.

TO ENHANCE REVIEWS

In Chapter 4, we discussed Giorgi Lozanov's theory of "Suggestopedia." There are some specific Suggestopedic techniques relevant to reviews. Lozanov created what he called "passive" and "active" concerts.

Lozanov believes that suggestion is more easily accepted when the student is in a deeply relaxed condition, both mentally and physically. He described this relaxed state as a "special internal setup of serene memorization without worry, strain or effort."[72] To achieve this level of relaxation in his learners, his reviews would include deep-breathing exercises, a comfortable and relaxed position, a calm, pleasant atmosphere, a background of classical music, and the recitation of critical information.

In an active concert, the learners recite the key points. In a passive concert, the instructor reads the points. In this application, slow Baroque or early Classic period music, pulsing at a rate parallel to that of the human heart, around 60 to 80 beats per minute, can be employed as background to a recitation review of critical information.

An effective passive concert review method is to place key review points into a PowerPoint style presentation. Simply create one slide for each review point. Set the timing of the presentation so that the questions change automatically every few seconds. Next, add music. Immediately prior to presenting this review to your learners, have them take a few deep breathes, and stretch their muscles out. Then invite them to sit back, relax, and read the statements that appear on the screen. The end result will be an automatic and effective review in which you don't need to say a word. For an active concert version, have your learners recite the review information as the music plays. If neither of these ideas appeal to you, you could play slow reflective music in the background while your learners silently review. Use Table 6-8 to help you select appropriate material.

REVIEW ENHANCING MUSIC ANALYZER

When selecting music for reviews, answer the following questions:

	Yes	No
▶ Is the music steady in its rhythm?	_____	_____
▶Can you easily walk in rhythm to the music?	_____	_____
▶Does the rhythm of the music pulse once or less per second?	_____	_____
▶Is the music devoid of lyrics?	_____	_____
▶Does the music maintain a steady volume level?	_____	_____
▶Is the music steady in its instrumentation?	_____	_____
▶Does the music tend to make you feel sad?	_____	_____
▶When you play the music, does it fade into the background?	_____	_____
Total (8 maximum)	_____	_____

The higher the Yes column score, the more effective the music usage will be.

TABLE 6-8

LENN'S TEN

Below, I have listed 10 of my favorite instructor-friendly music CDs. These CDs are ideal for learning situations. The ten, in alphabetical order, are:

- ▶ "Desert Rose"

- ▶ "Game Show Themes for Trainers"

- ▶ "Music for Accelerated Learning: Steven Halpern"

- ▶ "On the Wind"

- ▶ "Paint the Sky with Stars: The Best of Enya"

- ▶ The "Set Your Life to Music" Series

- ▶ "Trainer Sounds"

- ▶ "Touch"

- ▶ "Tropical Dreams"

- ▶ "Tunes for Trainers" and "Jazzy Tunes for Trainers"

"Desert Rose"

Artist: Peter Goslow

Label: Classic Press Recordings

Description: A peaceful collection of Baroque and Classic compositions ideal for solo reflection. The material is well chosen, the execution is flawless, and the recording captures every nuance of the acoustic guitar. The music maintains a constant approximate volume level with no jarring contrasts to distract learners.

Suggested Use: To create a state of relaxed awareness for a passive concert, or during reflection

Parameters: Higher initial cost, but purchase includes usage permission

Where to find it: MediaRider.com

"Game Show Themes for Trainers"

Artist: James & Lenn Millbower

Label: Offbeat Training Tunes

Description: A collection of original music written for instructors and inspired by favorite game shows. Selections range in style from jazz to country to rock, and include music for game show themes, quizzes, introducing prizes, TV commercials, and news breaks. For maximum flexibility, most of the selections are recorded in short, long, and "talk over" versions.

Suggested Use: Ideal for game style reviews, timed events, group interaction, and TV themed activities

Parameters: Higher initial cost, but purchase includes usage permission

Where to find it: Offbeat Training, Stylus Publishing, LLC, Trainer's Warehouse, Tool Thyme for Trainers

"Music for Accelerated Learning: Steven Halpern"

Artist: Steven Halpern

Label: Inner Peace Music

Description: Steve Halpern's works focus on the application of the Suggestopedia. Consequently, his music is ideally suited for the classroom. It is tuneful and emotive without distracting attention away from the learning task at hand. Selections feature acoustic and electronic instruments in a thoughtful, reflective mix.

Suggested Use: This music is ideally suited for Lozanov style passive and active concerts

Parameters: Copyright permission is not granted by purchase

Where to find it: Steven Halpern's Inner Peace Music

"On the Wind"

Artist: "Mike Strickland"

Label: MSP Records

Description: This collection of light jazz is familiar without being exceedingly so. Different tracks are vaguely reminiscent of Yanni, George Benson, or Sergio Mendez. Learners will think they have heard this music before without knowing exactly where. It is comfortable, light, up-tempo music.

Suggested Use: For the in-between times: as learners enter, take a break, or exit, and during the afternoon

Parameters: Higher initial cost, but purchase includes usage permission

Where to find it: MediaRider.com

"Paint the Sky with Stars: The Best of Enya"

Artist: Enya

Label: Warner Music

Description: Heavily synthesized, but with a light feel, this collection features lilting melodies, sophisticated musicality, and up-tempo rhythms. Although music with lyrics is not recommended during thinking activities (see The Use of Pop Songs in the Learning Environment below), the lyrics are mixed into the music in such a way as to make them indistinguishable from the synthesizers. Consequently, the collection provides up-tempo, seemingly lyrical pop music that functions as a modern learning equivalent to Mozart.

Suggested Use: Ideal for afternoon use, during reflection, and group discussions

Parameters: Copyright permission is not granted by purchase

Where to find it: Most CD retail outlets

The "Set Your Life to Music" Series

Artist: Various

Label: Phillips Classics, PolyGram Classics & Jazz

Description: The "Set Your Life to Music" series consists of several classical music recordings designed to complement daily activities. Titles include "Bach for Breakfast," "Bach for Book Lovers," Mozart for Meditation," and "Mozart for Morning Coffee." Each CD features music intentionally chosen to compliment the activity listed in its title. The music it is not boisterous. The selections are mostly minor key, pensive works that pull learners toward relaxed awareness. Never too loud, or too soft, fast, or slow, these selections allow you to start and stop the CD at will. In addition, the music provides a level of musical sophistication that engages both hemispheres of our brains by displaying both structural complexity and emotional depth.

Suggested Use: Ideal for use before noon, during reflection, study, and small group discussions

Parameters: Copyright permission is not granted by purchase

Where to find it: Most CD retail outlets

"Trainer Sounds"

Artist: Various

Label: Performance Insight, Inc.

Description: "Trainer Sounds" is different from the rest of the selections in this listing. It is not a CD. Rather, it is a royalty-free software collection of music and sound effects designed for us with any computer. Once the "Trainer Sounds" CD-ROM is placed into the CD-ROM drive of a computer, it is a simple matter to select and play any specific sound upon demand. The selections offer a wide variety of tempos and styles, with selections fitting virtually every musical need.

Suggested Use: Any situation where music or sound effects are required

Parameters: Requires 100MB of computer memory to run properly

Where to find it: Offbeat Training

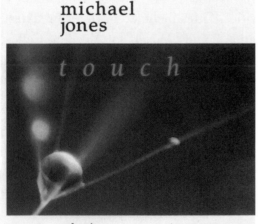

"Touch"

Artist: Michael Jones

Label: Narada Productions

Description: A light, soaring, reflective collection of original compositions played on a grand piano. The music has a new-age feel, backed by a spirituality that propels it forward. Its lightness makes it an ideal classroom companion.

Suggested Use: During passive reviews, reflection, and study

Parameters: Copyright permission is not granted by purchase

Where to find it: Narada Productions.

"Tropical Dreams"

Artist: Scott Moulton

Label: Revere Records

Description: Tropical Dreams is a light, mellow, melodic, meditative, minor key based collection of material. The selections are interconnected, flowing easily from piece to piece. A hint of ocean surf connects the whole. All the takes feature the same light, pensive touch, allowing you to pause and restart the CD at will.

Suggested Use: Ideal for reflection

Parameters: Higher initial cost, but purchase includes usage permission.

Where to find it: MediaRider.com

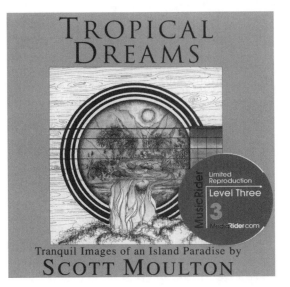

"Tunes for Trainers" and "Jazzy Tunes for Trainers"

Artist: Various

Label: Network Music, LLC

Description: "Tunes for Trainers" and "Jazzy Tunes for Trainers" are mixed-use collections. "Tunes for Trainers" features various campy training related songs, fifties through eighties pop rock, and light jazz selections. Among the pieces is a delightfully zany, campy and sickeningly sweet vocal selection called "Good Morning." This song, and

other selections in the training related section, aids in framing a learning environment. "Jazzy Tunes for Trainers" is also a compilation album, featuring various big band, cool jazz, funk, rock, Mexicana, and comedic and patriotic selections. The big band selections alone make the CD worth buying

Suggested Use: Before beginning, to introduce a break to lunch, to welcome the learners back from break or lunch, and to say goodbye at the end of a session

Parameters: Higher initial cost, but, as in the case of "Game Show Themes for Trainers," purchase includes usage permission

Where to find it: Trainer's Warehouse

THE USE OF POP SONGS IN FILMS

In *A Celebration of Neurons,* Robert Sylwester reported that "songs go far beyond words in their ability to insert emotion into communication."[73] Film makers know this, and often integrate familiar songs into their movies. Pop songs are so successful that movie producers will pay exorbitant sums, in some cases as much as $100,000, to acquire the rights for the song.[74]

Sylwester went on to explain:

> **"The songs of our adolescent years often become the beacons of our adult life because they can help us to recall the important developments of our adolescence. We often listen to this music to relive the memories in the extended reverie of song. The song slows the simple message so that we can savor all the emotions of the experience."[75]**

In a film composer's hands, pop songs are chosen and linked to those memories in a way that adds emotional texture to the film. Films with pop music scores function on two distinct levels. The first is the application of the song in the film. Every song lyric tells a story and a well placed song's story will dovetail with the film's visual.

The second, and deeper level, is the emotional meaning the use of specific songs brings forth within the listener. The songs become metaphors, placing the subject in the context of the listener's prior experience. Malcolm Knowles wrote that adults have an accumulated reservoir of experiences.[76] Familiar songs draw on those experiences. When people hear songs they know, and have personal memories of, they immediately are drawn back into those memories, and the experience is enhanced. In essence, pop music helps us relate to the story being told in a deeply personal, highly emotional way.

Many films use this technique. Three of the most successful at the use of pop songs are *American Graffiti, The Big Chill,* and *Forrest Gump.*

American Graffiti

Although movies have always featured pop songs, *American Graffiti* (1973) was the first to treat successfully a whole film as a series of pop music vignettes. *American Graffiti* tells the stories of a group of high schoolers, in the early 1960s, experiencing their last summer before adulthood. George Lucas, the film's director, developed the storyline, and selected the songs almost simultaneously. According to Jeff Smith, writing in *The Sounds of Commerce*, Lucas tried to match songs to a story-based "mood and melody."[77]

Lucas paced the film's individual scenes in such a manner that each scene was the length of the song that accompanied it. For example, Bill Haley's "Rock Around the Clock" plays during the opening credits. The song sets up the "innocence of summer" theme of the movie. The Crests' song "Sixteen Candles" accompanies a young girl's 16th birthday. "Teen Angel" by Mark Dinning is played when a character is killed in a drag race. Finally, the film ends with the Spaniels' "Goodnight, Well It's Time to Go."

Through it's almost two-hour running time, the film continues, one song after another. Each commenting on the visual being shown, and adding to the audience's personalization of the characters and their world.

The Big Chill

The Big Chill tells the story of a group of former 1960s radicals turned 1980s yuppies, who gather for a weekend to mourn the passing of an old friend. Like *American Graffiti, The Big Chill* uses pop songs, although the songs function in a different manner. The film is not built around the songs. Instead, the songs add commentary to the on-screen occurrences.

Examples of song placement includes the use of Marvin Gaye's "I Heard It Through the Grapevine" as individuals hear about their friend's passing. "You Can't Always Get What You Want" by The Rolling Stones is played as an ironic commentary on the friend's death. As the friends discuss relationships, The Young Rascals' "Good Lovin'" is performed. Finally, "Bad Moon Rising" by Credence Clearwater Revival is played immediately after a former lover proposes that she and her old flame reunite for an evening.

The best subconscious music placement occurs in a supermarket between the two former lovers, but before they get back together. Although their desire for each other is palpable, both hold back, and converse only about the shopping task at hand. Meanwhile, the Muzak system in the background symbolically plays Frank Sinatra's "Strangers in the Night."

Forrest Gump

Forrest Gump is the last of the three films we'll examine for pop music placement. *Forrest Gump* tells the story of a developmentally challenged man, Forest Gump, as he experiences a series of life adventures over several decades. Because of the film's extended time frame, the music serves to establish the time and place.

Credence Clearwater Revival's "Fortunate Son" sets up Gump's Vietnam tour. To state that Forrest's girlfriend has moved to California, "California Dreaming" by the Mamas and Papas is used. "San Francisco" by Scott Mackenzie frames Forrest's 1960s visit to San Francisco. When Forrest returns home to Alabama, Lynyrd Skynyrd's "Sweet Home Alabama" is played. These music placements help the films listeners comprehend the different locations and eras represented in the film.

American Graffiti, The Big Chill, and *Forrest Gump* were all highly successful films, and the pop song application played a huge part in creating that success. All three films appealed to people at a deeply personal level.

THE USE OF POP SONGS IN THE LEARNING ENVIRONMENT

In *Training with a Beat,* I discussed at length the application of pop songs in the learning environment. In part, I said:

> **"Concert halls, ballrooms, parties, and yes, the classroom, can be uncomfortable environments. When people hear a song they've listened to in the privacy of their home, they relax. Comfortable music emotionally warms the training room, placing learners in a receptive frame of mind for learning. Songs with lyrics, especially popular hits of the last 50 years, are extremely useful for this reason. They are old, well worn, welcome friends."[78]**

Songs with lyrics have distinct learning advantages. We have already examined the remembrances they bring forth. Lyrics also help people memorize information. The words and rhythm of a song are largely processed in the brain's left hemisphere, where the melody is largely processed by the right hemisphere. By using songs with lyrics, you help your learners engage both hemispheres. In the process, they gain a deeper meaning than is possible with one hemisphere alone.

Song lyrics can, as was the case in *The Big Chill,* speak directly to the learning topic. Aretha Franklin's "Respect" could be used for sexual harassment classes. "Short People" by Randy Newman might serve as a frame for a discussion about diversity. Kool and the Gang's "Celebration" is an effective graduation song. Given the large number of pop songs available, the options are limited only by your imagination and the musical preferences of your learners. Simply use Table 6–9 to determine the song you need.

Another helpful technique for engaging both hemispheres is to take a well known song and change the lyrics so that they fit your need. Most children learn their ABCs this way.

POP MUSIC PLACEMENT ANALYZER

Step 1: Use the following questions to select a pop song.
▶ What is the purpose for using a pop song?

_____

▶ What pop songs will best serve that purpose?

1. _____

2. _____

3. _____

Step 2: Use the following questions to determine the most appropriate pop song.

	Yes	No
▶ Do you want the learners to focus on the song?	_____	_____
▶ Can you easily walk or sway in rhythm to the music?	_____	_____
▶ Do the song's lyrics relate to your class subject matter?	_____	_____
▶ Do you know the meaning of the song's lyrics?	_____	_____
▶ Is the meaning of the song's lyrics consistent with your message?	_____	_____
▶ Will your learners positively relate to the song?	_____	_____
▶ Will the use of the song be inoffensive?	_____	_____
▶ Do you have the legal rights to use the song?	_____	_____
Total (8 maximum)	_____	_____

The higher the Yes column score, the more effective a pop song will be.

TABLE 6-9

The same techniques can be applied in adult learning, if you rewrite a song's lyrics to reflect your key lesson points and have your trainees sing along. The Create-A-Lyric Template Samples (Table 6.10) will start you on your way to writing your own lyrics.

DIFFICULTIES ASSOCIATED WITH THE USE OF MUSIC

Music does have a number of difficulties associated with it. Fortunately, these difficulties can be addressed easily if you are aware of them. They are as follows:

▶ Music must be used judiciously.

▶ Music must be integrated into the whole.

CREATE-A-LYRIC TEMPLATE SAMPLES

To create your own lyrics, follow three steps:

1. Write out the lyrics to the song you intend to use
2. Based on those lyrics, write out a Create-A-Lyric template
3. Fit your words into the template

To get you started, some sample templates are provided below.

Template key

—	A line indicates a one-syllable word.
— —	Multiple lines separated by small spaces indicate a multi-syllable word.
— —	Two lines separated by a large space indicate two different words.
=	Double lines indicates a phrase that repeats.
▬	Thick lines indicate words that must rhyme.
▬[1]	A number at the end of multiple lines indicates words that must rhyme with each other.
[	Brackets indicate repeated lines.

Template sample

"Mary Had a Little Lamb"

With lyrics   **Without lyrics**

First Verse

Mary had a little lamb,

Little lamb,

Little Lamb,

Mary had a little lamb,

Its fleece was white as snow.

Second Verse

Everywhere that Mary went,

Mary went,

Mary went,

Everywhere that Mary went,

The lamb was sure to go.

"Twinkle, Twinkle Little Star"

Verse

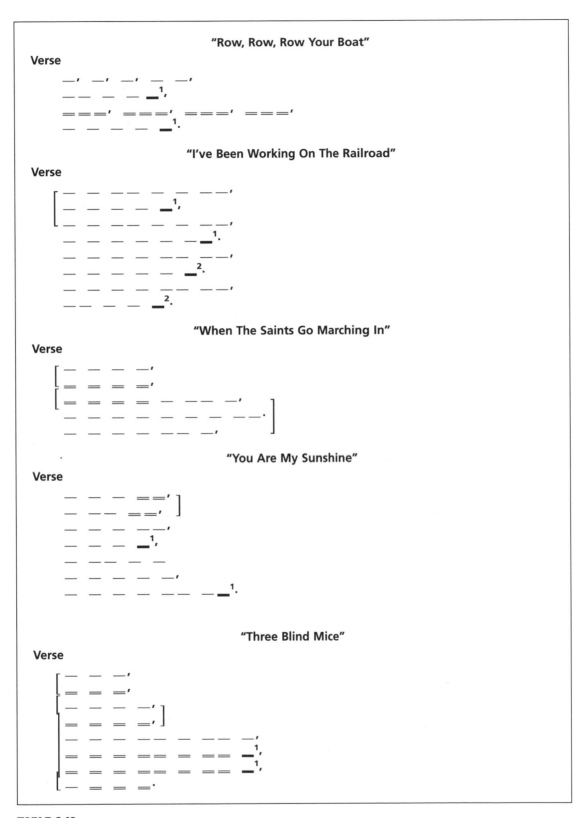

TABLE 6-10

▶ Music must be appropriate to the situation.

▶ Music must match the cultural norms of your learners.

▶ The meaning of a song's lyrics must fit the situation.

▶ Songs with lyrics should be used only when you want the song to be noticed.

Music Must Be Used Judiciously

Music Mania   By Millbower and Yager

Is the music loud enough?

In my Berklee College of Music days, I learned that it's not the notes that make the music. Rather, it is the silence between the notes. Just as you have to know ugly to appreciate beauty, silence helps focus your learners on the music. As composer Max Steiner stated, "My theory is that music should be felt rather than heard."[79] Author Tony Thomas explained that a composer: ". . . cannot make his effect if music is laid on with a trowel. The continuous flow of musical sound begins by merely irritating, and then the ear tends to ignore it."[80]

Select your musical moments for specific reasons, not just to create noise. Your musical moments should be allowed to sing.

Music Must Be Integrated into the Whole

When music is applied correctly, it is a seamless component of the learning, not an add-on. It should not be noticed. Composer William Alwyn explained: "I am a little worried if someone says to me, 'I liked your score for such and such a picture.' It makes me wonder whether I have stepped outside my brief, which is to provide music which is as indigenous to the film as the camera angles and the film sets."[81] Composer David Raskin concurred: "The purpose of film music is not to be noticed for itself. Its great usefulness is the way in which it performs its role without an intervening conscious act of perception. It is most telling when the music registers upon us in a quiet way, where we don't know it's actually happening."[82]

The music you select should be integrated into the whole. If it is not, remove it.

Music Must Be Appropriate to the Situation

In both the film and learning environments, music serves a support function. As Composer Leonard Rossenman explained: "Certainly, the music can contribute a great deal in support of an overall shape, but this shape originates with the film itself, not the music."[83] Composer Bronislau Kaper added: "At certain moments in films, nobody knows the difference between what is visual and what is acoustical. It all comes together. It's like seeing and hearing lightening—it's one effect."[84]

Pay special attention to the question of appropriateness. Avoid selecting a song because it is a favorite of yours. Particularly avoid changing out appropriately selected music because you grow tired of the music yourself. Select the best piece for your needs, and then fully integrate it into your instruction. And, once you know it works, stick by it with conviction.

Music Must Match the Cultural Norms of Your Learners

Although films like *American Graffiti, The Big Chill,* and *Forrest Gump* were big hits, there were some people who did not connect with those films owing to their personal tastes in music. Regardless of how appropriately you choose your music, and how successfully you integrate it into your instruction, music that your learners do not relate to will distract from your instruction. Oliver Sacks, in discussing the ways music connects with his patients, explained: "To help, however, the music must be the right kind for each patient—music that has meaning and evokes feeling for that individual."[85]

Obviously, you cannot know every cultural and personal factor related to each of your trainees. You can, however, ensure that the music you select fits your instruction. It should match so seamlessly that your learners focus on the instruction, not the music.

The Meaning of a Song's Lyrics Must Fit the Situation

One common mistake novices make is selecting material with inappropriate lyrics. Professionals pay attention to this detail. For example, Muzak does not play "Stormy Weather" during plane flights.[86] Muzak dropped "The Yellow Rose of Texas" during the aftermath of Kennedy's 1963 assassination in Dallas, Texas.[87] Two days after the attacks on the World Trade Center, I personally witnessed a situation where Bob Seeger's "Fire in the Sky" played over a restaurant's music system. I waited and watched. Within a minute, two different restaurant patrons left their seats, and in another 30 seconds, the music was turned off, no doubt due to strenuous customer objections.

I realize these examples are extreme, but they do prove an important point. If the song your are using has lyrics, know what those lyrics are. Do not allow yourself to be unpleasantly surprised.

Songs With Lyrics Should be Used Only When You Want the Song to be Noticed

Another common mistake is the misapplication of songs with lyrics. Instructors will ask learners to reflect or work in small groups, and then begin playing a song with lyrics. Lyrics are difficult to ignore, and the learners invariably are distracted from their learning. The only time songs with lyrics are appropriate is when you want your learners to notice the lyrics. In films, songs with lyrics do not compete with dialog. Neither should they in your classroom.

The Musical Difficulties Avoidance Analyzer in Table 6-11 may help you identify difficulties before they become the focus of your classroom.

MUSIC AND EMOTION

One of our core Learnertainment points is that emotional engagement makes learning meaningful and permanent. Film composers concur. Many of the film examples we have discussed are teeming with emotion. The terror the *Jaws* theme evokes, the sadness of

---

MUSICAL DIFFICULTIES AVOIDANCE ANALYZER

Use the following questions to avoid some of the difficulties associated with music.

	Yes	No
▶ Is your usage of music less than 40% of total class time?	_____	_____
▶ When you use music, do you have specific reasons for doing so?	_____	_____
▶ Is your placement of music integrated into the whole?	_____	_____
▶ Is the music usage appropriate to the learning situation?	_____	_____
▶ Is your music selection based on need, not on favoritism?	_____	_____
▶ Does your music match the cultural norms of your learners?	_____	_____
▶ Are the song's lyrics appropriate to the learning situation?	_____	_____
▶ If using songs with lyrics, do you want the song to be noticed?	_____	_____
Total (8 maximum)	_____	_____

The higher the Yes column score, the more you will avoid difficulties associated with the use of music.

TABLE 6-11

The Godfather ballads, the wonderment of the *Star Wars* theme, the adrenaline rush the "James Bond Theme" brings forth, and the horror of the knife slashes in *Psycho* are extremely, and intentionally, emotional moments.

Many composers have commented on the connection of emotion and music. For instance, Wagner stated: "What music expresses, is eternal, infinite and ideal; it does not express the passion, love, or longing of such-and-such an individual on such-and-such an occasion, but passion, love or longing in itself." Arthur Schopenhauser offered an almost identical observation: "[Music] does not express this or that particular or definite joy, this or that sorrow, pain, or horror, or delight, or merriment, or peace of mind; but joy, sorrow, pain, horror, delight, merriment, peace of mind themselves."[88] Fellow composer Elmer Bernstein added: "Of all the arts, music makes the most direct appeal to the emotions. It is a non-plastic, non-intellectual communication between sound vibration and spirit. The listener is generally not burdened with a need to ask what it means. The listener assesses how the music made him feel."[89]

From a completely different field, educator Robert Sylwester added, "Music doesn't even need words to communicate emotion."[90]

Music is perhaps the most emotional element of a film. You may not notice the music when you cry at a film, but the music has reached you in a deep, meaningful, moving way. Perhaps because music is free of the specificity that accompanies words, music is free to feel.

Heightening Emotional Reactions in the Learning Environment

Music can be emotionally beneficial in the learning environment. Although music is not a substitute for good instruction, music is a way to penetrate the info-fog. In *Music for the Movies,* Tony Thomas made this statement: "Music comes to bear when helping to define the meaning of the film by stimulating and guiding an emotional response to the visuals. Directly and pervasively appealing to the subconscious. . . It is this unique ability to influence the audience subconsciously that makes music truly valuable to the cinema."[91]

I suggest that although Thomas was speaking about Hollywood, the same dynamic applies to your classroom. Composer Jerry Goldsmith explained how when he commented that "The function of a score is to enlarge the scope of a film."[92] The function of music in the classroom is to enlarge the scope of the learning. Music speaks to a level deeper than words. It adds an extra track of information that layers meaning for your learners. In Elmer Bernstein's words: ". . . part of the fun of being a film composer, (is) that you are reaching people at a subliminal level, where they are relatively defenseless. That's an exciting thing because you can make people feel a certain way, even though they may not understand why they feel that way."[93]

CUE CARD: Music speaks to a level deeper than words.

Part of the fun of using Show Biz techniques is the ability to reach people at a subliminal level. For once you break through the cognitive info-fog, true learning occurs.

[1] Crofton, Ian, and Fraser, Donald, eds. (1985). *A Dictionary of Musical Quotations.* New York: Schirmer.

[2] Ayto, John (1990). *Dictionary of Word Origins.* New York: Arcade.

[3] Sylwester, Robert (1995). *A Celebration of Neurons: An Educator's Guide to the Human Brain.* Alexandria, VA: ASCD.

[4] Blacking, John (1987). *A Common Sense View of All Music.* Cambridge, UK: Cambridge University Press.

[5] *The 1995 Grolier Multimedia Encyclopedia* (1995). vr. 7.0.2. Grolier Electronic Publishing.

[6] Bruney, Charles (1935). *A General History of Music from the Earliest Ages to the Present Period.* London: Oxford University Press.

[7] Jourdain, Robert (1997). *Music, the Brain, and Ecstasy: How Music Captures Our Imagination.* New York: Avon Books.

[8] Ellis, Catherine J. (1985). *Aboriginal Music: Education for Living.* St. Lucia: University of Queensland Press.

[9] Grolier (1995).

[10] Keil, Charles (1979). *The Song.* Chicago: University of Chicago Press.

[11] Grolier (1995).

[12] Berg, Charles Merell (1976). *An Investigation of the Motives for and Realization of Music to Accompany the American Silent Film 1896–1927.* New York: Arno Press.

[13] Ibid.

[14] Ibid.

[15] Burt, George (1994). *The Art of Film Music.* Boston, MA: Northeastern University Press.

[16] Prendergast, Roy M. (1977) *Film Music, A Neglected Art: A Critical Study of Music in Film,* 2nd edit. New York: W. W. Norton.

[17] Lozanov, Giorgi (1978). *Suggestology and Outlines of Suggestopedia.* New York: Gordon & Breach.

[18] Grout, Donald, and Palisca, Claude (1996). *A History of Western Music,* 5th edit. New York: W. W. Norton.

[19] Ortiz, John, Ph. D. (1997). *The Tao of Music: Sound Psychology, Using Music to Change Your Life.* York Beach, Maine: Samuel Weiser.

[20] Sacks, Oliver. When music heals body and soul. *Parade* Magazine, March 21, 2002.

[21] Rawson, Hugh, and Miner, Margaret, eds. (1986). *The New International Dictionary of Quotations.* New York: E. P. Dutton.

[22] Prendergast, Roy M. (1977).

[23] Millbower, Lenn (2000) *Training with a Beat: The Teaching Power of Music.* Sterling, VA: Stylus.

[24] Ibid.

[25] Meyer, Leonard (1996). *Emotion and Meaning in Music.* Chicago: University of Chicago Press.

[26] Millbower, Lenn (2000).

[27] Schopnenhauer, Arthur (1966). *The World as Will and Representation,* Vol. I. New York: Dover.

[28] Millbower, Lenn (2000).

[29] Grout, Donald, and Palisca, Claude (1996).

[30] Berg, Charles Merell (1976).

[31] Smith, Jeff (1998). *The Sounds of Commerce: Marketing Popular Film Music.* New York: Columbia University Press.

[32] Smith, Jeff (1998).

[33] Burt, George (1994).

[34] Ibid.

[35] Millbower, Lenn (2000).

[36] Thomas, Tony (1997). *Music for the Movies,* 2nd edit. Los Angeles, CA: Silman-James Press.

[37] Burt, George (1994).

[38] Prendergast, Roy M. (1977).

[39] Ibid.

[40] Burt, George (1994).

[41] MuSICA Research Notes, 2/1 (Spring, 1995): <www.musica.uci.edu>.

[42] Millbower, Lenn (2000).

[43] Prendergast, Roy M. (1977).

[44] Lanza, Joseph (1994). *Elevator Music: A Surreal History of Muzak, Easy Listening, and Other Moodsong.* New York: Picador USA.

[45] Thaut, M., and de l'Etoile, S. (1993). The effects of music on mood state-dependent recall. *Journal of Music Therapy,* 30/2:70–80. Thaut, M. (1989). The influence of music therapy interventions on self-rated changes in relaxation, affect, and thought in psychiatric prisoner-patients. *Journal of Music Therapy,* 26/3:155–66.

[46] Lanza, Joseph (1994). *Elevator Music: A Surreal History of Muzak, Easy Listening, and Other Moodsong.* New York: Picador USA.

[47] Ibid.

[48] Ibid.

[49] Ibid.

[50] Borling, J. (1981). The effect of seductive music on alpha rhythm and focused attention in high-creative and low creative subjects. *Journal of Music Therapy,* 18/2:101–08.

[51] Blood D., and Feriss, S. (1993). Effects of background music on anxiety, satisfaction with communication, and productivity. *Psychological Reports,* 72/1:171–77.

[52] Prueter, B. and Mezzano, J. (1973). Effects of background music upon initial counseling interaction. *Journal of Music Therapy,* 10:205–12.

[53] Devlin, Hilton J., Sawatzky, D. Donald (1987). The effects of background music in a simulated initial counselling session with female subjects. *Canadian Journal of Counseling,* 21(2–3):125–32.

[54] Miller, Leon K, and Schyb, Michael (1987). Facilitation and interference by background music. *Canadian Journal of Counseling,* 21(2–3):125–32.

[55] Wolff, Florence I. (1989). An investigation of the effects of background music on learning of vocabulary and grammar and in public speaking. *Journal of Music Therapy,* XXVI(1):42–54.

[56] Mezzano, Joseph and Prueter, Bruce (1974). Background music and counseling interaction. *Journal of Counseling Psychology,* 21:page nos.

[57] Routhieaux, R. L., and Tansik, D. A. (1997). The benefits of music in hospital waiting rooms. *Health Care Supervisor,* 16(2):31–40.

58 Stratton, V. N. (1992). Influence of music and socializing on perceived stress while waiting. *Perceptual and Motor Skills,* 75(1):334.

59 Ibid.

60 Ibid.

61 Storr, Anthony. (1992). *Music and the Mind.* New York: Ballantine Books.

62 Adaman, Jill E., and Blaney, Paul H. (1995). The effects of musical mood induction on creativity. *Journal of Creative Behavior,* 29/2:95–108.

63 Wlodkowski, Raymond J. (1999). *Enhancing Adult Motivation to Learn: A Comprehensive Guide for Teaching All Adults.* San Francisco: Jossey-Bass.

64 Millbower, Lenn (2000).

65 Storr, A. (1992).

66 Blood, D. J., and Ferriss, S. J. (1993). Effects of background music on anxiety, satisfaction with communication, and productivity. *Psychological Reports,* 72/1:171–77.

67 Morton, L. L., Kershner, J. R., and Siegal, L. S. (1990). The potential for therapeutic applications of music on problems related to memory and attention. *Journal of Music Therapy,* 27/4:195–208.

68 Ibid. Thaut, M., and de l'Etoile, S. K. (1993). The effects of music on mood state-dependent recall. *Journal of Music Therapy,* 30/2:70–80.

69 Blood, D. J., and Feriss, S. J. (1993). Effects of background music on anxiety, satisfaction with communication, and productivity. *Psychological Reports,* 72/1:171–77.

70 Morton, L. L., Kershner, J. R., and Siegal, L. S. (1990).

71 Millbower, Lenn (2000).

72 Lozanov, G. (1978).

73 Sylwester, Robert (1995). *A Celebration of Neurons: An Educator's Guide to the Human Brain.* Alexandria, VA: ASCD.

74 *Chicago Tribune,* October 24, 1999.

75 Sylwester, Robert (1995).

76 Knowles, Malcolm (1984). *The Adult Learner: A Neglected Species.* Houston, TX: Gulf Publishing.

77 Smith, Jeff (1998).

78 Millbower, Lenn (2000).

79 Thomas, Tony (1997).

80 Ibid.

81 Ibid.

82 Burt, George (1994).

83 Burt, George (1994).

84 Thomas, Tony (1997).

85 Sacks, Oliver. *When Music Heals Body and Soul. Parade* Magazine, March 21, 2002.

86 Lanza, Joseph (1994).

87 Ibid.

88 Schopenhauer, Arthur (1883). *The World as Will and Idea,* vol. 1. R. B. Haldane and J. Kemp, eds. London: Trubner.

89 Burt, George (1994).

90 Sylwester, Robert (1995).

91 Thomas, Tony (1997).

92 Ibid.

93 Ibid.

CHAPTER SEVEN

LESSONS FROM MAGIC

HOCUS POCUS

The magician stands center stage as various assistants enter and exit. Usually a piece of exotic apparatus is introduced. The story line calls for the magician to don a hood. He does so, as do his assistants. The magician grabs the leading lady by the arm and places her, usually bound, into the apparatus and locks it shut. The assistants make a great show of tying ropes around the box. Once the box is thoroughly tied, the dancers strut around the stage. They turn the apparatus side to side and end to end as the magician walks around the box. When the box stops turning, the dancers prance around it. At an appropriately suspenseful moment, the box is opened. Surprise! It's empty. The magician takes his hood off. Surprise. It's the assistant. But where's the magician? At this moment, the magician appears, to the breathless amazement of the audience, at the back of the theater and runs down the center aisle of the theater. He runs to the stage and receives a well-deserved round of applause.

> "The first impulse of people
> is to believe." —DR. HARLAN TARBELL[1]

The Show Biz Training techniques in this chapter are based on the following Learner-tainment Principles:

Principle 3: Direct Attention—suggest the outcomes you expect.

THE FIRST ILLUSION

We don't know when man first performed magic. We can, however, assume that it occurred early in the history of humanity. The word "magic" is ancient. Where many words came about as derivatives of other words, magic is an original source word, from the ancient Greek, *mãgos,* which meant *sorcerer.*[2]

We can also assume that the first individual to perform a magic trick was viewed with awe and wonder. That person must have quickly become a powerful member of the community. In ancient times, conjurers were highly regarded, regardless of the charlatan nature of their miracles. Magicians communicated with the gods, celebrated tribal rituals, advised kings, and predicted the future. Traditions, myths, and legends are filled with stories of such sorcerers. Aladdin's genie of the lamp in *A Thousand and One Arabian Nights*[3], Merlin of King Arthur's court, and the healers of Tanzania's Maasai tribe[4] are three examples.

As humanity grew to understand science, magic gradually separated itself from its charlatan roots. Magic became less relevant as the source of miracles. It became instead what it should have been all along, an entertainment art form. The transition took hundreds of years, finally concluding in the early 20th century with the theatrical entertainments of magicians such as Keller, Blackstone, Robert-Houdin, and of course, Harry Houdini.

Houdini probably finished the debunking of magic's supernatural roots. In the late 1800s and early 1900s, people believed it was possible to communicate with deceased relatives through mediums. The mediums would use ringing bells and tambourines, lifting tables, and producing ghost written messages as proof of their connection with the after-life.

Even scientific-minded intellectuals such as Sir Arthur Conan Doyle, author of the Sherlock Holmes stories, believed in supernatural magic. It seems that Sir Arthur over-applied Holmes' most famous adage: "When you have eliminated the impossible, whatever remains, *however improbable* [original emphasis], must be the truth."[5] In this case,

Doyle concluded that a medium's shaking of a tambourine was impossible, and the medium's act, although improbable, must have been true. He was mistaken.

The demise of the medium cult began on July 29, 1913, when Houdini's mother died.[6] In a desperate quest to contact her, Houdini attended seance after seance. Unfortunately for the mediums, their tambourine shakings, bell ringings, table liftings, and ghostly writings did not fool Houdini. He felt betrayed, and this feeling of betrayal turned into a rage against all mediums. The result was a single-handed crusade that exposed the charlatan nature of the mediums. Although Houdini's efforts did expose some secrets of magic, they also completed the transition from magician-as-miracle-worker to magician-as-entertainer. It is a debt that magicians still owe him.

Magic's charlatan legacy has left the public with what psychologists would call a cognitive disconnect. We are suspicious of magicians. The very word *illusion,* from the Latin *illūdere,* means "to make fun of,"[7] and most people don't like to play the fool. We know there is a trick at work, and we want to discover its secret.

Yet, simultaneously, the lure of magic remains. We may have lost our belief in the divinity of magicians, but not the desire to believe. We watch a fake, and knowing its fakeness, still fall for the illusion.

Magicians have responded to this disconnect by downplaying the trick. Between 1940 and 1975, Dariel Fitzee wrote the three definitive volumes about magic psychology. In *Showmanship for Magicians,* he explained it this way: "The secret is NOT important. The ONLY [original emphasis] thing that is important is its favorable impression on the majority of the spectators."[8]

It may seem that the very nature of magic is trickery, but it isn't so. Granted, magic is performed through trickery, but audiences rarely leave a magical entertainment bragging about how well they were tricked. The trickery is a tool, not an end in itself. People do not want to be tricked; they want to be entertained.

The entertainment occurs *in spite of* the trick. In fact, magicians don't even refer to their magic routines as tricks. They avoid the devious sounding word *trick,* preferring to recast the word *illusion* into *fun with* instead of *fun of.*

MANIPULATION

When people watch magicians perform, they see the manipulation of cards, billiard balls, silk handkerchiefs, and other paraphernalia. There is a level of manipulation that the audience never sees: the performer's manipulation of the audience. The extraordinary effort that the magician puts into directing the audience's attention is hidden from view. The audience sees magic. The magician sees deception.

In *Magic by Misdirection,* Fitzee explained: "The real secrets of magic are those whereby the magician is able to influence the mind of the spectator, even in the face of that spectator's definite knowledge that the magician is absolutely unable to do what that spectator ultimately must admit he does do."[9]

Singer John Davidson, in partnership with Cort Casady, wrote a primer for musical performers called *The Singing Entertainer.* In it, they concurred with Fitzee: "Entertainment truly is an art form. The art lies in the fact the audience seldom [consciously] realizes it is being manipulated."[10]

The magician uses two fundamental principles to manipulate the audience: direction and suggestion. The story that opened this chapter made extensive use of both principles. Let's look at that story again. Only this time, we will examine the illusion from the magician's point of view, as a switch.

Hocus Pocus Exposed

The magician stands center stage as various assistants enter and exit.

The first time spectators see an assistant enter, they notice. They may even notice the second entrance. But soon, the comings and goings become routine, and no longer warrant attention. They become invisible. The magician directs attention away from these entrances, suggesting their lack of importance.

Usually a piece of exotic apparatus is introduced.

The box is not the focus of this illusion, the upcoming switch is. By directing attention toward the box, the magician directs the spectator's attention away from the various personnel on stage, and suggests the box is important. This false focus makes the switch a total surprise.

The story line calls for the magician to don a hood. He does so, as do his assistants.

No magician wants to wear a hood. It's hot, sweaty, and unattractive. The nature of this illusion is a switch, and a switch cannot occur if the magician is easy to spot on stage. The magician dons a hood so that the switch can occur, but audience knowledge of that purpose would telegraph the illusion. A story line that suggests a logical explanation is invented for the hood.

> *The magician grabs the leading lady by the arm and places her, usually bound, into the apparatus and locks it shut. The assistants make a great show of tying ropes around the box.*

The ropes are inconsequential as a barrier to escape, but important as a directing tool. They play no role in the illusion, except to suggest that escape is impossible. In addition, the rope by-play allows the leading lady time to escape her bonds, take off her outer layer of clothes to reveal an assistant's costume and hood, and slip out a trap door in the back of the box. As the last of the ropes are tied, the leading lady, now dressed as an assistant, exits stage left with the other assistants, who are by now not important enough to watch, as the hooded magician directs attention to him by walking toward the audience.

> *Once the box is thoroughly tied, the dancers strut around the stage. They turn the apparatus side to side and end to end as the magician walks around the box.*

With all the whirling, twirling, circling, and strutting, it is hard for spectators to remain focused on the critical details. There is just too much stimuli directed at them. At this point, while the spectators are in stimuli overload, the magician boldly walks toward the wings.

> *When the box stops turning, the dancers prance around it.*

The alluring dancers direct attention away from the magician, who, having reached the wings, exits stage left. At that precise moment, the dancers execute their most provocative dance step. Almost immediately, the leading lady enters from the exact area where the magician exited, and by manner of walk and attitude, suggests that she is the magician.

> *At an appropriately suspenseful moment, the box is opened. Surprise. It's empty. The magician takes his hood off. Surprise. It's the assistant.*

The suggestion is that the switch occurred at that instant. Of course, the switch is minutes old, but, because the magician purposely directed the spectators' attention away from the critical events, they completely missed it. They now begin focusing on possible solutions for the switch, but it is too late. The trail has already gone cold. In addition, their attention is about to be directed away from the puzzle with an even more enticing stimulus.

> *But where's the magician? At this moment, the magician appears, to the breathless amazement of the audience, at the back of the theater and runs down the center aisle of the theater. He runs to the stage and receives a well-deserved round of applause.*

To the spectator, the switch is made all the more miraculous by the appearance of the magician at the back of the theater. The unstated suggestion is that the magician has just now magically appeared behind the audience. A closer look would reveal his fast breathing. For, he has just run all the way around the theater. But the magician isn't the only one gasping for air. The audience has been left breathless.

What seemed like a true miracle was accomplished through direction and suggestion. We will overview each of these fundamental principles in turn, and examine the ways they relate to the learning environment.

Direction

To create magic, magicians must bend the laws of nature. Or rather, they must seem to bend the laws of nature. Control isn't necessary; the *appearance* of control is enough. The appearance of control comes from directing the audience's attention away from items that would destroy the illusion, and toward those that reinforce it. Direction can take many forms, but is invariably a physical action: a nod, a gesture, a change in posture, or a verbal statement.

There is an old saying from the training community, "Tell them what you're going to tell them, tell them, and then tell them what you told them." Direction operates in a similar manner, but in reverse. Magicians tell the audience what the magician wants them to see, tell them what

Flash Appearance   By Millbower and Yager

TADA!

POOF!!

He's good!

Copyright © 2002 Stylus Publishing, LLC. Reprinted by permission from Cartoons for Trainers, Stylus Publishing, VA.

they should be seeing, and tell them what they just saw. Where trainers *direct attention* toward positive learning outcomes, magicians *misdirect attention* away from truth.

A simple example is the magician's statement, "Nothing up my sleeve." This is an intentional ploy. Calling attention to the obvious preempts future "It was up his sleeve" comments. It also gives the audience something irrelevant to think about, thus pulling their attention away from the bulge in the magician's pocket. Or, in the case of the switch, away from the critical events of the illusion.

Attention was directed toward the box, and away from the assistants. The hoods are explained in the story. Because no extra attention is paid to them, they seem unimportant. The attention placed on the tightness of the ropes implied importance when there is none, and stalled for time while the assistant changed clothes and slipped through the trap door. The alluring dance steps directed attention away from the switch. The appearance of the magician at the back of the theater directed attention away from the true secret of the illusion. All these events were planned to control what the audience saw. Without this direction, the illusion could not have happened.

Suggestion

The second of our two fundamentals is suggestion. In discussing the importance of suggestion, Sam Sharpe stated: "Suggestion is a very potent force in the conjurer's armoury [sic]; indeed without it his magical effects would be impossible to accomplish."[11]

Where direction is often physical, via gestures, posture, and verbal statements, suggestion is the art of implication. Dariel Fitzee elaborated: "The magician's suggestion is a subtle but positive act of putting something into the mind of the spectator. This biased stimulus instigates a mental process by means of which a spectator responds to the desires of the performer."[12]

These statements parallel Giorgi Lozanov's comments about his theory of learning, Suggestopedia. In Chapter 4, we discovered Lozanov's definition of suggestion: "A constant communicative factor which chiefly through paraconscious mental activity can create conditions for tapping the functional reserve capacities."[13]

In the Hocus Pocus switch example, several suggestions were employed:

▶ The comings and goings of the assistants were not important.

▶ The box was a major focus of the illusion.

▶ Hoods needed to be worn because of the story.

▶ Ropes make escape from the box impossible.

► The hooded assistant was the magician.

► The switch occurred in an instant.

► The magician magically appeared at the back of the theater.

Each of these suggestions was false, but accepted as true by the audience.

As we also discovered in Chapter 4, Show Biz Training is based on the tendency of the brain to shut down if danger is perceived. Suggestion is a powerful tool for calming the anxious right hemisphere, and creating positive emotion. The end result is a more attentive brain. Regardless of the field, be it magic, vocal performance, or instruction, the goal and the technique for reaching that goal are the same. Subtle, positive, focused suggestion creates an atmosphere of trust. Once that atmosphere is created, the audience will accept the stimuli offered to them.

Acceptance of Manipulation

The audience subconsciously condones and willingly accepts the manipulation as long as two factors remain in place:

► The manipulation must be clearly for the audience's benefit.

► The audience must not be reminded of the manipulation.

THE MANIPULATION MUST BE CLEARLY FOR THE AUDIENCE'S BENEFIT.

Magicians place great emphasis on communicating benevolence to the audience. They suggest supernatural powers, but with their tongues firmly planted in their cheeks. They present their illusions as harmless concoctions for the audience's enjoyment. The audience, knowing the intent is pleasurable emotion, allows itself to be fooled.

Davidson and Cort added the following explanation:

> **"You are the only one who knows what your show is designed to do and where it is designed to go. Without revealing your techniques—your devices and tricks—you must be the one who lets the audience know (a) that you have a plan for their enjoyment, a map for the journey you're taking them on; and (b) what that plan is as your journey progresses."[14]**

Show business agent Bob Vincent in his book *Show Business is Two Words* added: "In order to be truly involved deeply with the audience, you must not be conscious of 'self' and only be totally committed to the 'word.'"[15]

This advice is applicable to the learning environment. For learning to occur, an instructor must focus the learners on the subject at hand, keep the focus on the subject throughout the learning process, and create an environment in which the learners amaze themselves with what they have learned. Instruction is manipulation for the learner's benefit.

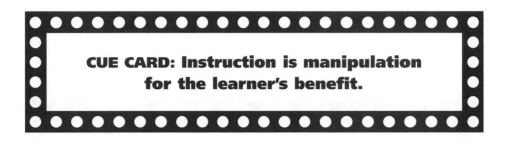

CUE CARD: Instruction is manipulation for the learner's benefit.

Trainees allow themselves to be controlled, as long as they trust the trainer. The moment they suspect the trainer is more concerned with his or her ego than with their benefit, the level of trust plunges.

I believe this is one of the reasons that securing role-play volunteers is difficult. Unless learners perceive an environment of implicit trust for the trainer's motives, volunteers are hard to find.

THE AUDIENCE MUST NOT BE REMINDED OF THE MANIPULATION.

A willingness to be manipulated is not the same as a conscious awareness of that manipulation. Learners will accept manipulation only if they are not consciously aware of it.

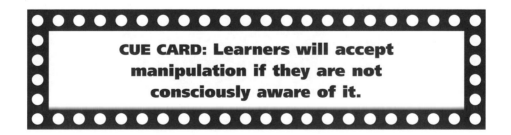

CUE CARD: Learners will accept manipulation if they are not consciously aware of it.

To manipulate the audience without calling attention to that manipulation, suggestion must be employed. The audience's reluctance to be tricked, and the learner's reluctance to be coerced, dictate the need for suggestion. Both Fitzee and Lozanov felt that dictates would be doomed to failure. Fitzee stated: "It is utterly impossible to force the spectator's reason or judgment directly. *The spectator must believe he has made his own decision* [original emphasis]. This makes it necessary for the magician to use inducement rather than persuasion."[16]

Lozanov believed that adult suspicions about the classroom, like those about the magician, block learning. He viewed a joyful attitude on the part of the facilitator, one in which the facilitator positively suggests relaxed and tension-free learning, as the key to transcending inhibitions.

CUE CARD: Suggestion allows manipulation to occur without attention.

USING MAGIC IN THE LEARNING ENVIRONMENT

Now that we have an understanding of the dynamics that simultaneously pull people away from and toward magic, let's turn our attention to the placement of magic in the learning environment. Magic can serve a number of learning purposes. Use magic to:

- ▶ Begin the learning.
- ▶ Refocus attention.
- ▶ Illustrate key points.
- ▶ Conclude the learning.

Use Magic to Begin the Learning

As we shall discover in Chapter 8, the purpose of an opening activity is to capture attention and build curiosity about the subject to follow. Fast-paced, showy illusions are highly effective in this "kick-off" spot. They capture attention quickly. In addition, illusions presented as metaphors tied to the learning topic build curiosity and frame the discussion that follows.

Use Magic to Refocus Attention

When performing in nightclubs, I often found that the audience's attention would wander. It's not that the audience wasn't enjoying the show. Rather, there were more stimuli present than the average person could absorb. Occasionally, we would be required to perform a flashy illusion. Often, these illusions would have no intended effect beyond recapturing the audience's focus.

That situation is similar to the info-fog that classroom learners face. It is occasionally necessary to remind them of the subject they are supposed to be focused on. A well placed magic trick captures attention, so that you can make your point. Use them any time the learners have lost their focus.

Use Magic to Illustrate Key Points

A magic routine built around key learning points creates a strong visual of the point you wish to make. In the process, you present your learners with a holistic image of the subject that will stick with them beyond the classroom event. In Chapter 9, we shall more fully explore the power of visual mnemonics.

Use Magic to Conclude a Learning Segment

As we will discover in Chapter 10, The Script, three-act structure concludes with a celebration of learning. Magic is an ideal companion to these festivities. When presented as the last event of the learning, a magic illusion functions as the exclamation point. It concludes the event in a special, memorable manner.

PROFESSIONAL VS. HOUSEHOLD ILLUSIONS

Some magicians strive to create magic using household items. They believe that people are more amazed when ordinary, everyday items become magical. This is true for professional magicians. It is not true for trainers performing magic. Magicians are perceived as magicians, and expected to perform miracles with previously prepared props. When the magician performs a miracle with an everyday item, it is all the more magical.

On the other hand, there is no expectation of magic from trainers. Trainers who perform homemade illusions run the risk of seeming amateurish. A sharp, clean, professional magic prop suggests the instructor knows something about magic. Professional illusions imply competence, and thus make the acceptance of the illusion more likely. In short, go professional.

LENN'S TEN

Below, I have listed 10 of my favorite instructor-friendly illusions. None of the 10 require the skill of a master magician, but they are professional illusions, using readily available professional props. The 10, in alphabetical order, are:

- ▶ Blendo Bag
- ▶ Burned
- ▶ Domino Card
- ▶ Fresh Fish
- ▶ Hot Book
- ▶ Hot Cup
- ▶ Magic Coloring Book
- ▶ Needle Through Balloon
- ▶ Creative Finance
- ▶ Square the Circle

Blendo Bag

The action: Three silk handkerchiefs blend into one multicolored scarf.
Suggested use: Diversity awareness
The Patter: "I have here three different silks."

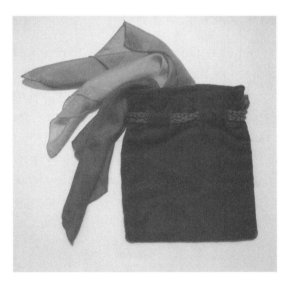

(Display silks bunched up.)

"Inwardly, they are much the same. They are all the same size, and they all are made out of the same material. But from outward appearances, they look very different; one is red, one is yellow, and the last one is green."

(Display each silk individually.)

"All three are great colors."

"But imagine a world in which only one of these colors existed. Take traffic lights for instance. If red was our only color, we'd be stopped at traffic lights all day."

(Place the red silk into the blendo bag.)

"If we only had yellow, we wouldn't have an excuse for accelerating through the light."

(Place the yellow silk into the blendo bag.)

"And, if green was the only color, no one would stop!"

(Place the red silk into the blendo bag.)

"Clearly, we need all three colors."

(Shake the bag.)

"And when those colors work together, like they do on a traffic light, they achieve more than one can do alone, for they blend into a beautiful mosaic of color."

(Display blended silk.)

Alternative uses: Any situation in which people or items must work together.

Parameters: Can be performed surrounded, in any size room. The silk handkerchiefs are usually sold separately from the blendo bag.

Where to find it: Hank Lee's Magic Factory ("Change Bag/Deluxe"), Trainer's Warehouse ("One-Hand Change Bag")

Burned

The action: The participants write their negative emotions on individual pieces of paper. The facilitator collects the paper, places them in a trashcan, and burns them up in a flash.

Suggested use: To define leadership

The patter: (Pass out sheets of paper, one per learner.)

"Think back through your work life, and picture the worst boss you ever worked for. Then, please draw a picture that represents that boss."

(Learners draw their pictures. Once complete, the instructor leads a discussion defining what poor leadership looks like.)

(Have all the learners place their drawings into a metal trashcan.)

"Because we don't want to work for these leaders again, let's get rid of them."

(Light the papers up, and stand back.)

"Now, let's learn how to be great leaders."

Parameters: Can be performed surrounded, but the trashcan must be free of all other trash.

Where to find it: Hank Lee's Magic Factory (Flash Paper)

Domino Card

The action: The number of black dots on a domino card changes every time the card is turned over, until the domino is covered in eight dots.

Suggested use: Communication

The patter: "There once was a button manufacturer called 'Black Dots.' 'Black Dots.' were the favorite of people the world over, but the business was losing money. And it was no wonder, for each manager had his or her own idea of how many dots should be placed on each shipping card. One manager directed employees to pack each dot on a separate card."

(Show side one of the domino.)

"Another told the employees to put four on each card."

(Show side two of the domino.)

"A third manager directed the employees to place three per card."

(Show side one of the domino.)

"The fourth manager felt that the company was wasting cards, and directed that the number be six."

(Show side two of the domino.)

"And so it went. One day, the employees were told to pack one per card."

(Show side one of the domino.)

"The next day, it was four."

(Show side two of the domino.)

"The next, three."

(Show side one of the domino.)

"Then six."

(Show side two of the domino.)

"Well, the employees had had enough. They complained to the general manager, who immediately directed that the managers communicate with one another, and come up with one system. This should have solved the problem, but half of the managers argued that two was the proper number."

(Show side one of the domino.)

"The other half argued for five."

(Show side two of the domino.)

"At this point, the general manager stopped production and called a meeting of all the employees. At the meeting, it was decided to try six dots to a card."

(Show side one of the domino.)

"Six worked pretty well, but there was more space available, so the employees upped the number to eight."

(Show side two of the domino.)

"This higher number saved costs because fewer packing cards were used. As a result, the Black Dot company regained financial success. The company's open communications model became a legend in corporate America. In fact, you may have heard of it. They were celebrated as the first 'dot-com business.'"

Alternative uses: Any situation in which a multitude of options are present.

Parameters: Can be performed three-quarters surrounded, in any size room, and is especially visible from a distance.

Where to find it: Hank Lee's Magic Factory ("What's Next"), Trainer's Warehouse ("Dubious Domino")

Fresh Fish

The action: A paper sign saying "Fresh fish sold here today" is torn up one word at a time, only to be fully restored.

Suggested use: To build teamwork

The patter: "There once was a team that functioned poorly. This team had been tasked with the challenge of creating a sign for a fish market owner. The first team member came up with a sign that said, 'Fresh Fish Sold Here Today.'"

(Display sign.)

"The team could have stopped right there. But each member of the team felt that his imprint had to be on the final product so they all offered suggestions. The second team member said, 'We don't need the word 'Today.' It's obvious that we're selling fish today.'"

So, the first team member tore off the word, "Today."

(Tear off "Today.")

"The third team member took one look at the sign and said, 'You don't need to say 'Here.' Of course it's here. Where else would we sell the fish?'"

"So, the first team member tore off the word, 'Here.'"

(Tear off "Here.")

"The third team member added, 'You wouldn't need to say, "sold." It's obvious that fish are for sale.'"

"So, the first team member tore off the word, 'Sold.'"

(Tear off "Sold.")

"The fourth team member felt the need to contribute and said, 'You could also do away with "Fish." Anyone could smell the fish.'"

"So, the first team member tore off the word, 'Fish.'"

(Tear off "Fish.")

"And, the team, satisfied that everyone's imprint was now on the sign took it to their boss, who said, 'All it says is 'Fresh!?'"

(Display "Fresh")

"'Who could write such a stupid sign?' exclaimed the boss. With that, the boss disbanded the team, and set up a new team to create a sign. That team, in one 10-minute session came up with the idea for a sign that said, 'Fresh Fish Sold Here Today.'"

(Display reconstituted sign.)

"The boss loved this sign, and because the second team stayed focused on the goal, they all got promoted. Meanwhile, all the first team could do was talk about the one that got away."

Alternative uses: Any situation that involves more than one person or step.

Parameters: Can be performed three quarters surrounded, with a previously prepared piece of paper, and may be hard to see in a very large room.

Where to find it: Hank Lee's Magic Factory

Hot Book

The action: A book is opened, and flames shoot out of it.

Suggested use: To gain attention

The patter: "Today's subject is really 'hot,' so please pay close attention, and we won't get 'burned.'"

(Open book.)

Alternative uses: While passing out workbooks
Parameters: Can be performed surrounded, in any circumstance.
Where to find it: Hank Lee's Magic Factory

Hot Cup

The action: Similar to the Hot Book, flames
    rise from a cup of coffee.
Suggested use: To introduce a break
The patter: "We do have coffee available."
    (Display coffee cup.)
    "It is a little hot."
    (Display flames.)
    "So be careful before you drink it."
    ("Take a sip from the cup.)
Alternative uses: Prior to lunch
Parameters: Can be performed surrounded,
    with any coffee cup, except Styrofoam, but is hard to see in a very large room.
Where to find it: Hank Lee's Magic Factory

Magic Coloring Book

The action: A coloring book is displayed with blank pages. The next time it is displayed
    it has black and white drawings. The third and final time it is displayed, the black and
    white drawings have become colorized.
Suggested use: Customer service
The patter: "When customers approach you
    with a problem, your mind should be a
    blank page."

    (Display blank pages.)
    "Listen to what they say, and focus on
the nature of the problem. A customer will
tell you what he feels is necessary to solve
the problem, and expect you to do that for
him."

    (Display black and white pages.)
    "Once you determine the nature of the
problem, provide the solution the customer

wants. But, because we are known as a service leader, we want you to do more. Once you have solved the problem, give the customer something extra as a thank you for being patient while you solved the problem. Your goal should be for that customer to leave feeling better than if the problem had never occurred."

(Display colored pages.)

Alternative uses: Use for situations in which additional information or steps offer improvement.

Parameters: Can be performed surrounded, in all but the largest rooms.

Where to find it: Hank Lee's Magic Factory ("Coloring Book"), Tool Thyme for Trainers ("Magic Coloring Book"), Trainer's Warehouse ("3-Way Magic Coloring Book")

Needle Through Balloon

The action: A needle is pushed all the way through a balloon. The needle is then removed and the balloon stays inflated. Finally, the balloon is punctured with the same needle.

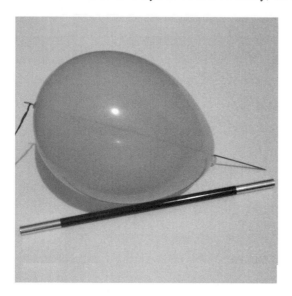

Suggested use: Orientation

The patter: (Display balloon and needle.)

"As you absorb more . . ."

(Begin blowing up the balloon.)

". . . and more information . . ."

(Continue blowing up the balloon.)

". . . over the next several days,"

(Tie the balloon.)

". . . your head may begin to feel like it's going to explode."

(Put the needle into the balloon.)

"It won't."

(Display needle in the balloon.)

"Instead, you will soon find that you comprehend all that information."

(Remove the needle from the balloon.)

"And, unlike this balloon, your brain did not pop."

(Pop the balloon.)

Alternative uses: Any situation in which concentration is critical, or people are likely to feel pressure

Parameters: Can be performed surrounded, in any size room; also purchase the Super Needled Balloon Wand as a carrying case and protector for the wand.

Where to find it: Hank Lee's Magic Factory (Super Needled Balloon)

Creative Finance

The action: A repeated counting bill effect, in which a sum of money grows from $4.00 to $80.00, and back down to $5.00

Suggested use: As a setup to Financial Training

The patter: "I'd like to tell you how I broke the budget and still managed to stay within it. I needed to purchase an office supply that cost $56.00. The petty cash drawer had only $4.00 in it."

(Count out $4.00.)

"So, I borrowed what I could from my boss, $19.00."

(Count out $19.00.)

"With $23.00 in my pocket, I went to the office supply store."

(Count out $23.00.)

"But by the time I got there, something amazing had happened. My $23.00 was now $80.00."

(Count out $80.00.)

"So, I bought the item for $56.00."

(Count out $56.00)

"I paid my boss his $19.00."

(Count out $19.00.)

"And I was left with $4.00, or so I thought. But then my boss pointed out that $56.00 plus $23.00 plus $4.00 equals $79.00. I should have a dollar left. And sure enough, when I counted my change,"

(Count out $5.00.)

". . . there was one . . . two . . . three . . . four . . . and five dollar bills. The extra dollar, I put in the petty cash drawer. Who knows . . . Maybe it'll multiply again."

"Now, can we rely on our finances multiplying by magic? No, clearly not. But with some hard work, and a lot of financial awareness, we can stretch our $4.00 too. So, let's get started."

Alternative uses: Any subject related to finances

Parameters: Can be performed surrounded, in any size room.

Where to find it: Hank Lee's Magic Factory (Creative Finance)

Square the Circle

The action: A shiny metal circle is displayed and then tossed into the air. On catching it, the performer transforms it into a square.

Suggested use: Career development

The patter: (Display the circle.)

"Have you ever felt like a square peg trying to fit into a round hole?"

(Toss the circle in the air.)

"Careers can be like that. We get placed in a job we don't like, or don't do well in, and yet we stay."

(Toss the circle in the air again.)

"Successful career management requires knowing what you do best, so that you can find a career you can fit into."

(Turn the circle into a square.)

Alternative uses: Any situation where one item or person can be viewed in multiple ways.

Parameters: Can be performed surrounded, in any size room.

Where to find it: Hank Lee's Magic Factory

Where to Buy Magic

The appendix provides a listing of magical resources, as well as explanations about the specifics involved in purchasing magic.

ORCHESTRATION

The magic routines just previewed seem simple. But, think back to the level of detail and coordination involved in creating the switch that began this chapter. Every element of the performance had to be in place for the illusion to work. This is true for the routines in this chapter, and of any entertainment presentation. Without proper orchestration of the details, the whole enterprise is doomed.

In Act Three, we will strip away the details behind the performance. As you will soon discover, magicians must deal with a wide variety of challenges; and many of those challenges parallel situations in any classroom. We will examine the solutions magicians have concocted, and determine their relevance to the learning environment. In the process, we'll discover the techniques that allow ordinary people to become wizards, in both the theater and the classroom.

[1] Tarbell, Dr. Harlan (1927). *Tarbell Course in Magic.* New York: Louis Tannon.

[2] Ayto, John (1990). *Dictionary of Word Origins.* New York: Arcade.

[3] <www.middleeastuk.com/culture/mosiac/arabic.htm>

[4] <www.globalvolunteers.org/1main/tanzanialegends.htm>

[5] *Webster's Dictionary of Quotations* (1992). New York. Smithmark.

[6] Cox, Clinton (2001). *Houdini: Master of Illusion.* New York: Scholastic.

[7] Ayto, John (1990).

[8] Fitzee, Dariel (1943). *Showmanship for Magicians.* Pomeroy, OH: Lee Jacobs Productions.

[9] Fitzee, Dariel (1975). *Magic by Misdirection.* Pomeroy, OH: Lee Jacobs Productions.

[10] Davidson, John, and Casady, Cort (1979). *The Singing Entertainer: A Contemporary Study of the Art and Business of Being a Professional.* Los Angeles: Alfred.

[11] Sharpe, Sam H. (1988). *Conjurers' Psychological Secrets.* New York: Hades Publications.

[12] Fitzee, Dariel (1975).

[13] Lozanov, Giorgi (1978). *Suggestology and Outlines of Suggestopedia.* New York: Gordon & Breach.

[14] Davidson, John and Casady, Cort (1979).

[15] Vincent, Bob (1979). *"Show-Business" Is Two Words.* Studio City, CA: Main Track Publications.

[16] Fitzee, Dariel (1975).

ACT THREE

STAGECRAFT

CHAPTER EIGHT

THE STAGE

HARRIET AND THE HOUSEKEEPERS: SCENE TWO

The Technical Skills classroom was one Harriet rarely used. She wondered what shape it was in, and decided to look it over. "A walk-through of the room might give me some ideas," she thought.

She walked toward the room as if she were a housekeeper required to attend her class. What she saw surprised her. The hallway outside the training room was dirty. She would get it cleaned.

The door to the room had old notices taped to it. She removed them.

When she turned the corner to enter the room, she saw a wall of files, left-over computer cables, and other junk. It was the first thing the learners would see. "What message does this mess send?" she exclaimed under her breath, "It's certainly not professional. I'll have to clean this up."

The walls of the room were dirty. She could not get the room painted, but she could put posters over the dirt spots, she thought.

She absorbed the atmosphere of the room itself. Beyond the air conditioning humming cold, the room felt cold and sterile. "The posters will help," she reasoned, "So would some music. Maybe I can create a theme song."

She sat down in a chair. The chairs were comfortable, but arranged in school house style. She preferred half rounds, and would rearrange them the day of the class.

Finally, she looked at the area she would stand in during the class. She discovered that the viewing was partially obscured by a post. She would have to move a little to her left.

With her walk-through complete, she left the room. She still didn't know how she would structure the class, but at least she knew her stage.

"All the signals in a classroom should be in concert with the learning goal." —GIORGI LOZANOV[1]

The Show Biz Training Principle most applicable to this chapter is:

Principle 6: Stage the environment—Orchestrate every detail of the environment.

Another Learnertainment Principle applicable to this chapter is:

Principle 2: Layer meaning—Present your message on several levels.

AN INTRODUCTION TO STAGECRAFT

There is magic in every illusion show, but it's not where you expect to see it. The real magic can be found in the extraordinary stagecraft that the conjurers employ to control themselves and their surroundings. For if you can control yourself and your environment, then you can imply control over nature, and by inference the gift of supernatural powers, and thus influence the spectator.

When speaking about trainers in their book *The Creative Trainer's Handbook*, Michael Lawlor and Peter Handley stated: "If the information we are receiving comes from a source which is lacking in authority or which has a negative emotion connected to it, we will tend to reject it on a subconscious level and not allow it to go in to our long-term memory."[2]

In the performance arena, if with the wave of a hand the magician can levitate the assistant, shouldn't the same magician be able to command the workings of a piece of fabric; or scenery; or his own person? The answer is that the magician should be able to control these elements, and sets out to do so.

Influencing the mind of the spectator depends on stagecraft: the skills, techniques, and devices of the theater.[3] The magician, through careful stagecraft, aligns every possible facet toward the illusion of supernatural control. Dariel Fitzee elaborated in *Magic by Misdirection:*

> **"Throughout the presentation of every trick there are hundreds of factors that shape the course of the spectator's thinking. These may range from the obvious and significant to the most intangible and trivial. All of these details, even the most minor, even the very order in which they occur, shape the spectator's concept. The expert deceptionist deliberately colors all the details, both major and minor, to accomplish his purpose."[4]**

One excellent example is the Hocus Pocus illusion discussed in Chapter 7. As you read the description from the magician's viewpoint, you may been struck with the level of coordination and detail involved. The detail was critical. Without the detail, the performance would appear ordinary, not magical, and the detail comes in the stagecraft.

There are five specific areas of stagecraft that the magician must control. In this chapter, and the four that follow, we will explore the stagecraft that magicians and other performers use to create their entertainment magic. Those areas are as follows:

- ▶ The Environment

- ▶ The Properties

- ▶ The Script

- ▶ Rehearsal

- ▶ The Performer

In Chapter 9, we will examine the use of props in performance. Chapter 10 will focus on script writing, and Chapter 11 on rehearsal. We will explore basic Three-Act structure, and learn what is entailed in a show biz rehearsal. Finally, in Chapter 12, we will continue the persona discussion we started briefly in "Lessons from Comedy." But first, we begin with the environment that the magician must control.

THE ENVIRONMENT

From the theater lobby to the stage to the seating arrangement itself, everything in the environment must suggest magic.

The Lobby

Lobbies are designed to be functional. Theater owners want to get you through the lobby and into the theater as quickly as possible—that is, of course, once you have purchased some refreshments. To encourage sales, the refreshment stand is front and center, with its popcorn enticing you into the theater experience. Off to either side of the refreshment stand, in the areas the patrons will face as they walk toward the auditorium, lobbies will often be set with posters, props, and other displays that foreshadow the show.

For the purpose of this discussion, let us assume that two different magicians are to perform. The first intends to tell a story of an epic fight with the forces of evil. The second intends a comedic story about miscommunication, referred to in the theater as a comedy of errors. As the spectators enter the theater, both magicians will attempt to establish an initial mood. For them, the show begins the moment the spectator enters the theater.

The sinister presentation may choose to set a slightly foreboding environment, with a sinister poster, and if the space is available, mood lighting or props. The comedic presentation may choose a poster display advertising the comedic nature of the performance combined with zany music or props. In both cases, great performers will foreshadow their performance to the full extent the theater owner will allow.

The Seating Arrangement

Stage magicians cannot control this element, but assume they will perform in front of a theater style arrangement. Club magicians such as myself have some ability to move chairs around, but must pay close attention to the sight lines. Many magic illusions can be presented only when the entire audience is in front of the illusion. This leaves club magicians at a disadvantage. Every illusion must be carefully chosen and routined so as to conceal its secret. In addition a buzz saw illusion, where an unlucky assistant is sliced in half, may look great from the stage, but close-up it looks fake and, frankly, disgusting.

In the case of our two magicians, the intimate setting of a three-quarters environment lends itself to comedy, but not to epic struggles. The comedy act can be performed in either environment, but the sinister performance risks becoming humorous if it is presented up close.

Stage Preparation

The stage itself requires close attention. Most stage shows mark their floors with tape so as to connote exact placement of props, people, and movable scenery. This taping prevents performers from bumping into each other. In addition, it documents sight-line problems, and helps position movable set pieces. It also allows the performers to rehearse anywhere space is available. By simply taping the floor of a rehearsal room, the performers can re-create their stage space.

Stage technicians also ensure that the stage is clean, well maintained, and free of any unnecessary materials. Both of our magicians would follow the same procedures regarding the taping and maintaining the stage.

Lighting

Lighting is a major component of the magical atmosphere, and consists of two different light grids, house lighting and stage lighting.

HOUSE LIGHTING

House lighting refers to the lighting over and around the audience. They are the lights that dim as the performance is about to begin, and brighten when the performance is over, or when the audience is brought directly into the action and the performer requires audience illumination.

STAGE LIGHTING

All the lighting that is dedicated to enhancing the performance is considered stage lighting, even if the lighting should happen to be in the audience. Lighting functions as an illuminator of the stage and the performers' faces. As Alan Wurtzel and Stephen Acker explained their work, *Television Production:* "When we light a scene we are painting with light to create shape, texture, highlight and shadow, accent and detail."[5] There are three types of lights used during a stage performance. They are called "key," "fill," and "backlight."

> ▶ Key: The word "key" implies importance, and key lighting is the principle illumination for a stage, and as such, is usually hung from the ceiling in front of and facing the performers.

> ▶ Fill: Fill lighting is used to compensate for the shadows created by key lighting. It is usually positioned on the sides of a stage, facing on-stage.

> ▶ Backlight: Backlight separates the foreground from the background. It provides contrast, and illuminates background items such as backdrops. These lights face scenic items that must be illuminated.

Although the purpose for each is decidedly different, these three types of lighting work together to create the unified effect the audience sees.

MOOD LIGHTING

Lighting is an added indicator of the emotional content of the performance. It is often so critical to success that performances staged outdoors in the daylight will use still lighting. Where white lighting will suggest harshness, amber adds warmth. Red can portray a nighttime city scene, and blue can remind of water, or melancholy moods.

In the case of our two magical presentations, the sinister performance would not be believable if the lighting were bright and vivid. On the other hand, the comedy would have difficulty getting laughs were the stage lighting to be dark and foreboding. Both performances will have created lighting plots, or diagrams, that identify and build the mood required by that performance.

Scenery

The scenery determines what the stage will look like, and what atmosphere is to be portrayed. Our two magicians would require two very different looking stages. The sinister fight with the forces of evil would require a dark, somber treatment. This stage might utilize oversized set pieces and lurking shadows that induce a mood of foreboding. On the other hand, for our magician presenting a comedic farce, the dark, overblown treatment would seem out of place. The implications of the scenery would be in conflict with the stated theme. That magician's comedic presentation requires a light, lilting feel, with details that suggest whimsy.

CLASSROOM-IN-THE-ROUND

In the learning environment, the stage you set has great impact on the learning that occurs. Sharon B. Merriam and Rosemary S. Caffarella summarized the importance of the environment in their book, *Learning in Adulthood,* when they said: "The most common explanation (for how the brain handles incoming information) is that information from our environment is registered within sensory memory through our visual, auditory, and tactile senses."[6]

The stage you set in your classroom should provide rich sources of information for your learners' visual, auditory, and tactile senses. In *Making Connections,* brain researchers Renate Nummela Caine and Geoffrey Caine added: "Because the learner is constantly searching for connections on many levels, educators need *to orchestrate the experiences* [original emphasis] from which learners extract meaning."[7]

To create this orchestrated experience, you should think of your classroom as your stage. In fact, the origin of the word *stage* can be found in the vulgar Latin word *staticum*, meaning "a standing place." [8] The classroom is your standing place. It is your "theater-in-the-round."

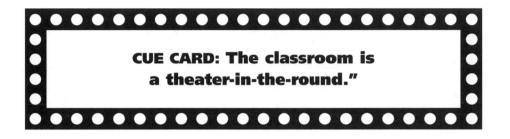

CUE CARD: The classroom is a theater-in-the-round."

A properly set stage, with supportive reminders strategically placed throughout the classroom, reinforces learning. As Nummela Caine and Geoffrey Caine explained: "The teacher can and should organize materials that will be outside the focus of the learner's attention."[9]

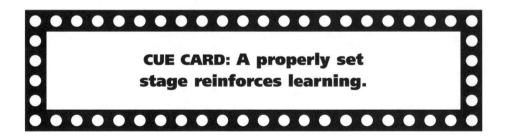

CUE CARD: A properly set stage reinforces learning.

The Lobby

When we first meet someone, our initial impressions of that person are formed within seconds, and linger long afterwards. This dynamic is equally true in the classroom. The first impression presented to your trainees as they enter your learning environment will establish or diminish your credibility and that of your instruction.[10]

As the learners enter, they should be enticed into an exciting exploration of learning. Everything about the entryway should suggest invitation. The first visual images a learner

CLASSROOM SHOW READINESS FORM

Part 1: Outside the Classroom

The approach to the classroom	Yes	No	Corrective Action to Take:
▸ Is the hall carpet/flooring clean?	_____	_____	_____
▸ Are the walls dirty?	_____	_____	_____
▸ Are all posted signs neat and orderly?	_____	_____	_____
▸ Do posted signs undercut your message?	_____	_____	_____
▸ Can the hallway be more inviting?	_____	_____	_____
▸ Can the hall support your content?	_____	_____	_____

The classroom door

	Yes	No	Corrective Action to Take:
▸ Are old notices taped on the door?	_____	_____	_____
▸ Is the door dirty?	_____	_____	_____
▸ Will the door stay open if you need it to?	_____	_____	_____
▸ Does the door squeak?	_____	_____	_____
▸ Can the door be more inviting?	_____	_____	_____
▸ Can the door support your content?	_____	_____	_____

Part 2: Inside the Classroom

At first glance	Yes	No	Corrective Action to Take:
▸ Does the room look inviting?	_____	_____	_____
▸ Can you make it more inviting?	_____	_____	_____
▸ Can the room support your content?	_____	_____	_____

The stage

	Yes	No	Corrective Action to Take:
▸ How can the platform be more inviting?	_____	_____	_____
▸ How can the platform support your content?	_____	_____	_____

The room

	Yes	No	Corrective Action to Take:
▸ Is the lighting adequate?	_____	_____	_____
▸ Are the walls clean?	_____	_____	_____
▸ Is the floor clean?	_____	_____	_____

▶ Is the room cluttered?	_____	_____	_____
▶ Does the room smell pleasant?	_____	_____	_____
▶ Is the temperature comfortable?	_____	_____	_____
▶ Will sound travel well?	_____	_____	_____
▶ Can the room be more engaging?	_____	_____	_____
The seating			
▶ Are the seats comfortable?	_____	_____	_____
▶ Is the seating arrangement appropriate?	_____	_____	_____
▶ Can the stage be seen from every seat?	_____	_____	_____
▶ Are the tables clean?	_____	_____	_____
▶ Do the chairs and tables wobble?	_____	_____	_____
The scenery			
▶ Can you decorate the room?	_____	_____	_____
▶ Will the decorations support your content?	_____	_____	_____
Lighting			
▶ Will your face be lit?	_____	_____	_____
▶ Will the learners see their notes?	_____	_____	_____

TABLE 8-1

sees in the hallway before he or she enters should be clean and orderly. No stepping around file cabinets or trash cans. The hall should smell fresh, not mildewed. The classroom door should be open in invitation.

Once the participants walk through the open doorway, the trainer should be waiting, personally serving as a welcoming presence, not covered in sweat while scrambling to set up. As the trainees look past the trainer, and into the room, the environment should beckon them forward and into the enjoyment of learning. If it is morning, the smell of fresh coffee should surround them. Music should comfort their ears. The learning environment should be alive with items to touch. In short, the learning should begin the moment the learners enter the classroom. Use the Classroom Show Readiness Form in Table 8-1 to help you set your stage.

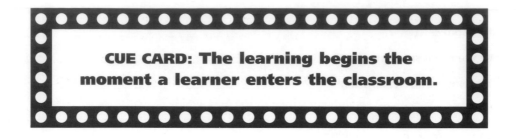

CUE CARD: The learning begins the moment a learner enters the classroom.

The Seating Arrangement

Just as magicians contend with the theater layout they are given, instructors may not have control over the seating arrangements in their classroom. You are likely to encounter a number of seating arrangements:

▶ U-shaped

▶ Conference Room

▶ Schoolhouse

▶ Rounds

▶ Half-rounds

▶ Theater

▶ Amphitheater

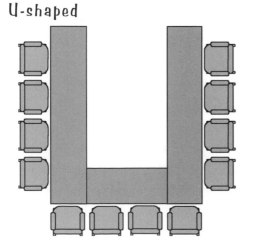

U-shaped

U-SHAPED

In a U-shaped arrangement, learners sit on the outer sides of a "U" shaped table with the instructor in the middle. This arrangement works best in situations in which the focus is on learner interaction, not instructor presentation.

CONFERENCE ROOM

A conference room table places the trainees on three sides with the trainer at the head of the table. I find this environment more conducive to

Conference Room

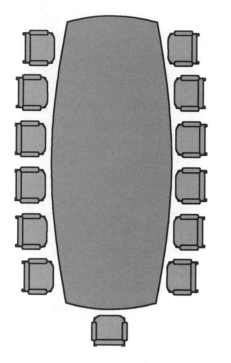

Schoolhouse

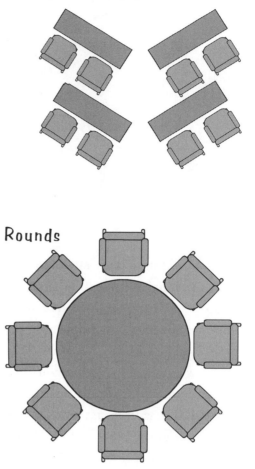

Rounds

meetings than to learning. Although I have conducted a number of trainings in these style rooms, they are not ideal for entertainment techniques.

SCHOOLHOUSE

Two or three learners are placed at a table, facing front, in a Schoolhouse arrangement, with the instructor standing at the front of the room. This arrangement has two major drawbacks. It feels like school, potentially resurrecting learner fears as discussed in Chapter 1. Schoolhouse seating also tends to discourage group discussions by in effect limiting the number of people a learner can consult with to one or two.

ROUNDS

Rounds place participants, in groups of seven to nine, at a rounded table, with the facilitator in front of the room. Rounds, if the tables are not too large, provide opportunities for learners to converse directly with each other. The drawback comes in sight line problems. Regardless of his or her position, the facilitator is always speaking to someone's back.

Half-rounds

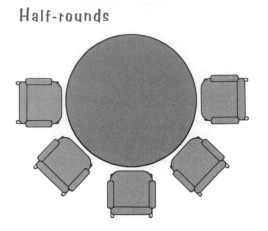

HALF-ROUNDS

Learners, in groups of five or six, sit at the back of a rounded table in half-rounds, while the instructor stands in front of the room. Half-rounds have a number of advantages, and is my preferred smaller venue seating style. They allow learners to confer with each other, while also avoiding the sight line problems inherent in rounds.

THEATER

Theater seating places attendees shoulder to shoulder, facing forward, in side-by-side seats. Although not ideal for group discussions, this arrangement, owing to its traditional nature, is ripe for show biz techniques. Illusion sight line issues are not a problem, and audience visibility can be assured by the use of a platform or video projection equipment.

This style has become a preferred arrangement for learning conferences. Some facilitators worry that the seating arrangement makes group activities impossible, but that assumption is faulty. It is true that theater style seating makes small group activities more difficult. But, within easy reach of every participant are eight other people to form a group. (Three in front, three in back, and one on either side.) Theater style seating does not prevent activity, but it does require more careful planning on the part of the instructor.

Theater

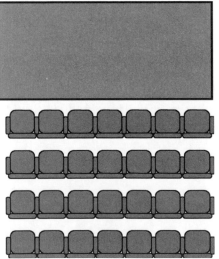

A factor to consider in theater seating is the placement of the aisleways. Try to have the aisles placed on either side, not in the center. If the aisle is in the center, you will find yourself looking down a big chasm in the classroom as you speak. Rather than engaging the majority of the audience with your eyes every time you look straight ahead, you will be forced to look either left or right, but never at all your learners at once. You also run the risk of people walking in front of you as they come and go from the classroom.

You may also discover that the majority of attendees choose to sit further back, leaving the first few rows empty. This makes communication harder for you, and forces latecomers to walk up front for a seat. A smarter technique is to rope off or place tape across the back rows, so people are forced forward. This will also save those back rows for the latecomers.

AMPHITHEATER

In amphitheater style seating, learners are slightly wrapped around the facilitator on the left and right. Amphitheater seating is my personal favorite for large-scale presentations. It places the instructor in the center of the action. It feels less formal than theater style seating, and it allows audience members, owing to the wraparound seating, to make eye contact with other audience members. Because of its great similarity to theater style seating, the same descriptions apply.

Regardless of the arrangement you decide on, or must contend with, show biz techniques add value. You should account for those factors in advance, and design your presentation accordingly. While advance planning, ask yourself the questions listed in Table 8-2.

The Stage

A major difference between theatrical performances and instruction is the fact that theatrical audiences are often separated by the theater's "fourth wall," where classroom audiences are within this wall. They are on the stage. In other words, the classroom stage is not the podium, or the area in front of the room, it is the *entire* room. The classroom *is* your stage, and, as such, it should be staged.

Amphitheater

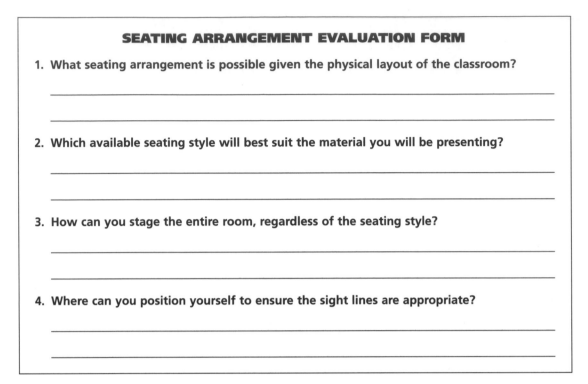

SEATING ARRANGEMENT EVALUATION FORM

1. What seating arrangement is possible given the physical layout of the classroom?

_____

_____

2. Which available seating style will best suit the material you will be presenting?

_____

_____

3. How can you stage the entire room, regardless of the seating style?

_____

_____

4. Where can you position yourself to ensure the sight lines are appropriate?

_____

_____

TABLE 8-2

Room Lighting

Just as theatrical lighting establishes a mood and tone, the classroom lighting will either aid or distract from learning. The fact is that many learning conference rooms, especially in supposedly state of the art hotels, have poorly designed lighting schemes. Often, the stage area is placed with little to no attention to lighting, and with no key, fill, or backlight lighting available. The result is an instructor whose face is in shadows because the only available light comes from available ceiling lighting.

If you have any control over the location of the stage area, place it where the lighting will pick up your face. If you cannot control the location, consider hanging additional lighting. During my road years, we traveled with portable lights that could be clamped onto the ceiling and controlled from the stage. It is a habit I continue to this day. This may seem like extra work for little gain, but it can be critical. If the venue is large, and the learners cannot see your face, your props, or your hand gestures, how can they comprehend the meaning of your message?

Adequate lighting is obviously required for reading and note taking, but studies demonstrate that too much light can be stressful. The goal should be for a well lit, but not bright, environment. An excellent technique is to alternate areas of bright and dark lighting. If, like the seating arrangement, you have no control over your lighting, you should still take extra care when adjusting light levels for videos. My advice would be to never turn the lights off. Most videos can be viewed quite adequately without fully darkening the room. If you turn the lights off, how will you know if your learners are paying attention? If you must turn the lights off, allow adjustment time when you turn them back on. Turn them on gradually if possible, or call a break so that people have time to readjust.[11]

Room Scenery

Few trainers would argue that they have too much time with their trainees, and yet do not take advantage of all the teachable moments available to them.

CUE CARD: Use every teachable moment available to you.

What learners see when they look away from you, and they will, is a teachable moment. If the visual your participants see is a pile of junk in storage along the side wall, you have unintentionally suggested something about the value of your instruction. In the words of Renate Nummela Caine and Geoffrey Caine, "The subtle signs and surface indicators reflect what we actually are and not what we try to be."[12]

These kind of extraneous stimuli negate an opportunity to reinforce learning. Scientists tell us that 90 percent of all information is taken in visually.[13] Your classroom should be alive with visual stimuli that support the key learning points. You should set the stage with food for the eyes.

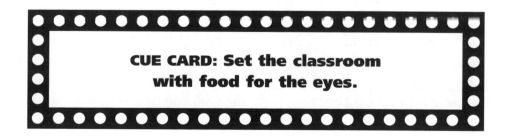

CUE CARD: Set the classroom with food for the eyes.

Adorning the Walls

Place posters that align with your learning points on the walls. Renate Nummela Caine and Geoffrey Caine explained:

> **"The brain absorbs information and signals that lie beyond the field of attention. These may be stimuli that one perceives 'out of the side of the eyes,' such as gray and unattractive walls in a classroom. Peripheral stimuli also include the subtle signals that are within the field of attention but are not consciously noticed (such as a hint of a smile or slight changes in body posture). This means that the brain responds to the entire sensory context in which the teaching or communications occurs."[14]**

Another technique is to place quotes on the walls. For my own sessions, I have a collection of quotes printed on oversized colored paper, laminated, and cut in odd shapes. Before a class begins I will select laminated quotes appropriate to the subject being taught and spread them out on the learners' tables. As the learners enter the classroom, I instruct them to select their favorite quotes and tape them to the walls. In this way, I have begun the session before actual instruction begins. The activity is holistic, engaging, moves people around the room, and provides a quick reference point for discussion as the learning unfolds.

Projection Viewing

Projection equipment should be placed so that all the attendees can view the presentation. You should also consider the danger posed by electrical cords that stretch across the area in which you will be standing. There are occasions in which theatrical productions must run cables across the floor. In such cases, the resulting wires are securely duct taped to the floor. The danger to any instructor is not so much from electrocution as it is from foolishness. Performers, including Dick Van Dike and Chevy Chase, have made careers out of tripping over things. Trainers should leave pratfalls to the professionals. Tape those wires down.

A Tangled Web   By Millbower and Yager

Did he mean to do that?

SLIDES AND OVERHEADS

When creating slides and overheads for training environments, three factors should be considered:

► The effects of color

► Text usage

► The placement of graphics

The Effects of Color

You should pay special attention to the colors you choose for overheads. Colors are influenced by the colors that surround them. For instance, a light color against a dark background will draw more attention than a dark color against a light background. In their book *Television Production,* communications professors Alan Wurtzel and Stephen R. Acker make this very point:

> **"Important foreground elements ought to be lighter in color and brighter than the background so that they will stand out more prominently and attract the viewer's attention. Nearly all graphics prepared for television use light lettering on a dark background. Because of this design decision, the words come toward the audience, while the background recedes."** [15]

Scientists have discovered that the brain reacts differently to different color frequencies. Of special interest is their discovery that people see color before content, and that yellow is usually the first color that people distinguish. Yellow is also conducive to positive moods. These factors make yellow the ideal color for highlighting critical information in electronic presentations.[16] Table 8-3 provides additional color-related information.

CUE CARD: Yellow is the first color people see.

COLOR PLACEMENT TABLE

General tendencies:

Bright colors: Spark energy, creativity

Light colors: Enhance learning

Dark colors: Lower stress, increase feelings of peacefulness

Specific colors:

Red

Effect: Engages, elicits emotion

Use: To elicit creative thinking and boost short-term energy, may trigger aggressiveness during stress

Yellow

Effect: First color the brain distinguishes, creates positive moods

Use: To attract attention and elicit positive feelings

Orange

Effect: Exhibits characteristics halfway between red and yellow

Use: To elicit creative thinking, boost short-term energy, to draw attention

Pink

Effect: Restful and calming

Use: To create a soothing environment

Blue

Effect: Calming, increases sense of well being

Use: To enhance study, deep thinking, concentration, when combined with red frames will create keener insights

Purple

Effect: Creates tranquilizing moods

Use: To induce relaxation

Green

Effect: Calming

Use: To enhance productivity and long-term energy

White

Effect: Bright, disruptive, and hard to look at

Use: Avoid where possible, substitute off-white or beige

Black

Effect: Inhibits learning

Use: Avoid, substitute off-white or beige

Gray

Effect: Little effect

Use: In situations where no emotional response is intended

Source: André Vermeulen, Neuro-Link. <www.neurolink.co.za>

TABLE 8-3

Text Usage

Just as magicians pay careful attention to sight lines, ensuring that everyone in the audience can see, the facilitator should ensure that everyone can see, and understand, the words placed on the projection screen. Visibility will be increased greatly if you observe a few simple guidelines:

► Restrict yourself to one thought idea per slide. A magician would not perform two illusions at once. The resulting dual focus would confuse the audience.

► Edit the words you place on any slide to the absolute minimum. Make the remaining words as clear and succinct as possible.

► The text font should be readable from a distance.

► Avoid ornate, scriptive fonts.

► Maintain a minimum font size of 24 points.

► 18-point is readable, but does require more effort on the part of your participants.

► Font sizes of 28 to 32 are easily readable.

► The larger the font, the less text you can place on a slide.

► Limit slide text to six or seven words per line.

► Avoid lettering that's entirely in uppercase. It is more difficult to read than lowercase text.

The Placement of Graphics

"Try to avoid verbal approaches. Start with images. Stay with images."[17] Luke Sullivan offered that advice for advertisers. It is equally valid for instruction. Graphics are an ideal way to make your point without words, or to reinforce the words you use. They provide a deeper, holistic level of meaning than words can achieve alone, while fully supporting the message of the words. The trick is to select graphics that coincide with the meaning of your text. Ensure, however, that the graphics you select closely relate to the text. Loosely related graphics will only confuse the focus, and may send different messages than those you intend.

Sensory Stimulants

Victor Hugo once commented, "Nothing awakens a reminiscence like an odor."[18]

In *Conjurers' Psychological Secrets*, Sam. H. Sharpe advised magicians that "we judge things according to our senses."[19] A similar comment comes from Joseph Pine and James Gilmore. In *The Experience Economy*, they advise businesses to enhance their environment through the use of the five senses: "The sensory stimulants that accompany an experience should support and enhance its theme. The more effectively an experience engages the senses, the more memorable it will be."[20] With these comments in mind, a few sensory factors should be considered.

ROOM TEMPERATURE

One dynamic that affects a number of senses is the training room's temperature. An empty room should be cooler than you intend it to be. When the learners arrive, their body heat will heat up the room for you. The room temperature should be comfortable: neither warm or cold, but comfortably cool. Studies have shown that the brain performs better when it is cooler.[21] Keep your temperature ranges between 66 and 72 degrees Fahrenheit, but slightly on the cool side.

AUDITORY, VISUAL, AND KINESTHETIC APPROACHES

In learning theory, auditory, visual, and kinesthetic approaches use three of the senses, but ignore the learning potential of smell and taste. I have always felt that an auditory, visual, and kinesthetic approach is too simplistic. Virtually everything that occurs in the learning environment can be seen and heard, and if the participants are taking notes, a lazy instructor can claim that all three are covered, and thus everything possible is being done to aid learning. I believe in a more expansive approach in which you utilize all five senses, including taste and smell.

ROOM ODOR

The classroom should give forth an attractive odor. We know intuitively that a foul smell distracts attention. It is not a stretch to believe that the opposite is also true, and that a pleasant odor aids learning. It is also reasonable to suppose that, much the way popcorn draws us into the theater lobby, other odors may draw us into learning.

Although research is ongoing, we do know that our sense of smell is directly linked with our limbic systems, and that smell has a "subtle effect on our level of relaxation or agitation."[22] In addition, neurolinguistic programmers recommend the smell of peppermint or lemon to enhance productivity.[23] Just as magicians use the smell of fire to draw us a spectacular illusion, trainers can use coffee to draw us into an early morning learning room.

Odors can also detract when overused. If your classroom becomes heavily perfumed, and one of your learners suffers from allergies, the classroom time might become extremely uncomfortable. Commercial room sprays are available, but most only cover existing odors with other odors. Until the researchers can tell us more, it is sufficient to be aware of the odors present in your classroom, and to make every attempt to establish an "odor friendly" environment.

ROOM TASTE

For centuries, people have regarded the breaking of bread as a major rite of communal humanity. When people eat together, they feel a sense of community and belonging. Although learning room feasts are unnecessary and can be financially prohibitive, providing basics such as coffee, tea, sodas, candies, popcorn, and other light snacks engages the sense of taste and in this way increases the sense of belonging.

AN OUNCE OF PREPARATION

By now you have no doubt realized that staging the environment requires advance planning. In *Poor Richard's Almanac,* Ben Franklin once said that "An ounce of prevention is worth a pound of cure."[24] Planning allows you to prevent problems before they become catastrophes. So, plan for the unexpected. Control what you can, and plan for the uncontrollable. Design your instruction in such a way that you are never surprised by the circumstances that confront you. Have a backup plan for your backup plan. And then, back up your backup plan. Table 8-4 is provided to assist you.

MOVE IN

Your stage will be your home for the duration of the learning. Visit the learning environment well beforehand. Become comfortable with it. Walk up to the stage from as many different angles as possible. Walk onto it. Walk around it. Become one with it.

Meet with the people who control the room. Make friends with the technicians. They can make or break your performance. Ask for their help in meeting all of your logistical needs, and thank them when they assist.

On the day of the event, arrive early. Pick up the mood of the room. Become one with it. For, in the eyes of your learners, the environment is an extension of you.

FIVE-SENSES ENHANCEMENT FORM

Use this form to enhance the classroom environment through the five senses.

Sight
▶ What visuals are present in the classroom?

_____

_____

▶ What visuals should be present in the classroom?

_____

_____

▶ How can you add those visuals?

_____

_____

Smell
▶ What odors are present in the classroom?

_____

_____

▶ What odors should be present in the classroom?

_____

_____

▶ How can you add those odors?

_____

_____

Touch
▶ What touchable items are present in the classroom?

_____

_____

▶ What touchable items should be present in the classroom?

_____

_____

▶ How can you add those touchable items?

_____

_____

Taste
▶ What tastes are present in the classroom?

_____

_____

▶ What tastes should be present in the classroom?

_____

_____

▶ How can you add those tastes?

_____

_____

Hearing
▶ What sounds are present in the classroom?

_____

_____

▶ What sounds should be present in the classroom?

_____

_____

▶ How can you add those sounds?

_____

_____

TABLE 8-4

[1] Lozanov, Giorgi (1978). *Suggestology and Outlines of Suggestopedia.* New York: Gordon & Breach,

[2] Lawlor, Michael, and Handley, Peter (1996). *The Creative Trainer: Holistic Facilitation Skills for Accelerated Learning.* London: McGraw-Hill.

[3] *The American Heritage College Dictionary,* 3rd edit. (1997). Boston: Houghton Mifflin.

[4] Fitzee, Dariel (1975). *Magic by Misdirection.* Pomeroy, OH: Lee Jacobs Productions.

[5] Wurtzel, Alan, and Acker, Stephen R. (1989). *Television Production.* New York: McGraw-Hill.

[6] Merriam, Sharan B., and Caffarella, Rosemary S. (1999). *Learning in Adulthood: A Comprehensive Guide.* San Francisco: Jossey-Bass.

[7] Caine, Renate Nummela, and Caine, Geoffrey (1991). *Making Connections: Teaching and the Human Brain.* Parsippany, NJ: Dale Seymour.

[8] Ayto, John (1990). *Dictionary of Word Origins.* New York: Arcade Publishing.

[9] Caine, Renate Nummela, and Caine, Geoffrey (1991).

[10] Brydon, Steven R. and Scott, Michael D. (2000). *Between One and Many: The Art and Science of Public Speaking,* 3rd edit. Mountain View, CA: Mayfield.

[11] Vermeulen, André (May 22, 2000). ASTD International Conference. Session M508.

[12] Caine, Renate Nummela, and Caine, Geoffrey (1991).

[13] André Vermeulen, of Neuro-Link.

[14] O'Keefe and Nadel 1978 quoted by Caine, Renate Nummela, and Caine, Geoffrey (1991).

[15] Wurtzel, Alan, and Acker, Stephen R. (1989).

[16] Howard, Pierce J. (1994). *The Owner's Manual for the Brain: Every Day Applications from Mind–Brain Research.* Austin, TX: Leornian Press.

[17] Sullivan, Luke (1998). *Hey Whipple, Squeeze This: A Guide to Creating Great Ads.* New York: John Wiley & Sons.

[18] *Webster's Dictionary of Quotations New York: Smithmark.*

[19] *Sharpe, Sam H. (1988). Conjurers' Psychological Secrets.* New York: Hades Publications.

[20] Pine II, Joseph B., and Gilmore, James H. (1999). *The Experience Economy.* Boston: Harvard Business School Press.

[21] Howard, Pierce J. (1994).

[22] Kallan, 1991 as reported in Howard, Pierce J. (1994).

[23] Vermeulen, André (May 22, 2000).

[24] *Ben Franklin's Wit and Wisdom* (1987). White Plains: Peter Pauper Press.

CHAPTER NINE

PROPS

AN INTRO TO TIME MANAGEMENT

It was my turn to teach the time management class. And because it was a time management class, I wanted to start the class on time. I also knew that there would be some stragglers. (Anyone who arrived on time probably didn't need the class anyway.) I decided to frame up the discussion with an attention-getter that would honor the trainees who had arrived on time, while giving the stragglers more time to arrive. I grabbed a couple of props and headed into the classroom.

I began at the exact class start time. After introducing myself, I said, "Today's topic is time management. To help us out, I've brought in an arrow. Can anyone tell me how an arrow relates to time management?"

No one responded.

"How quickly does an arrow fly?" I asked.

One student took the bait and responded, "Fast."

"That's right. In fact, you could say that time flies like an arrow."

They all nodded.

I next produced a banana. "How about the banana? How does it relate to time management?"

There was no answer. I think they were stunned.

Finally, a quiet voice responded, "Err, bananas don't stay fresh long?"

"That's right. How long will an uneaten banana last before it spoils?"

"A few days" was the reply.

"What would happen if I peeled the banana and let it sit on the counter?" As I asked the question, I peeled the banana.

Warming to the discussion now, another student joked, "It would stink."

I nodded. "And attract flies. Why though?"

"Because it spoiled" responded another student.

I then asked, "How does that relate to managing your time?"

Finally one learner got it. "You never know how long you have before you spoil?"

"That's correct." I smiled. "We don't know how much time we have." Then, looking as if the idea had just occurred to me, I stated, "This reminds me of a quote from Marx." I paused before adding, "Groucho Marx that is."

They laughed and I knew I had them. I displayed the quote.

"Time flies like an arrow, but fruit flies like a banana."

With that, they all groaned.

"So remember," I continued undaunted, "Be an arrow, not a banana. Let's learn how to manage our time."

With that, I began the class.

"Let your concept be so visually powerful that a viewer would get it with the sound turned off."—LUKE SULLIVAN[1]

The Show Biz Training techniques in this chapter are based on the following Learnertainment Principles:

Principle 7: Use mnemonics—Provide visual learning cues.
Principle 2: Layer meaning—Present your message on several levels.

Other Learnertainment Principles applicable to this chapter are:

Principle 1: Make it fun—Create an atmosphere of playfulness.

Principle 4: Evoke emotion—Engage your learners emotionally.

PROPS AND THEIR USAGE

We have discussed the major elements in the performance environment, with the exception of two: the performer and the performer's props. In this chapter, we will focus on the use of props.

A prop can be defined as any article that a performer handles to make his or her point. Props are inseparable from staged performances. Imagine the magician without a magic wand, or a rabbit, and you see the point.

In general there are five common entertainment uses for props:

► As a visual aid

► To frame the environment

► To capture attention

► As a metaphor for the subject at hand

► As a pacing device.

We will first discuss each of these uses in the performance arena, and then explore ways that props can be applied to the learning environment. Then, we will examine the OFF-BEAT™ Prop Placement Matrix. Finally, we will conclude by discussing specific props, and their potential use applications.

Props as Visual Aids

There's an old saying: "A picture is worth a thousand words." It's certainly true in regard to props. They are visual clues that convey information without words.

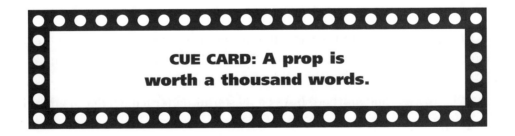

CUE CARD: A prop is worth a thousand words.

Often, when a book is made into a live production or a film, whole sections of the book are omitted. Whereas in a book an author can describe every circumstance in great detail, an entertainment can only be a few hours long. There is limited time to make each point.

If a script calls for an actor to read a newspaper, the very act of holding a newspaper in front of her face tells the audience what the actor is doing. With this clear visual, little explanation is required. The prop saves words. When performers can use props to replace words, they have in essence freed up time. This in turn allows the audience to focus on the larger points being made in the entertainment.

Advertising faces an accelerated version of this time crunch. Where a movie or a live entertainment is typically two hours long, a commercial has only 30 seconds to tell its story. To communicate quickly, advertisers often rely on props. The commercials we explored in Chapter 3 offer some great examples:

▶ The Timex commercials visually demonstrated the toughness of the product so effectively that the tag line, "Timex, it takes a licking and keeps on ticking," functioned as a punch line to the visual. The phrase ended the commercial, but was not necessary as a statement of fact. The visual had already proven the point. The phrase simply verbalized what the audience had already viewed.

▶ The visual of squeezably soft Charmin states, without the needs for words, that the tissue is soft.

▶ The Energizer bunny is a highly visual prop that suggests long-lasting batteries.

Chapter 5 taught us that many comedians rely on props. We also discovered that some items are inherently funny. Table 9-1 features a listing of performers. See if you can match each performer with the prop that helped them become famous.

Different performers have become identified with specific props. Perhaps the best usage of props as visual aids can be seen in Charlie Chaplin's portrayal of the Little Tramp. Chaplin, in that silent film era, could not use dialog. He had to impart information visually. Consequently, his character portrayals relied heavily on props. Chaplin used his undersized bowler hat, twirling cane, and shoes worn on the wrong feet to create a funny, inoffensive personality.

He would also interact with the items he found around him. In one famous example, *The Gold Rush* (1925), Chaplin portrayed a down-on-his-luck gold prospector trapped in a desolate Alaskan cabin for the winter. With no food to eat, Chaplin's character ate his shoe. He ate the shoe leather as if it were a steak, and the shoe laces became spaghetti noodles that he twirled and slurped. It was a masterful performance, and a great demonstration of prop usage.

THE COMEDIAN'S PROP

See if you can match the performer with the prop(s) that performer used to become famous.

Charlie Chaplin	Cigar and glasses
Gallagher	Cane and derby
Michael Jackson	Oversized glasses
Elton John	Pencils
Larry King	Sequined glove
David Letterman	Suspenders
Groucho Marx	Watermelon

ANSWER KEY: CHARLIE CHAPLIN—CANE AND DERBY; GALLAGHER—WATERMELON; MICHAEL JACKSON—SEQUINED GLOVE; ELTON JOHN—OVERSIZED GLASSES; LARRY KING—SUSPENDERS; DAVID LETTERMAN—PENCILS; GROUCHO MARX—CIGAR AND GLASSES

TABLE 9-1

Props as Visual Learning Aids

Named after the Greek goddess Mnemosyne, the mother of the Muses, a mnemonic is a devise that aids in the memorization through the arts.[2] In the learning environment, props are effective mnemonics.

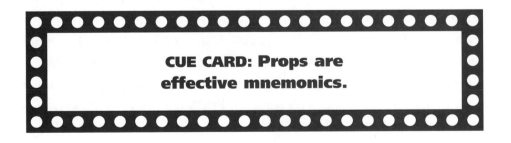

CUE CARD: Props are effective mnemonics.

People process and react to data on many levels. Where traditional learning methods appeal to the logical neocortex, props work on a peripheral level, appealing to the emotional limbic system. They help people process your learning points holistically. They attract attention, offer appealing visuals, indicate fun, and give your learners a metaphorical anchor for remembering the material.

In addition, 90 percent of the information people absorb is taken in visually.[3] It is no accident that the introduction of television sounded the death knell for radio drama. When given a choice, people preferred to see the information being presented. Yet, many instructors rely on their voices to carry the day. Imagine what would happen if you conducted your classes with the learners sitting facing the back of the classroom. It would be a short class.

Use this need for visual information. Harness it to your advantage. Bring your classroom to life with visual mnemonics that support key learning points. To emphasize those points, hold up items that say visually what you are saying verbally. Give your learners something to look at, and their minds something to anchor the learning to. Set your stage with food for the eyes.

Props as Frames for the Environment

Another entertainment function of props is as a framing device. Magicians make extensive use of framing devices. At any illusion show, audience members expect to see swords, tables, colorful silks, bouquets of flowers, saws, cards, and all sorts of other devices. Consequently, magicians populate their show with such items. The props visually affirm the expectation of magic to follow.

Movies frame their scenes with props too. For example, *Shakespeare in Love* (1998) is a fictionalized story of the Bard's experiences while writing *Romeo and Juliet*. The movie often shows Shakespeare writing with a feather pen. Imagine the confusion that would occur if he instead used a computer. As small a matter as a writing utensil can disrupt, or frame, a scene.

Props are so effective at framing a scene that non-entertainers have used them too. One example comes from the political arena. American president Franklin D. Roosevelt (FDR) was elected during the Great Depression. It was a time of great uncertainty, with approximately 25 percent of the population out of work. FDR made it a point to flash a smile whenever possible—and not only to smile, but also to display a can-do aura of jaunty activity. Considering an early bout with polio left FDR's legs paralyzed and confined him to a wheelchair, this was no small feat. FDR had to show activity without walking. He did so through the use of a prop, a cigarette holder. Any cigarette holder would not have worked. This was a long-stemmed one. The very act of clutching it in his teeth made him smile, and, by wiggling it with his tongue, he could display extra bodily movement. The length of the cigarette holder allowed its movement to seem bigger than it was, and gave FDR an aura of movement when there was none.[4]

Props as Frames for the Learning Environment

Just as swords, tables, colorful silks, bouquets of flowers, saws, cards, and all sorts of other devices frame a magical environment, the entertainment savvy trainer props the classroom with items that draw attention. As learners walk into the classroom, they should immediately comprehend the nature of the environment they are entering.

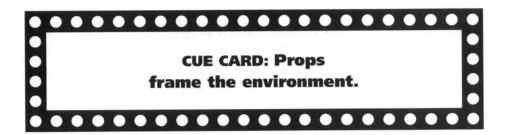

**CUE CARD: Props
frame the environment.**

In their excellent book about the placement of entertainment in business service environments, *The Experience Economy,* Joseph B. Pine II and James H. Gilmore describe just such a way to enhance any environment: "Perhaps the most straightforward approach to making goods more experiential is to add elements that enhance the customer's *sensory interaction* with them."[5]

Frame the classroom as an enjoyable place to be. Create a festive, inviting environment. Make the room seem like a party with a purpose. Put the subject of your class on display. For machinery training, display the tools the learners will use. If the subject is leadership, place leadership quote plaques around the room. For a diversity presentation, display culturally appropriate materials. Regardless of your subject, find small, inexpensive items indicative of that subject, and place them on the learners' tables as centerpieces.

Capturing Attention with Props

Props are great attention-getters, and performers use props to set themselves apart from the crowd. The props made them different. Here are some examples:

▶ Charlie Chaplin used his cane and hat to mimic, and thus lampoon, the pompous mannerisms and attitudes of the pretentious rich.

▶ People would go to Elton John concerts in part because of the outrageousness of his outfits.

▶ The one sequined glove helped Michael Jackson break through to superstar status.

▶ Larry King's suspenders helped differentiate him from other talk show hosts, and helped propel his CNN show to success.

For those performers, props provided immediate identification. Even if a member of the public could not recall their names, especially true of parents trying to remember the names of current rock stars, those performers could be identified by their signature prop.

Capturing Learners' Attention with Props

In my own nightclub performance career there was a constant need to capture attention. The audience had so much stimuli available to them that their attention was usually split. To pull distracted people into the activities, we would display an unexpected prop. The audience members would become interested in the prop and its purpose. As they thought, "What in the world is that for?" we would refocus their attention.

In a similar manner, it is often necessary to refocus learners' attention once they become comfortable in the learning environment. To capture your learners' attention, display an item related to your subject matter. In the process, you will be establishing a mnemonic connection to the learning point. If the prop is small enough to handle, engage your learners' sense of touch by passing it around the room.

CUE CARD: Props capture attention.

Props as Metaphors for the Subject at Hand

Props provide great metaphoric examples. Perhaps the world's most famous play, Shakespeare's *Hamlet,* features a scene in which lead character Hamlet holds the skull of his former mentor and court jester, Yorick, as he ponders human mortality. Yorick's skull is a metaphor for the human condition as Hamlet explains it: "A man may fish with the worm that hath eat of a king, and eat of the fish that hath fed of that worm."[6]

Metaphoric prop usage is not limited to show biz. Political leaders have used them too. In some cases, the usage was so effective that the verbal mnemonic tied to the usage has entered our language. Two examples come from different American presidential campaigns featuring relatives.

In 1840, William Henry Harrison won the U.S. presidency from incumbent Martin Van Buren. Harrison's supporters would make "Harrison balls" of 10 to 12 feet in diameter. They would plaster the balls with Harrison campaign slogans. The balls would then be rolled down the street to the phrase, "Keep the ball rolling." In the process, they added a mnemonic to our language.[7]

Forty-four years later, Harrison's grandson contributed another phrase. In the 1888 American presidential election, Benjamin Harrison ran against, and beat, incumbent Grover Cleveland. One of the success factors was the symbolism his followers employed when they carried large brooms to rallies and parades. Supporters would "sweep" the streets with their brooms, while promising to "deliver a clean sweep." Although it took about 50 years for brooms to disappear from the campaign trail, electoral "sweeps" are still with us.[8]

The use of props as political metaphors is not limited to campaigns. In the mid-1980s, American president Ronald Reagan wanted to demonstrate visually what he considered to be an out-of-control United States budget. At his State of the Union speech, he produced the entire budget, all 6,000 pages of it, leather bound in seven volumes, and dropped each volume onto the podium with a thud. The visual was of a preposterously long document that no one could read or understand.

Props as Metaphors for the Learning Subject at Hand

In the learning environment, metaphors are potent tools. As advertising expert Luke Sullivan explained: "What makes metaphors particularly useful is they're a sort of conceptual shorthand and say with one image what you may otherwise need 20 words to say. They get a lot of work done quickly and simply."[9] He goes on to explain the use of metaphors in advertising: "Part of what makes metaphors in ads so effective is that they involve the reader. They use images already in the reader's mind, twist them to our message's purpose, and ask the reader to close the loop for us."[10]

These same observations are true in learning environments. Metaphors can provide visual mnemonics that learners will remember long after the learning event has passed. This is especially important when you consider that the average listener remembers only about half of what was said immediately after it was said. After 48 hours the average listener remembers only about one quarter of what was said.[11]

Props, when used as classroom metaphors, increase retention by providing visual shorthand representations of the learning.

One method is to tie a prop to a story with a pun as an ending. The story that

Prop Mix-up   **By Millbower and Yager**

Alas, poor Yorick. He had a-peel.

started this chapter offered an example of how this technique might work. The OFFBEAT™ Prop Placement Matrix (Table 9-2) beginning on page 250 provides additional examples.

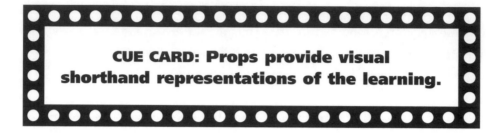

CUE CARD: Props provide visual shorthand representations of the learning.

Props as Pacing Devices

The final common use for props is as pacing devices. Comedian George Burns' use of his cigar is an excellent example. Burns was known for his subtle wit. Often, his wit was so subtle that the audience needed time digest the meaning of his words. This required Burns to wait for people to laugh. Rather than just stand there, he would puff on a cigar while he waited. This gave the appearance that the act was moving forward, when it was really at a stop.

Groucho Marx used the same technique. In addition to being intellectual, his wit was risqué. The Hollywood of the 1920s felt an obligation of self-censorship, and would not allow off-color comments to be filmed. Groucho would circumvent the censors by playing with his cigar as he lifted his eyebrows and leered at the object of his comments. This gave the audience time to process the more obscure, risqué meaning of the joke. This technique is not limited to these two performers. Two other examples are Johnny Carson and David Letterman. Both drum pencils to stall for time, or highlight a comment just made.

Comedians aren't the only well known figures to pace events with props. In Clinton v. Jones, the infamous Paula Jones sexual harassment lawsuit against President Bill Clinton, Clinton was deposed for six hours. The president paced his answers quite effectively through the use of soda cans. Every time the president was asked a tough legal question he would pause to sip a soda. This pause gave him time to process his answers without speaking.[12]

Props as Classroom Pacing Devices

When placed on the trainees' tables, props function as hand amusers. They give learners something with which to occupy their fingers and mind during the moments when they are having difficulty focusing on the instruction. Unlike the way comedians control the pacing through props, classroom props allow trainees to pace their own learning focus.

CUE CARD: Table props help learners release pent up energy.

Breaks are a second pacing opportunity. Pierce Howard, in his book, *The Owner's Manual for the Brain,* suggests providing activity games for use during breaks. He explained: "The ideal break involves some level of exercise. This can dissipate the results of over-arousal or stimulate people out of boredom or under-arousal."[13]

Carla Hannaford, in her book *Smart Moves,* recommended building frequent movement into learning. Movement aids learning, enhancing the thinking regions of the brain and increasing the speed of electrical transmissions in the brain.[14]

CUE CARD: Games that involve props speed electrical transmissions in the brain.

The placement of bowling pins, plastic horseshoes, beanbag, and other harmless play devices will bring your learners back to the classroom early from break, and wear down any excess energy.

Bruce Posgate, in *Kid-Show Showmanship,* discussed this very point in regard to controlling the excessive energy levels of children during children's show performances. He would begin his performances by getting the children to shout on cue two or three times. In the process, the children would get the rambunctiousness out of their systems. Although I realize that the needs of children are different than those of adults, the need to release excess energy still exists, and should be honored.[15]

THE PLACEMENT OF PROPS

Having completed an overview of how props aid learning, let's turn our attention to their selection. The props you select may be partially dictated by your topic, but the other opportunities may present themselves if you run your selection through a filter: The OFF-BEAT Prop Placement Matrix™. The letters of this acronym stands for:

*O*riginal
*F*ascinating
*F*un
*B*uild Upon
*E*laborate
*A*ppropriate
*T*asteful

The Props You Select Should Be Original

The usage you select for a prop should place it in an original situation. Just as comedians create humor by turning conventional thought patterns inside out; your usage should place the prop in an unexpected context. As Walt Disney said, "Give them what they want, but surprise them on how you present it."[16]

Of course, there are those learning props that are exactly what they seem. When learners are being exposed to a cash register that they will use in their job, there is no point in camouflaging the usage. Those uses are expected and legitimate. But because they are expected, their enjoyment value is limited. Seek out additional props your learners do not expect to see.

One example might be the use of a blender for diversity awareness. You could display the blender and suggest that each person brings a unique "flavor" to the group, and that, when people work together, they become stronger because of the blending of ideas. Or, use the same blender to indicate the need for teamwork. Turn the handles and state that our attitudes dictate how well we "blend" together as a team.

Another example could be the use of a suitcase to vent participant complaints you cannot fix, but must air before the learning can proceed. You could have the learners anonymously write down their complaints. Next, you could collect the complaints, read them to the class, and lead a discussion about the comments. Finally, you would put all the pieces of paper in the suitcase, close the suitcase, and place it in a corner. You could then conclude by saying, "I can't help you with this baggage. But could we at least set it aside for the duration of this session?"

The key point in the last three examples is not the specific usage, but rather the idea that you should select and use props that surprise your audience, and connect with them in unexpected ways. The surprise of the connection will work in much the same manner as a joke. It will create connections that the learners never considered before, and remain with them as a mnemonic.

The Props You Select Should Be Fascinating

According to Lawrence S. Munson, "Getting the commitment of your participants becomes possible only after you have captured their interest."[17] The prop you select will serve this end if the use is fascinating. An effective prop will immediately draw the learners' attention. They should want to know more about it as soon as they spot it.

The best props are those that seemingly have no connection to the subject being taught. Props that do not relate incite curiosity. This curiosity draws the participants in as they try to discover what the item has to do with the subject at hand. The ideal prop should not display its connection to the subject too readily. It should draw attention and curiosity while the learners attempt to guess its connection.

The blender and suitcase examples already offered function in this manner. Another example might be the use of a road map to discuss future career paths. Simply produce and display the map, and after a few seconds, ask the trainees if they know what the significance of the map is. After honoring all replies, state the following: "Most people look at a road map before they plan a long trip. Yet, in life, many people do not. Do you have a road map for your life? Do you know where you're going?" By using this simple, readily available map, you will have made a powerful, and unexpected, point.

The Props You Select Should Be Fun

In Chapter 5, we discovered that some items bring forth a feeling of fun. Items such as bananas, broccoli stalks, cream pies, glasses with an attached nose and mustache, plastic fish, hand buzzers, noisemakers, plungers, potatoes, and hats are fun props. If there is a way to use one of these items in your classroom, do so. Your goal should be to evoke a feeling of positive emotion through fun.

Michael Michalko, in *Cracking Creativity*, stated: "An environment of playfulness and humor is highly conductive to creativity. Playfulness relaxes the tension in a group. In a state of relaxation, individuals show less fixation and rigidity in their thinking."[18]

Props that bring forth a feeling of fun enhance an environment, making it more playful and less threatening. Undersized and oversized items work especially well. Items of odd size are visually humorous, and place the item out of its everyday context. For this reason, toys make some of the best props. Play phones, fake food, and even fake vomit have their place in the pathaneon of fun.

The Props You Select Should Build Upon What Has Already Occurred

Joseph Pine and James Gilmore, in *The Experience Economy.* explained: "The sensory stimulants that accompany an experience should support . . . its theme."[19]

The prop should support what you are saying and illustrate what has come before. It should not disrupt the flow of instruction. Rather, it should seem to your learner that the props fit in some odd, and as yet undiscovered, manner. When the meaning of the item is revealed, the prop should be easily recognized as adding value to matters already discussed, and perhaps building a bridge to other topics.

The Suitcase example offered under *"Fascinating"* demonstrates how a prop can be used to build upon what has already occurred. The suitcase is presented almost as an afterthought. The flow of the presentation builds logically out of the content being discussed. It requires little explanation, and serves as a bridge to other topics. When done properly, it is, as Bronislau Kaper explained about film music, an effect like lightning.[20]

The Props You Select Should Elaborate on the Prior Learning

The prop should add new insight into the subject. It should offer a deeper explanation than what has been explained verbally. At the juncture when you reveal the meaning of the prop, it should not just fit with what has already occurred, but should add new information. It should say visually what you are communicating verbally, and should add a holistic layer of meaning.

In the prior roadmap example, the metaphor of life as a road map is one example. The map adds a depth of meaning not possible with the words alone. It is the perfect visual representation of career planning.

The Props You Select Should Be Appropriate to Your Audience

Cultural expectations are different around the world. Items appropriate for one group of people may be poorly received by another. For example, a prop that might appeal to front line employees may not work for senior executives.

The only way to avoid cultural misunderstandings is to know your audience. Think through the negative comments you might receive and plan around them.

The Props You Select Should Be Tasteful

The final point in regard to prop placement is a caution. Use common sense and good taste. If the usage of a prop offends your learners, the underlying point will be lost.

One example from my own career centers on a funny prop I discovered in a novelty store. It was a burlap bag that was tied shut, with a cat's tail sticking out of the top of the sack. Squeezing the sack would cause it to vibrate and emit the sounds of a trapped cat. My specific usage for the prop was as a verbal complement for the phrase, "I guess I can let the cat out of the bag now."

My fear was that a cat lover would be offended. I could have avoided the situation altogether by not using the prop, but the prop was so funny that I couldn't resist. Instead, I prepared for the worst. I added a second gag to the routine. After the cat sack was introduced, I put down the sack, and held up a second prop. This one was a sign, like those you see added to movie credits, disclaiming that any animals were hurt in the production of this event. The sign got a laugh, and lightened the situation in a such a way that everyone relaxed.

In summary, when you are preparing to add a prop to your classroom, ask yourself, "Would the average person consider the prop to be offensive?" If the answer is yes, come up with an alternate prop, or find a way around the offense.

LENN'S TEN

Below, I have listed 10 of my favorite props. All 10 are readily available, and none require skill to use. The 10, in alphabetical order, are:

- ► Clapboard
- ► Clapping hands
- ► Dirty hand gag
- ► Giant bandage
- ► Goodie bag
- ► Hats/costume pieces
- ► Hoberman sphere
- ► Noisemakers
- ► Skyliner
- ► Whine sticks

Clapboard

The action: The instructor displays a director's clapboard and claps it to begin the action.

Suggested use: To frame a role-play activity

The patter: "Take one, scene one, and action"

Parameters: Remember to remove your finger before you clap down.

Where to find it: Trainer's Warehouse ("Slate Clapper"), Tool Thyme for Trainers ("Director's Clap Board")

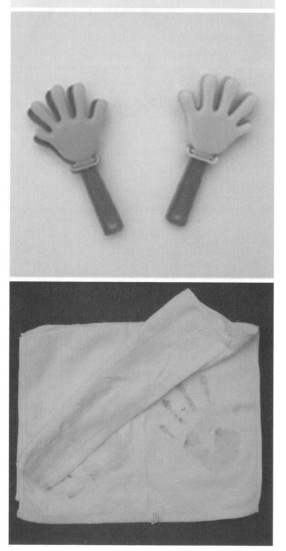

Clapping Hands

The action: The instructor holds up two plastic hands on a stick. As the instructor shakes the hands, they applaud.

Suggested use: To lead and encourage classroom applause

Parameters: Overuse can become annoying.

Where to find it: Tool Thyme for Trainers ("Clapping Hands")

Dirty Hand Gag

The action: When a learner is about to handle a prop, the instructor asks the learner to wipe his or her hands on a cloth. The learner does so, and leaves black handprints on the cloth.

Suggested use: As a throwaway joke when a volunteer is about to handle a prop

Parameters: Be careful not to embarrass the volunteer. Strive for good-natured humor.

Where to find it: Hank Lee's Magic Factory ("Black Hand Gag")

Giant Bandage

The action: The instructor displays a giant bandage.

Suggested use: As a metaphor for not fixing problems

The patter: "We could put a bandage on the problem, but after a while, the problem grows to the point where you need a pretty big bandage."

Alternative uses: When the instructor or a learner jokes that he or she has been "emotionally wounded."

Parameters: This is a throwaway prop, and comes in multiple quantities.

Where to find it: Hank Lee's Magic Factory ("Wand-Aid"), Trainer's Warehouse ("Giant Band-Aid")

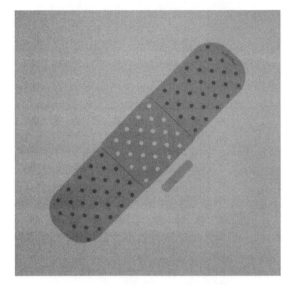

Goodie Bag

The action: Learners reach into a special bag for a treat or a reward.

Suggested use: Whenever a learner says something worthy of acknowledgement, let him or her take a reward out of the goodie bag.

Parameters: Rewards can range from treats to small trinkets to items tailored to reflect the learning situation. For instance, a reward for a leadership program could be a compass, or a pencil for financial awareness, or a roadmap for career planning.

Where to find it: A magician's Change Bag works well. So does any bag themed to the training subject. A hat that will not tip over when placed upside down also works.

Hats/Costume Pieces

The action: The trainer places hats and costume pieces on participants to convey specific characters.

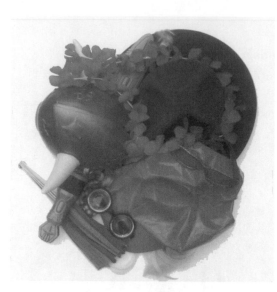

Suggested use: To enhance role plays and other character-specific activities

Sample items: Fake eyeglasses, hats, canes, wigs, mustaches, wardrobe pieces

Parameters: May distract from learning if overused.

Where to find them: Various toy stores, costume shops, novelty stores

Hoberman Sphere

The action: A plastic sphere expands and contracts as the instructor manipulates it.

Suggested use: To demonstrate that problems can be large or small, depending on your viewpoint

The patter: (Display fully expanded Hoberman Sphere.)

"Sometimes, a problem confronts us, and we think that it is too big to solve."

(Contract the Hoberman Sphere.)

"But, when you look closer, you realize that it's really a small problem. It's often a matter of perception. Big problem . . ."

(Display fully expanded Hoberman Sphere.)

". . . or little problem.

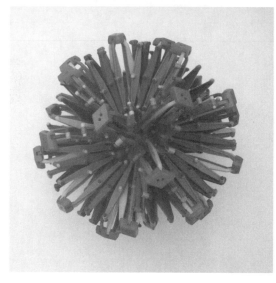

(Contract Hoberman Sphere.)

"You decide."

Parameters: This item does not pack flat, and thus takes up some space.

Where to find it: Trainer's Warehouse, Tool Thyme for Trainers ("Hoberman Square"), and children's science stores

Noisemakers

The action: At an appropriate moment, the trainer utilizes a noisemaker.

Suggested use: To bring a group back together after an activity, or to add a mnemonic sound effect to any presentation

Sample items: Train whistle, referee whistle, siren, triangle, and various other noise-makers

Parameters: Must make a noise loud enough to be heard in a room full of people.

Where to find them: Trainer's Warehouse, Tool Thyme for Trainers, various toy stores and novelty shops

Skyliner

The action: The instructor holds up, and twirls, a black rod that emits a series of laser lights. The lights spell out words and phrases.

Suggested use: To generate applause, to help learners remember key words, and to attract attention

Parameters: This is a great prop that can be seen in a large room. The room lights do not need to be turned off. Best of all, the phrase spelled out can be changed by the facilitator.

Where to find it: Tool Thyme for Trainers ("Skyliner")

Whine Sticks

The action: One colorful rod with a whiny sounding noisemaker inside is placed on each table.

Suggested use: As a device for preventing participants from overtalking any subject

The patter: "You may have noticed a colorful stick on each of your tables. They are our whine sticks. There are some rules about their use. (1) You can touch it only if you intend to use it. (2) When you pick

THE OFFBEAT PROP PLACEMENT MATRIX™

Use this matrix to determine the effectiveness of the props you select.

The props you select should be:	Yes	No
Original		
▶ Will the usage place the prop in an original situation?	_____	_____
▶ Will the placement surprise your audience?	_____	_____
▶ Will the prop connect with your learners in unexpected ways?	_____	_____
▶ Will the connection create a mnemonic learning tool?	_____	_____
Fascinating		
▶ Will the prop command your learners' attention?	_____	_____
▶ Will the learners want to know more about it when they see it?	_____	_____
▶ Will the prop have no apparent connection to the subject?	_____	_____
▶ Will the learners attempt to guess the connection?	_____	_____
Fun		
▶ Will the prop bring forth a feeling of fun?	_____	_____
▶ Will it encourage an environment of playfulness?	_____	_____
▶ Will it evoke a feeling of positive emotion?	_____	_____
▶ Will the usage be humorous?	_____	_____
Build Upon		
▶ Will the prop usage build upon what has already occurred?	_____	_____
▶ Will the usage fit naturally within the flow of instruction?	_____	_____
▶ When the usage is revealed, will it add value to the subject?	_____	_____
▶ Will the prop provide a bridge to the next topic?	_____	_____
Elaborate		
▶ Will the prop usage add new insight into the subject?	_____	_____
▶ Will it say visually what you are communicating verbally?	_____	_____
▶ Will it add a holistic layer of meaning?	_____	_____
▶ Will the learners comprehend the subject more completely as a result of the usage?	_____	_____
Appropriate		
▶ Is the prop usage appropriate to the learners?	_____	_____
▶ Will the prop meet the learners' cultural expectations?	_____	_____
▶ Will the prop engage the learners at their intellectual level?	_____	_____
▶ Will the learners understand the meaning of the prop?	_____	_____
Tasteful		
▶ Will the prop be inoffensive to the learners?	_____	_____
▶ Will they react positively to the usage?	_____	_____
▶ Can potential problems be addressed in advance?	_____	_____
▶ Will the usage cause your organization any legal challenges?	_____	_____
Total Score (24 maximum)	_____	_____

The higher the Yes column score, the more effective the prop usage will be.

TABLE 9-2

it up, you must make it 'whine'. (3) Once someone has "whined" the room, I will stop all conversation, and together, we will decide if it is time to change the subject."

Parameters: Requires one per table

Where to find it: Tool Thyme for Trainers ("Noise Stick")

WHERE TO FIND OTHER PROPS

Props are everywhere. Many of the funny food props are as close as your kitchen. Toy stores are another excellent resource. Some of my best ideas come to me while walking along the toy aisles. Novelty stores are another good resource. Entertainment supply companies can also help, as can magic supply companies. Some are listed in the appendix.

The main point to remember with regard to the use of props is to have fun. Introduce props to lighten the mood; keep the learning environment light and positive; keep your learners guessing what you will do next, and they will pay attention. Present your learners with props that add relevance, and their learning will increase.

[1] Sullivan, Luke (1998). *Hey Whipple, Squeeze This: A Guide to Creating Great Ads.* New York: John Wiley & Sons.

[2] *The American Heritage College Dictionary,* 3rd edit. (1997). Boston: Houghton Mifflin.

[3] Vermeulen, André (May 22, 2000). ASTD International Conference. Session M508.

[4] Johnson, Paul (1997). *A History of the American People.* New York: HarperCollins.

[5] Pine II, Joseph B., and Gilmore, James H. (1999). *The Experience Economy.* Boston: Harvard Business School Press.

[6] *Hamlet.*

[7] Boller, Paul F. Jr. (1984). *Presidential Campaigns.* New York: Oxford University Press.

[8] Ibid.

[9] Sullivan, Luke (1998).

[10] Ibid.

[11] Steil, Lyman K., Barker, L., and Watson, Kittie W. (1993). *Effective Listening.* New York: Random House.

[12] <www.washingtonpost.com/wp-srv/politics/special/pjones/docs/clintondep031398.htm>

[13] Howard, Pierce J. (1994). *The Owner's Manual for the Brain: Every Day Applications from Mind-Brain Research.* Austin, TX: Leornian Press.

[14] Hannaford, Carla (1995). *Smart Moves: Why Learning Is Not All in Your Head.* Arlington, VA: Great Ocean.

[15] Posgate, Bruce (1961). *Kid-Show Showmanship.* Colon MI: Abbott's Magic.

[16] *Walt Disney's Famous Quotes,* compiled by Dave Smith, 1994.

[17] Munson, Lawrence S. (1992). *How to Conduct Training Seminars: A Complete Guide for Training Managers & Professionals,* 2nd edit. New York: McGraw-Hill.

[18] Michalko, Michael (1998). *Cracking Creativity: The Secrets of Creative Genius.* Berkeley, CA: Ten Speed Press.

[19] Pine II, Joseph B., and Gilmore, James H. (1999).

[20] Thomas, Tony (1997). *Music for the Movies,* 2nd edit. Los Angeles: Silman-James Press.

CHAPTER TEN

THE SCRIPT

HARRIET AND THE HOUSEKEEPERS: SCENE THREE

With her walk-through complete, Harriet now turned her attention to the task of making Asbestos Awareness something more than a required chore. "How can I get them to pay attention, and to enjoy the class?" she thought. She tossed and turned for three nights straight trying to figure out some sort of fun angle, but to no avail.

Finally, while thumbing through a magazine in her doctor's waiting room, she stumbled on a weight loss ad. The ad purported to show a woman before beginning the weight loss program, and after supposed weight loss success. It looked so silly. The before picture was old and grainy. The after picture was a glamorous shot. The jeans she wore in the before picture were too tight. The after shot showed the woman wearing what were supposed to be the same jeans, and yet the jeans were at least six inches too large in the waist. It was obviously a setup. But the photo did give Harriet an inspiration; she would write a story for her class. In the story, she would compare and contrast two "sisters" who handled asbestos differently.

With this inspiration, she sat down at her computer, and began to write
"A Bess–Tess Story."

"There is but one art,
to omit." —ROBERT LEWIS STEVENSON[1]

The Show Biz Training techniques in this chapter are based on the following Learner-tainment Principles:

Principle 6: Stage the environment—Orchestrate every detail of the environment.
Principle 8: Stage the performer—Orchestrate every detail of your performance.

TO WRITE, OR NOT TO WRITE

There often is a debate within training circles regarding the need for scripting. Some instructional designers argue that the words will never be spoken, so there is no point in writing dialog. Others proclaim that the only chance of documenting what should occur in the class is to write it all down, even if the trainers don't say the words. Still others argue that an outline is the most functional solution. There is value in each of these positions. But, these arguments miss the point. There is a transcending reason to script.

Magic is a carefully scripted alternate reality, one in which humans have the ability to work miracles. The performer knows better, but the audience will suspend belief if that alternate reality is believable. Therefore, every detail of this alternate reality must be worked out. It must ring true. It cannot be an alternate reality. It must, for the time the audience is present, be THE reality.

A show biz production contains a myriad of details that are not readily apparent in an outline. The scripting process forces the show director to evaluate every second of the performance, to make choices based on logical criteria. The very act of scripting places a discipline on the performance that cannot be obtained in any other way.

To offer an example from music, Johann Sebastian Bach was a master improviser. He also placed on himself an intricate set of rules that governed every note he played. Sometimes, he would break his own rules. But when he did so, it was an informed choice made to create better music. Bach was a better improviser *because* he worked through all the details. His structure made him a better improviser. The result was some of the finest music ever created.

Another example comes from the legal profession. The stakes in a courtroom can literally be life and death. Often, lawyers script their opening and closing arguments, witnesses script their testimony, and judges script the explanations of their rulings. They rehearse so that what they say in the courtroom will be factually correct, and logically thought through.

Perhaps the best lawyer/script writer ever was also a political figure, America's 16th president, Abraham Lincoln. Lincoln's writings and speeches are marvels of simplicity and clarity. This was no accident. Lincoln's assistants reported that "He never considered anything he had written to be finished until published, or if a speech, until he delivered it."[2] Lincoln would research, analyze, and rewrite his speeches to the point of annoyance. He wanted to be absolutely certain his words rang true when he did speak them.

In *Lincoln on Leadership,* Donald Phillips shared this observation: "Lincoln's practice of writing his speeches before he delivered them gave him the time to think about what he wanted to say and insured that his message would come across the way he intended."[3]

The result was some of the finest political speeches the world has ever heard.

Another way to look at script writing is through the eyes of a coach. Scripting is the show biz equivalent of a professional football team's preparation. Between games, football teams study their next opponent and design a game plan targeted at their opponent's weaknesses. If the plays are brilliantly conceived and executed, the team wins. If, during the game, it becomes apparent to the team's quarterback that a specific play won't work, the quarterback calls an "audible," changing the play. The quarterback, because he knows all the options, can adapt the plan as circumstances warrant. Imagine the situation that football team would be in if they had no game plan.

One must learn the rules in order to break them. Scripting provides you with a set of rules. It helps you determine exactly what you mean, how what you mean connects with what you've already said, and how what you will say leads inevitably to a grand finale where every detail of the performance connects. The answer to the discussion I posed at the start of this section is simply, *you script to plan!*

CUE CARD:
Script to plan.

HOW TO WRITE

The following are specific points to consider when writing a script:

- ▶ Write a speech, not a book.

- ▶ Keep it pithy.

- ▶ Write for your audience, not yourself.

- ▶ Stay focused.

- ▶ Be logical.

Write a Speech, Not a Book

A script is a written document, but it should be written to be said, not read.

CUE CARD: Write to be said, not read.

Heavy Workload   By Millbower and Yager

Here's your script. Good luck!

Your learners will never read it. They will hear the words once, and from the auditory signal alone, will comprehend, or be confused by, your words. Avoid complexity. Keep your words simple. In the words of Henry David Thoreau, think "Simplicity!"[4] Limit yourself to one thought per sentence, and ensure that each sentence flows logically from the one before it.

I script the minimum number of words I intend to say, even though I know I'll miss lines in the spontaneity of the classroom environment. The process is more akin to documenting what I am likely to say naturally, rather than forcing a false style of speech. This approach is similar to that of most politicians. American presidents do not have time to write their own words. Instead, they hire speechwriters who write sentences that match the president's natural vocal cadence. In this same manner, match your script to your natural cadence, or the cadences of those who will be delivering it for you.

Keep It Pithy

In 1991, The Walt Disney film studios released the animated feature *Beauty and the Beast*. The film was an immediate hit with both filmgoers and critics. The film was so well received that it received a Best Picture nomination from the Academy of Motion Picture Arts and Sciences, the first and only animated feature to receive the honor. It also won a Golden Globe Award for Best Comedy/Musical.

What was not widely known at the time was that the entire film had not been released. Music composers Howard Ashman and Alan Menken had written a beautiful waltz called "Human Again" for the film, but cut it before the premiere. Editing a film before its debut is an old Hollywood story. What makes this cut remarkable is that "Human Again" was cut in spite of the writers' and film makers' strong desire to keep it in the film. As the movie's producer Don Hahn explained, "We tried valiantly to put it in. We could never fit it into the movie where it didn't stop the plot short." Rather than risk an inferior movie, the team exercised self control and reluctantly cut "Human Again."[5]

Fortunately, the story doesn't end there. Owing to the film's initial success, *Beauty and the Beast: The Broadway Musical* was created. The need to fill the longer time period of a Broadway show led to the reinsertion of "Human Again." And, as the original film team knew it would, the song became a highlight of each performance.

In 2002, when the animated *Beauty and the Beast* was re-released, Hahn and directors Kirk Wise and Gary Trousdale used the Broadway experience as a guide to place the song in its appropriate place in the film. The result was, in Hahn's words, a "greater emotional depth to the story" and strong audience reaction.[6]

The point is that great artists subject themselves to rigorous self-control. Greatness is possible without self-control, but is infinitely more likely with it. As advertising expert Luke Sullivan commented, "If you leave too much out, you'll mystify your audience. If you put too much in, you'll bore them."[7]

Much of this self-control involves distilling thoughts down to their essence. Maurice Saatchi, of the London advertising firm M&C Saatchi, explained it as follows: "Simplicity is all. Simple logic, simple arguments, simple visual images. If you can't reduce your argument to a few crisp words and phrases, there's something wrong with your argument."[8] Magician Dariel Fitzee echoed that point of view:

> "Make your act just a bit **shorter** than the length of time you are confident you can hold the audience's **highest** [original emphasis] attention. If they haven't had enough they'll applaud for more. If they've had enough—or too much—they won't want more. ALWAYS LEAVE THEM WANTING MORE" [original emphasis].[9]

So did magician Sam Sharpe: "Brevity is the soul of art. One test of an artist is to decide whether his work could be simplified without loss of effect."[10]

CUE CARD: Leave your learners wanting more.

When scripting for the classroom, distill your thoughts down to their essence. If you counted yourself among the readers who believes that the trainers will never say the words you write, you may be correct. If your script is too long, too stylized, or too ornate, your assumptions will be proven true. If, however, you deliver a pithy script that hits all the high points, chances of a correct delivery rise greatly.

Write for Your Audience, Not Yourself

A second lesson can be gleaned from the *Beauty and the Beast* story. You should please your audience, even at the risk of displeasing yourself. In the case of *Beauty and the Beast*, the film makers cut what they knew was some of their best work. But instead of becoming temperamental artists, they decided in the audience's favor.

Steve Hayden, author of the famous "1984" Apple Computer commercial, agreed when he said: "If you want to be a well-paid copywriter, please your client. If you want to be an award-winning copywriter, please yourself. If you want to be a great copywriter, please your reader."[11]

CUE CARD: Please your
audience, not yourself.

Musical acts know this all too well. One of the common complaints from musicians is that they must perform the same songs over and over. In my day, those songs included, "Proud Mary," "Celebration," "Tie a Yellow Ribbon," and "Bad, Bad Leroy Brown." I hope to never play them again. But on stage, my preferences didn't matter to the audience. If they wanted "Celebration," they got "Celebration." Dariel Fitzee echoed that opinion: "A magician should not necessarily select the tricks he likes to do best. He should select those the AUDIENCE [original emphasis] likes best."[12]

Stay Focused

Every script has a point of view. Attend any successful movie, and you can discover the film maker's point of view for yourself. In the *Star Wars* films, the point of view is that a force for good or evil exists within each of us. If we listen to that inner voice, the force will be with us. In the aforementioned *Beauty and the Beast,* the point of view is that beauty comes from within. *Forrest Gump* takes the point of view that it isn't the supposed intelligence of a person that matters; it is the behaviors that person exhibits. Or as Forrest Gump said, "Stupid is as stupid does."

All three of these films were box office gold, and deservedly so. They had a focus, and stayed focused throughout the entire film. Entertainments that stay focused on their point of view succeed. As magic historian Sam Sharpe explained: "The first thing a producer should do is to decide what atmosphere he wishes to create. Then he has to arrange all the influences at his disposal appropriately . . . See that nothing occurs to draw attention from the centre [sic] of action during a presentation. Where there is no focus, attention wanders."[13] Fitzee also discussed focus, which he defined as unity, at length:

"Unity is the maintaining of a single idea from beginning to end. It is the stressing of this idea to the subordination of any other suggestion. To achieve unity, somewhere, in some manner a connecting thread, whether based on similar objects, an idea, on character work, or the attitude of

the performer, or on effects, must tie the whole act together from begin-ning to end."[14]

If there is a point you'd love to make, but it isn't directly related to THE point, leave it out, or re-center your whole script around it.

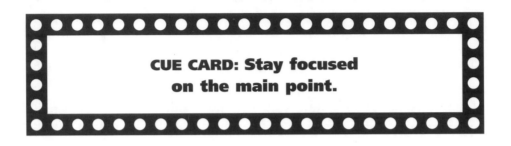

CUE CARD: Stay focused
on the main point.

Be Logical

Each sentence you write should make sense. The logic of the sentence should be readily apparent to your audience. Likewise, each successive sentence should fit logically with the one that proceeded it.

Every sentence, every activity, and every joke should, step by step, enhance your case, propelling the learning ever forward. By writing in this manner, you will ensure fi-delity to your point of view. You will also guarantee the logic of your argument, and thus aid your learners' comprehension. The script will also be easier for your trainers to re-member. They'll get the point, and thus be able to articulate it without the false challenge of memorizing a script.

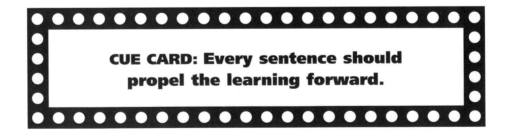

CUE CARD: Every sentence should
propel the learning forward.

THREE-ACT STRUCTURE

Now that we know some key script writing points, let's turn our attention to the organi-zational layout of most performances. Regardless of the performance medium, some com-monalties exist.

A show is structured to achieve maximum audience interest and involvement. It usually begins with an event that captures the audience's attention. From this initial splash, the pace gradually slows until all the relevant situational points have been presented, or in a live performance, where the performer communes one-on-one with the audience. From here, the pace accelerates, building slowly but steadily, until a point of resolution is reached. The resolution soon proves to be a false conclusion, and the pace drops to the lowest level of the performance.

From this point forward, the performance crescendos, building in tension and intensity, until past the breaking point. After the moment when the audience thinks the tension has become intolerable, the resolution occurs. All the information presented throughout the entire performance comes together in a tidy and, to the audience, extremely satisfying, package.

This model is called the Three-Act Structure.

Prologue

The prologue's function is to set a mood, peak curiosity, and prepare the audience for the story to come. It usually hints at characters and situations without offering much definition. Its purpose is not to inform, but to entice.

Act One

Act One is critical. The audience must become engaged in the performance. If not, there will be no audience for the later acts. As magician Max Dessoir explained, "The dramatic part of the presentation is the most important, because it excites the imagination."[15] Fellow magician Sam Sharpe concurred. "When an audience has absorbed a magical atmosphere it will be in a state of passive expectation for wonders."[16] In a movie, Act One introduces the main characters, displays their motivations, and provides all the necessary details for the story to unfold. In a live entertainment, Act One establishes a performer's credibility with the audience.

Act Two

Act Two puts the plot lines in motion. The information presented in Act One is acted upon, or set in motion by events, in such a way as to bring the characters together. It leads up to a happy ending that proves unsustainable owing to the complications laid out in Act One. This tension-release mechanism is intentional. The tension cannot continually build over a period of two hours. At some point, the audience has to catch its collective breath. John Davidson and Cort Casady elaborated on this point when advising singers on pacing: "The audience cannot maintain the same level of intensity all of the time. From time to time, you must let them off the hook, allow them to recharge their enthusiasm."[17]

Act Three

Act Three works all the challenges presented in Act Two to a feverish pitch where the tension seems unbearable. At the precise moment when the audience feels like they are about to explode because of the tension, the resolution occurs. Suddenly, all the details are resolved, and the characters are united in an emotional climax.

THREE ACT STRUCTURE EXAMPLES

This structure can be observed by reviewing the plotting of a few different entertainments.

Three-Act Structure in a Romantic Movie

THE PROLOGUE

The Prologue hints at the film to come. The audience would still be distracted with the logistics of arriving, finding a seat, and eating their popcorn. Consequently, they are not attentive, and no critical information is presented. Instead, the prologue displays visual and auditory indicators of the performance to follow. Because this film is a romantic comedy, the music would be light and the look of the film bright.

ACT ONE

Act One would introduce the hero and heroine, explain the situations they both find themselves in, and provide the opportunity for them to share their hopes and desires with the audience.

ACT TWO

Act Two would begin with the hero and heroine meeting each other. They would develop a romantic but uneasy relationship. The act would end with difficulties set up in the first act that would break the couple apart.

THREE ACT MOVIE EXAMPLES

MOVIE	PRESHOW	ACT ONE	ACT TWO	ACT THREE
Beauty and the Beast	A tale is told of a prince who could never love another.	The main characters are introduced, Belle expresses her desire for "something more," ends up at the Beast's castle.	Belle and the Beast argue, fall in love; Belle's father is imprisoned; the Beast frees Belle rather than become human.	The villagers attack the castle; Gaston attacks the Beast; Belle admits her love for the Beast; the Beast becomes human again.
Independence Day	July 1: The aliens approach, the main characters are introduced.	July 2: The aliens arrive; the main characters react as events pull them into the action.	July 3: The aliens overpower humanity; the main characters come together.	July 4: Humanity fights back, declare independence, and destroy the aliens.
Jaws	The shark attacks a midnight swimmer.	The characters are introduced; the chief is prevented from closing the beach until a young boy dies.	The three main characters go to sea, fight the shark, and tell tall tales around a nightime table.	The shark attacks, destroys the ship, and is in turn destroyed.
Raiders of the Lost Ark	Indiana Jones escapes multiple perils to capture a relic.	Information is provided about Indy; the ark is explained; Jones and Marion form a partnership and travel to Egypt; Marion is killed in an explosion.	The Ark is discovered; Marion is alive; a fight for control of the ark ensues; a romantic moment ends with the capture of Marion and the Ark.	The ark is opened; the bad guys are destroyed; the ark is stored.
Titanic	A research vessel begins exploring the wreck of the Titanic.	The Titanic leaves Europe; Jack explores the ship; Rose's desire to escape high society is revealed; Jack and Rose meet.	Jack and Rose develop a love affair; the romance concludes when Jack is accused of stealing; the Titanic hits an iceberg.	The Titanic sinks; Jack saves Rose; Rose concludes story and tosses the diamond overboard.

TABLE 10-1

ACT THREE

Act Three would focus on surmounting the complications introduced in Act Two. Eventually, all the complications would be solved, our couple would forgive each other, and they would live happily ever after.

Three-Act Structure in a Magic Show

THE PROLOGUE

In an illusion show, a warmup performer usually occupies the Prologue spot. This gives the audience time to settle down before the illusionist begins. Usually, the act presented is a novelty or comedy act. This act will not duplicate the main act to follow. It will avoid building tension, focusing instead on creating warm emotion, so that the audience embraces the performance to follow.

Occasionally, a magician will perform without an opening act. In that situation, the first illusion builds curiosity about the performance to come, while establishing the magician's credentials. The opening effect would relate holistically to the illusions that follow. For instance, if a magician were to present a performance of playing card illusions, an opening illusion utilizing doves, unless the dove illusion involved cards as well, would be counterintuitive. It would not build curiosity in the correct direction.

The first illusion is usually a throwaway. The vast majority of the audience has not fully settled in, and they may actually miss the magic. In that first spot, magicians place some highly interesting, but not critical, illusion. That way, the portion of the audience who noticed the opening effect would evidence interest, and thus pull the other audience members into the action. Often, magicians will present two or three opening illusions with no expectation of them being remembered, beyond gaining attention and piquing curiosity.

ACT ONE

Once the audience's attention has been focused on the entertainment, the first act begins in earnest. For several minutes, the activity would be nonstop. The illusions would be big, showy, and high energy, with little pause in between. The total effect would be breathtaking. The production would build to a peak of excitement that ends at a high energy level.

ACT TWO

Act Two is more intimate. Act One would have proved the magician's skill. Act Two's intent is to establish a personal connection with the audience, to prove that the performer is human too. This is the place where the performer comes off the stage, or invites volunteers onto the stage. Either way, the intent is to commune with the audience. The illusions are more intimate, with less hype. Where Act One was energetic, Act Two is warm and personal.

ACT THREE

Act Three starts at the low energy level established in Act Two, and gradually, but purposely, accelerates in pacing. The act becomes faster and faster, with each illusion building on the one before. In contrast to Act One, the illusions presented here are longer. They tell a story. The cumulative effect is to build the level of tension beyond the level achieved at the conclusion of Act One. The act finally ends with an illusion so grand, amazing, and memorable, that all the pent up tension is released in a torrent of applause.

A more complete description of the Three-Act Structure can be found in Table 10-1, with examples from some well known films showcased in Table 10-2.

THREE-ACT STRUCTURE IN A CLASSROOM

While Houdini was escaping chains the world over, and Sir Arthur Conan Doyle was, through his creation Sherlock Holmes, solving crimes, another contemporary was constructing a model of human learning. Carl Jung (1875–1961), a disciple of Sigmund Freud, suggested that there are four different ways in which people relate to the world: feeling, thinking, sensing, and intuiting (Table 10-3).[18]

Jung's work inspired a wealth of learning style theories. From David Kolb to Gordon Lawrence, from the Myers-Briggs Type Indicator to the DiSC Personality Profile, four-quadrant models have become prevalent among learning professionals. One specific application of Jung's idea deserves a higher profile. 4MAT is an instructional design method utilized in education but little known in the training community. Educator Bernice McCarthy designed 4MAT as an instructional design system with the four learning styles categorized as Types One through Four. The four categories are:

- ▶ Imaginative learners seeking personal meaning through their feelings

- ▶ Analytic learners seeking intellectual competence through thoughtful reflection

- ▶ Common sense learners seeking solutions to problems through trial and error

- ▶ Dynamic learners seeking hidden possibilities through visioning future applications[19]

THREE ACT COMPARISON CHART

MEDIUM	PRESHOW	ACT ONE	ACT TWO	ACT THREE
Movie	Visual sequence; sets a mood; piques curiosity; provides information about the upcoming story.	Introduces characters; shares characters hopes; explains current situation.	Puts the plot in motion; the characters come together; complications ensue; ends in despair.	Plot lines introduced in Act One come together to overcome Act Two complications.
TV show	Before the first commercial; captures attention; hints at story to come.	Introduces characters; shares characters hopes; explains current situation; ends with suspense.	Puts the plot in motion; the characters come together; complications ensue; ends with a crisis.	Plot lines introduced in Act One come together to overcome Act Two complications.
Broadway show	Music overture introduces music; sets mood; builds curiosity.	Introduces characters; shares characters hopes; explains current situation.	Puts the plot in motion; the characters come together; complications ensue; ends in despair.	Plot lines introduced in Act One come together to overcome Act Two complications.
Illusion show	A warm-up act; focuses the audience; draws attention; sets a mood of illusion.	Starts exciting; demonstrates magical ability; features snappy routines.	Features novelty or comedy; close-up magic; one-on-one contact with the audience.	Builds gradually, constantly faster and more intense, ending with an astounding illusion.
Nightclub singer	A warm-up act; relaxes the audience; draws attention; sets a mood.	Starts exciting; demonstrates performance ability; slows slightly in the center; ends strong.	Begins with dialog; features humor or novelty number; ends with serious ballad.	Builds gradually, constantly faster and more intense, ending with a high level of excitement.

TABLE 10-2

FOUR WAYS PEOPLE RELATE TO THE WORLD			
FEELER	**THINKER**	**SENSOR**	**INTUITOR**
Information processed through the emotion of the experience	Information processed rationally based on the logic of what they see	Information processed through concrete sensation	Information processed instinctually based on future possibilities

Source: Jung, Carl (1976). *Psychological Types.* Princeton, NJ: Princeton University Press, Bollingen Series.

TABLE 10-3

The power of 4MAT comes from its balancing act. It has one foot solidly planted in science, and the other in show biz. From the standpoint of science, 4MAT sequences the four-quadrant learning styles model. It then overlays alternating analytical left hemispheric and holistic right hemispheric activities. 4MAT also follows the contours of basic Three-Act Structure (Table 10-4). Using 4MAT, let's explore what a Three-Act structure might look like in a classroom.

A CLASSROOM IN THREE ACTS

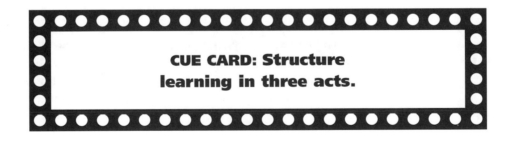

CUE CARD: Structure learning in three acts.

McCarthy did not speak in the terminology of show biz. Nevertheless, the similarities are so striking that I will interchangeably use the 4MAT term "quadrant" and the corresponding show biz terms as I describe how a 4MAT might relate to Show Biz Training techniques. As an overview, the steps of a 4MAT design are listed below.

> ► Prologue
> Step 1. Capture attention.
> Step 2. Discuss the opening activity.

4MAT THREE ACT STRUCTURE CHART			
PROLOGUE (PERSONAL MEANING)	ACT ONE (INTELLECTUAL COMPETENCE)	ACT TWO (SOLUTIONS TO PROBLEMS)	ACT THREE (HIDDEN POSSIBILITIES)
Initiates problem solving before instruction	Deepens the connection to what the learners already know	Provides hands-on practice	Seeks out usefulness
Begins with the familiar	Provides a metaview of the concept	Checks for under-standing	Encourages original applications
Builds on what students already know	Transforms the concept into an image	Encourages tinkering with the concept	Helps mistakes become learning opportunities
Guides reflection and analysis of the experience	Emphasizes the most significant aspects of the concept	Sets up situations where learners have to discover information	Summarizes by reviewing the whole
Encourages learners to share their opinions	Presents information sequentially	Provides opportu-nities for learners to design their own explorations	Celebrates shared learning
Clarifies the reason for the learning	Draws attention to important, discrete details	Requires person-alized synthesis	Leaves the students wondering about future applications

TABLE 10-4

▶ Act One

  Step 3. Picture the concept.

  Step 4. Share the key points.

▶ Act Two

  Step 5. Practice the concept.

  Step 6. Add complications.

▶ Act Three
  Step 7. Seek personal meaning.
  Step 8. Celebrate the learning.

Prologue (Quadrant One)

The introductory quadrant honors *imaginative learners* seeking personal meaning through their feelings. As in a movie, this quadrant sets a mood, peaks curiosity, and foreshadows the upcoming story. It provides the opportunity for the learners to settle in, become comfortable in the classroom, and develop a commitment to the learning.

The Learning Cycle　　　　By Millbower and Yager

Huh? Hum. Uh huh. Aha!

STEP 1. CAPTURE ATTENTION

The training begins by capturing learner attention with an activity that builds curiosity as it sets up the reason for the learning. The activity should hint at the instruction to come, with a focus on gaining the learners' attention. Show business agent Bob Vincent explained it this way: "Your opening . . . should almost be like an overture. It should start with an exciting intro."[20]

It has been said that you should switch instructional methods every 15 or 20 minutes. I believe that, given the info-fog, either is too long. Instead, I suggest that you structure your learning so that constant surprises are the norm. Keep the environment enlivened enough that learners do not want to look away. Keep the room energized, the pacing fast, and the tone light.

STEP 2. DISCUSS THE OPENING ACTIVITY

Once the opening activity concludes, the learners reflect on the experience, and share observations with each other. As a result, the learners develop a personal interest in continuing into the first act. Show biz agent Bob Vincent continued: "The end of the opening . . . should build to an exciting climax, with an obvious, clearly designed, finish, so there is no doubt in the audience's mind that they should 'get ready to applaud!'"[21]

Of course, in the case of classroom instruction, your goal is learning, not applause. Instead the opening should end with the audience having no doubt that what they are about to learn will be useful to them. This is where you establish the value of, and gain participant commitment to, the learning that will occur in Act One.

Act One (Quadrant Two)

Now that the learners are engaged by the subject, the topic is fully explored. This quadrant honors the *analytic learners* seeking intellectual competence through thoughtful reflection. This is where, as in the movies, the facts are presented.

STEP 3. PICTURE THE CONCEPT

To begin the act, the instructor leads a visualization activity. The learners conclude the activity with a metaview of the concept to be taught.

STEP 4. SHARE THE KEY POINTS

Once the learners have integrated their observations with the upcoming concept, the instructor presents the relevant concept points sequentially. This is the spot where the learners should become familiar with the conceptual ideas of the subject. The intent is to set up the "plot lines" for the hands-on practice with the concept that will occur in Act Two.

Avoid a lecture if at all possible. Instead, use a variety of instructional methods. Where your learners were focused by the end of the Prologue, complacency can set in once they become comfortable. Structure your learning so that the pace never slows long enough for complacency to set in. Magician Sam Sharpe addressed this point for magicians: "Few people are interested in conjuring presented like a scientific lecture. Add human interest by using attractive things to conjure with and patter that holds the attention of the audience."[22]

Sharpe was obviously referring to an illusion show. Substitute the word "learning" for the word "conjuring" and the classroom connection becomes evident. If your learners think that something interesting will be coming up, they will pay attention, for fear they'll miss it.

Act Two (Quadrant Three)

Now that all the plot elements have been introduced, it is time to put them in motion. This quadrant explores how things work. It is geared toward *common sense learners* seeking solutions to problems through trial and error.

STEP 5. PRACTICE THE CONCEPT

In this act, the learners engage in hands-on practice. It is their opportunity to examine the concepts through problem solving situations. Simultaneously, the trainer can verify that the learners understand the concepts.

STEP 6. ADD COMPLICATIONS

Once the trainer determines that the learners comprehend the material, it is time to interject complications. Typically, the instructor will challenge the learners to solve a problem related to the concept without supplying all the relevant information. Through research, reading, conversations with experts, and other learner-directed activities, the learners discover additional information that allows them to synthesize their learning in a personal manner.

Act Three (Quadrant Four)

In the final quadrant, all the elements previously introduced come together and build to a conclusion, much as a show climaxes. This final act focuses on *dynamic learners* seeking hidden possibilities through visioning future applications. It provides the opportunity for the learners to teach new applications to themselves.

STEP 7. SEEK PERSONAL MEANING

The trainees begin the act by exploring possible personal applications. They then share their application ideas with the class.

STEP 8. CELEBRATE THE LEARNING

After all have shared, the instruction concludes with a celebration of the learning, and a commitment by the participants to carry their learning into their lives.

MAINTAINING ATTENTION

A final script writing consideration relates to the normal fluctuations in the human attentional cycle. Hobson reported that: "Our ability to maintain attention is affected by normal cyclical fluctuations in the efficacy of the neurotransmitter molecules that chemically regulate attention. These fluctuations occur in 90-minute cycles across the 24 hours."[23] Sylwester added:

"People differ in their rhythmic patterns, but at about 6 A.M. many people experience a sharp rise in the availability of these attentional molecules (which causes us to wake up), and the average level of molecules remains relatively high during the morning. The average levels begin to decline during the afternoon, and reach their lowest levels after midnight, when sleep becomes almost inevitable. We tend to do things that we *have* to do in the morning, when it's easiest to maintain attention—and the things that we *want* to do in the late afternoon and evening, when it's more difficult to maintain attention without the emotional support of personal interest."[24]

Maintaining attention throughout the whole of the performance isn't easy. Fortunately, when people are curious, they pay attention. As a nightclub performer, I was performing before the toughest audience imaginable, people who had been drinking. Our illusions had to be placed in such a way as to pull people toward us continually. After much trial and error, we stumbled on a formula of rapid-fire routining, with no single piece of entertainment taking more than two minutes. When distractions would draw them away, our flashiness and the quick pacing that we had built into our act would pull them back. Consequently, our illusions were highly visible with little explanation required, and told a story that could be resumed by the errant viewer. In this manner, we could keep the surprises coming, and the pacing so unpredictable that people would choose to watch rather than miss something.

Posgate concurred when he said the following: "Fill in every second of your show with something interesting, a flourish, a flash of color and of humor, but don't deliberately waste time. It does not pay."[25]

If your learners think that something interesting will be coming up, they will pay attention, for fear they'll miss it.

CUE CARD: Once you know
the script, improvise.

As a final word of caution, a script is only a plan, and like any plan, it is subject to change when circumstances dictate it. Even if the plan must be abandoned, the very act of scripting prepares you for the unexpected. For, if you've planned thoroughly, you will have already discovered those difficulties, and planned around them. Regard your script as Bach did his composition rules, or as a professional football team does its game plan. Script to plan. Then, knowing the plan, improvise. The true art comes not from reading a script, but from making the script your own.

1 *Webster's Dictionary of Quotations* (1992). New York: Smithmark.

2 Phillips, Donald T. (1992). *Lincoln on Leadership: Executive Strategies for Tough Times.* New York: Warner Books.

3 Ibid.

4 *Webster's Dictionary of Quotations* (1992).

5 Jay Boyer. *Orlando Sentinel* 1/02.

6 Ibid.

7 Sullivan, Luke (1998).

8 Quoted by Sullivan, Luke (1998).

9 Fitzee, Dariel (1943). *Showmanship for Magicians.* Pomeroy, OH: Lee Jacobs Productions.

10 Sharpe, Sam H. (1988). *Conjurers' Psychological Secrets.* New York: Hades Publications.

11 Sullivan, Luke (1998).

12 Fitzee, Dariel (1943).

13 Ibid.

14 Dessoir, Max (1893). The psychology of Legerdemain. *The American Journal of Psychology.* Vol. VI.

15 Sharpe, Sam H. (1988).

16 Davidson, John and Casady, Cort (1979). *The Singing Entertainer: A Contemporary Study of the Art and Business of Being a Professional.* Los Angeles: Alfred.

17 Jung, Carl (1976). *Psychological Types.* Princeton, NJ: Princeton University Press, Bollingen Series.

18 McCarthy, Bernice (1996). *About Learning.* Wauconda, IL: About Learning.

19 McCarthy, Bernice (1996). *About Learning.* Wauconda, IL: About Learning.

20 Vincent, Bob (1979). *"Show-Business" Is Two Words.* Studio City, CA: Main Track Publications.

21 Ibid.

22 Sharpe, Sam H. (1988).

23 Hobson, J. Allan (1995). *Sleep.* New York: Scientific American Library, W. H. Freeman.

24 Sylwester, Robert (1995). *A Celebration of Neurons: An Educator's Guide to the Human Brain.* Alexandria, VA: ASCD.

25 Posgate, Bruce (1961). *Kid-Show Showmanship.* Colon, MI: Abbott's Magic.

SEEING RED

"Florida," we thought as we headed southeast. "We've arrived!"

Well, almost arrived. The following week, we were booked to play the Dutch Americana Resort at Walt Disney World. In the meantime we needed somewhere between here and there to stay.

We had just finished a highly successful booking in St. Louis, Missouri. To cut travel expenses, and keep paychecks coming in, we had accepted a weeklong filler job at a Monroe, Louisiana hotel. The pay was low by our standards, but it fit our itinerary.

The hotel looked great. The accommodations were clean, the lounge was large, and the personnel were friendly. Everything was fine until the hotel manager told me that we could not rehearse in her lounge. This was unheard of. Our home was the road. And we practiced where we worked: in hotel lounges. I began expressing the need to keep our material current. She would have none of it.

"You mean you're not a fully rehearsed band?" she snapped. " Am I paying for amateurs?"

I tried to explain the reality of professional traveling bands to her. She just got angry.

"Well, if you're not ready to perform," she shouted, her face now red, "we'll get somebody else."

At this point, I backed off. The location was convenient, and it was only for a week. I decided to call off rehearsals, and told her so.

It was then that the other shoe dropped.

"By the way," she said. "My name is Georgia. "Georgia on My Mind" is my favorite song. She was referring to Willie Nelson's latest hit. "You know it, don't you?"

This, too, was unusual. Managers rarely cared what songs we performed, as long as their patrons were happy. Clearly, this manager was new to the business. Not wanting to engage in further pointless discussion, and knowing that we had intended to learn the song anyway, I replied, "Yes, we can play it for you." Hopefully, we could fake it without rehearsal.

The band did their part. The drummer learned the rhythms, I transcribed the chord changes, and the guitarist wrote out the lyrics for the bass player, in red pen "for emphasis", he said. The next night, with Georgia literally on our minds, we began the engagement.

As soon as I saw the manager, I called the song. "Let's get it over with." I muttered. We pulled out our cheat sheets and the bass player taped his lyrics to his mike stand. Once everybody was set, we began.

The intro sounded fine. It was the last part of the song that would matter. The bass player began singing something, but it wasn't "Georgia on My Mind."

"Georgia, Georgia, that old song, . . . it's sweet, . . . It's on my mind. Georgia."

Those aren't the lyrics, I thought.

"It's a sweet song. It's Georgia."

"Hummmm, hummm, hummm."

Something was definitely wrong, but I didn't want to stop playing and call even more attention to whatever the problem was.

"Georgia, . . . Georgia, . . . hummm, . . . sweet Georgia song. It's sweet."

"Georgia, . . . I said Georgia, . . . Georgia I said."

"That's a song. Georgia . . . It's on my mind."

Finally, it was over and I was the one turning red.

The bass player quickly explained what had happened. The stage lighting had washed out the red ink! The paper looked like blank and the lyrics were useless. He had made up what he could.

Mortified and hiding behind my keyboards, I noticed the manager charging the bandstand. She urgently motioning to our bass player.

"Where did you get those lyrics?" she shouted.

"Uh oh." I thought, "Looks like a fight coming on."

The bass player mumbled, "We wrote them out."

"I've been looking all over them." She smiled, "Can I have a copy?"

"Here, take these!" With that, he shoved the useless paper at the manager.

"That was great!" She exclaimed as she turned and left the lounge.

First, we were stunned. Then, we began to laugh. Our rendition had been awful . . . And yet she liked it! Now I knew why her bands didn't rehearse. (They probably needed to though.) I realized that our sound was better than most of the acts that performed in this hotel. I realized that the week would be no trouble for us.

As I thought it would, the week worked out. The band sounded great and the patrons responded. By mid-week, word about us had spread through town. Before the engagement was over, we had filled the lounge to capacity two nights straight.

I saw the manager once more, when she paid us. As she handed the money over, she said she had one more request. Given her last request, I braced myself for the worst.

"The owner told me that I have to do whatever it takes to get your group back here for New Year's Eve," she explained. "Now, how much will it cost?"

I quoted a price higher than she could afford. As she gagged on the price, I said, "Oh, and one more thing. The contract would have to state explicitly that we can rehearse in the lounge."

It was worth it, just to see her face turn red again. And of course, we never went back.

Next week, we played the Dutch Americana as scheduled. It was a great four-week run. During the whole of the stay, the only red we saw was our well deserved Florida suntans—after rehearsals of course.

> ## "Give strict attention to every detail."—DR. HARLAN TARBELL[1]

The Show Biz Training techniques in this chapter are based on the following Learner-tainment Principles:

Principle 6: Stage the environment—Orchestrate every detail of the environment.

Principle 8: Stage the performer—Orchestrate every detail of your performance.

WHY REHEARSE?

Rehearsal! My eyes glaze over at the thought: grueling run through after run through, with no audience to applaud and cheer you on is hard work. Most performers recognize the value of rehearsal, for it is relentless rehearsal that brings the extremely complicated details of a magical performance to life.

CUE CARD: Rehearsal brings the details to life.

Ed Eckl, in his forward from *The Professional Routines of Ron Fredrick*, backed this position with his description of master close-up magician Ron Zollweg:

> **"Ron Fredrick's (Zollweg's stage name) brand of entertainment, which is a blend of surprise, mystery, and a wry, off-beat humor featuring puns, at first appears extraordinarily technical. But close observation reveals this is achieved by careful routining and extensive practice to achieve a fluidity that completely disarms the spectators."[2]**

Sam Sharpe added: "Truly magical effects should seem to work themselves; or be worked by invisible forces, without the slightest sign of manipulative effort on the conjurer's part. A prominent sign of a master magician is his apparently effortless mastery of his magic."[3]

Performance, when done properly, is both extraordinarily technical and effortlessly fluid, and rehearsal bridges the gap between the two. In *The Stage Manager's Handbook*, Bert Gruver and Frank Hamilton discussed the purpose of rehearsal: "The production of a play may be likened to the manufacture of any complicated article. The various parts are created separately, are brought together at the proper time by careful planning and scheduling, and are assembled into a complete unit. After testing, the product is presented to the public."[4]

Rehearsal therefore is, before a dance is learned, before an arrangement is taught, and before a prop is picked up, about considering all the details and ensuring they all fit together. It is methodical, detailed, step-by-step planning, that works out every detail of the routine. This orchestration is absolutely necessary. There are so many details involved in an illusion show that flawless in-the-moment miracles are impossible.

The same can be said for any live performance, or for that matter, for the filming of a movie. The amount of detail that must be attended to can seem overwhelming. Unless those details are mastered, time and money are wasted as people stand around waiting for an unexpected detail to be sorted out.

REHEARSAL STEPS

In general, the steps to rehearsal are as follows:

- ▶ Gather the materials.

- ▶ Plot the stage.

- ▶ Walk the logistics.

- ▶ Add the dialog.

- ▶ Practice beyond endurance.

- ▶ Run a dress rehearsal.

- ▶ Debut the show.

Gather the Materials.

The first step in staging a performance is to gather all the necessary materials. Once your script is written, it is a simple matter to go through the script, line by line, and create a list of all the items you will need for your performance. For illusion shows, the list can be quite lengthy. It is not unusual for a traveling illusion show to fill one or more semi-trailers with magical apparatus. Fortunately, a trainer's needs aren't nearly as extensive. Table 11-1 will aid you in determining your materials needs.

Plot the Stage.

The second rehearsal task is to determine where all the props and other materials, and the performers who use them, should be placed throughout the performance, and how each

---

MATERIALS LIST FORM

Use this form to compile a list of all needed materials.

Prologue needs:

▶ **Props**

_____

_____

▶ **Participant materials**

_____

_____

▶ **Presentation materials**

_____

_____

Act One materials needed:

▶ **Props**

_____

_____

▶ **Participant materials**

_____

_____

▶ **Presentation materials**

_____

_____

Act Two materials needed:

▶ **Props**

_____

_____

▶ **Participant materials**

_____

_____

▶ Presentation materials

_____

_____

Act Three materials needed:
▶ **Props**

_____

_____

▶ **Participant materials**

_____

_____

▶ **Presentation materials**

_____

_____

TABLE 11-1

item and person will get from point "A" to point "B." To determine this basic placement, a moment by moment plot is drawn. In Table 11-2, you can see what a stage plot looks like.

A plot, or floor plan, is an overhead view of the stage, including the wings and backstage storage areas. A plot is usually drawn to scale, with 1/4 inch equaling 1 foot. It is critical for stage shows to diagram every stage movement. When you consider the traffic that occurs in a very small space, you begin to understand why. For instance, a typical illusion show will feature five or more performers; two or three technicians; a truckload of props, some of which can be quite dangerous if handled incorrectly; and animals that are, in some cases, wild. All these elements must be orchestrated in such as way as to prevent onstage collisions, get props to and from the required locations, and in the case of traveling shows, provide for the packing of show props during the performance after each item has completed its assigned task.

In the learning environment, the need for a stage plot is less critical. It is enough to consider which items you need, and then determine where the items should be placed before and after their use. You should be able to reach for the item you need at the moment you need it without having to look for, or at, the item. As children's show magician Bruce Posgate explained: "You must know where every prop is placed so there is no time lost, in the middle of a presentation, when you have to start looking around for something."[5]

Use Table 11-3 to help you plan prop placement.

STAGE PLOT FORM

UR	URC	UC	ULC	UL
R	RC	C	LC	L
DR	DRC	DC	DLC	DL

STAGE PLOT FORM EXAMPLE

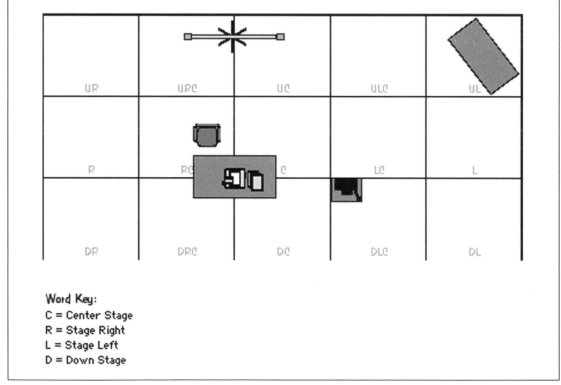

Word Key:
C = Center Stage
R = Stage Right
L = Stage Left
D = Down Stage

TABLE 11-2

Run the Logistics

Once the initial plotting is complete, the action begins on the stage. As Bert Gruver and Frank Hamilton explained, "The primary purposes of the run-through are to consolidate direction, establish tempo of the play as a whole, get a feeling of unity in the acting company, and establish the playing time."[6]

Often, the stage is not available for rehearsals. In that case, a rehearsal room is utilized. To simulate the dimensions and specifics of a stage, the floor is taped. This tape outlines the edges of the stage, the placement of each set piece and large prop, and the various locations where the performers should stand throughout the performance. These locations are called "marks" and are indicated by "Xs" taped on the floor. For an actor, marks are critical. If you "miss a mark" chances are your face will not be lit.

Practice Purgatory   **By Millbower and Yager**

Not quite. Let's try it again.

At first, run-throughs are tedious and frustrating. They involve frequent stops as the performers realize that the blocking is incorrect. The performer may be blocked in the wrong location for the action required. A prop may not be where it is supposed to be unless it is moved earlier. The lighting for a specific moment may be inadequate. This results in a correction to the mark, the prop placement, or to the lighting, and that takes time.

As time consuming and difficult as run-throughs are, they are critical. Run-throughs allow the performers to iron out all the annoying details. It is critical that these details fit. Actions devoid of purpose clutter an act and detract from the act's meaning. As Joseph Pine and James Gilmore suggested in *The Experience Economy:* "Each and every action contributes to the total experience being staged, no matter what the venue."[7]

In the classroom, the details of your performance can build the learning, or detract from it. Every moment in a classroom is a teachable moment. Some moments are straightforward and obvious. Others are subtle and obscure. It is easy to teach the obvious moments. Most facilitators do this quite effectively. Unfortunately, nonrehearsed moments can easily be at odds with the underlying intent. In *Magic by Misdirection,* Fitzee elaborated: "Departures from the usual become prominent because they disturb the harmony and unity of the whole. They are out of character. There is a jarring note. Dissonance results. This discord must attract specific notice."[8]

REHEARSAL QUESTIONS TO ASK

Here are some theatrical-based rehearsal questions. Use them to help you plan your performance.

The script:

▶ What is the message of the script?

_____

_____

▶ What is the point of view of each character?

_____

_____

▶ How does that point of view support the message of the script?

_____

_____

▶ How can the performers convey the point of view of their characters?

_____

_____

▶ What costume will best support the point of view of each character?

_____

_____

The props:

▶ What prop needs to be in what spot at what moment?

_____

_____

▶ Where should the prop be placed before the time it is needed on stage?

_____

_____

▶ How do I get the prop on stage? Off stage?

_____

_____

▶ Where should it be placed afterwards?

_____

_____

The performers:
▶ Who walks where, when?

_____

_____

▶ Where should each performer stand at any given moment?

_____

_____

Other:
▶ What lighting will best support the script?

_____

_____

▶ What music will best support the script? When should it be cued?

_____

_____

TABLE 11-3

Your run-through is the ideal opportunity to align all the elements and eliminate these departures. It is a chance to streamline your performance. Years earlier, in *Showmanship for Magicians,* Fitzee explained:

> **"The routine must be free from extravagance with time. It must be free from extravagance of movements or words. Your outlay of time, movement, words—and, yes, tricks—must be limited to the bare essentials necessary. Cut unnecessary things out of the routine. Retain only the bare essentials to sell the idea."[9]**

Although a classroom run-through is not as extensive as that of a staged performance, runthroughs help you teach every moment, even the subtle ones. Use your run-throughs to purposely point every action toward the learning goal.

Add the Dialog

Once the blocking is complete, it is time to add the dialog. Some show directors prefer to conduct dialog rehearsals before the blocking is done. Others do both simultaneously. Regardless of the approach you take, the dialog should be a part of the rehearsal as soon as it is feasible to do so. Once you add the dialog, you will discover that some lines will need to be extended, and others cut. The rehearsals will then pick up speed and begin to reflect what the real performance will look like.

Practice Beyond Endurance

By now, you have gone past the tedious blocking. YEAHHH! Unfortunately, hours of tedious practice lie ahead. The irony is that the more rehearsed a performer becomes, the more unrehearsed she looks.

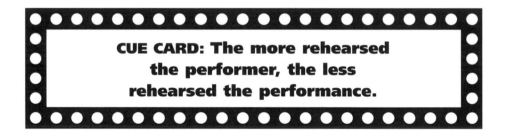

CUE CARD: **The more rehearsed the performer, the less rehearsed the performance.**

In entertainment, you can spot the true professional. That performer has mastered her illusion, her jokes, or her songs so well that she looks unrehearsed. Athletes call it getting in "the flow." The flow occurs when you know something so completely that you no longer concentrate on it. Your body takes over and you lose yourself completely in the moment, much as your car finds itself at work in the morning. It just happens, or so it seems. The reality is that flow isn't an accident. You've rehearsed that drive for months. All the particulars of the drive have become a "doing" memory.

The same advice holds true in the learning environment. You should know your instructional routine implicitly. Practice enough so that your doing memory knows what needs to be done, and then let the artistry take over. Do not practice to the point where your delivery appears stale. Focus on ideas, not words. Even in practicing jokes, where the exact wording is critical, strive to understand the meaning behind the punchline, not the words of that punchline. If your focus is words and you lose your place, you will find it difficult to continue. Focus instead on the ideas.

I have found that the best approach is to practice repeatedly, a couple of times a day, over a period of days and weeks. This sort of aggressive, disciplined, long-term practice will help you look professionally casual. It will tighten up your performance, giving the learners a clearer focus. It will allow you to concentrate on your primary goal, serving the learning needs of your participants. Finally, it will relax you. After all, you don't worry about driving your car. You know you know how. Strive to create the same inner peace with your instruction.

Run a Dress Rehearsal

Once you can present your routine implicitly, try it in real life. In a dress rehearsal, every item, bit of business, and technical detail of the performance is presented in real time. This is the opportunity to act out the entire performance before the intended audience sees it.

There is an old show biz expression that a bad dress rehearsal indicates a strong opening night. I don't believe it. I have never figured out how lousy suggests good. I recommend that you try for perfection in your dress rehearsal, while realizing that some level of energy will be missing owing to the lack of an audience.

Debut the Show

Congratulations. You did it! Break a leg! Score lots of Lightner Scale "5s!"

---

[1] Tarbell, Harlan, Dr. (1927). *Tarbell Course in Magic.* New York: Louis Tannon.

[2] Eckl, Ed, in foreword from Zollweg, Ron (1982). *The Professional Routines of Ron Fredrick: As Told to Ron Zollweg.* Beverly, MA: Unikorn Magik.

[3] Sharpe, Sam H. (1988). *Conjurers' Psychological Secrets.* New York: Hades Publications.

[4] Gruver, Bert, revised by Hamilton, Frank (1972). *The Stage Manager's Handbook.* New York: Drama Publishers, Quite Specific Media Group.

[5] Posgate, Bruce (1961). *Kid-Show Showmanship.* Colon, MI: Abbott's Magic.

[6] Gruver, Bert, revised by Hamilton, Frank (1972).

[7] Pine II, Joseph B., and Gilmore, James H. (1999). *The Experience Economy.* Boston, MA: Harvard Business School Press.

[8] Fitzee, Dariel (1975). *Magic by Misdirection.* Pomeroy, OH: Lee Jacobs Productions.

[9] Fitzee, Dariel (1943). *Showmanship for Magicians.* Pomeroy, OH: Lee Jacobs Productions.

CHAPTER TWELVE

THE PERFORMER

NO ESCAPE

It was July 15, 1914, and a family friend had arranged for me to date a pretty acquaintance. Impressing her was uppermost in my mind, so I decided to do something quite special. I picked her up in an auto I borrowed from my brother. We went from there to one of the best Italian restaurants in New York, Mama Leone's Restaurante. The meal went well, and the conversation was delightful. It appeared that we were attracted to each other. But, taking no chances, I had more surprises in store.

I next took her to the Hammerstein's Roof Garden Theater, where I had arranged front row seats to watch magician Harry Houdini perform. I knew this choice would find favor with her, because Houdini's exploits in New York had been a part of our dinner conversation.

We were both impressed with the show. Houdini performed one amazing feat after another. We laughed together; we cried together; we were amazed together. It was turning out to be a wonderful evening. One illusion in particular, Houdini's presentation of the Chinese Water Torture Cell, stands out in my memory. It changed my life.

A curtain slowly opened to reveal the Torture Cell. It was huge. It had a mahogany frame, metal framing, and a glass panel front that allowed us to see inside. In front of the box and off to the side was a chair and an ax, in case the worst might happen.

Houdini, wearing black evening dress, walked on stage. He announced, "Ladies and gentlemen, this is the climax of all my studies and labors. Never will I be able to construct anything that will be more dangerous or difficult for me to do."

Growing serious and sinister now, he continued, "I shall now attempt to cheat death by escaping from this, the Chinese Water Torture Cell."

With that bit of drama, he ran offstage. Almost immediately, two male assistants began adding water to the cell, filling to overflowing. Soon, Houdini reentered, this time in bathing trunks.

He then asked for a volunteer committee to ensure that no trickery was involved. And this was one of my little surprises. The stage manager was a friend of mine. It had already been arranged for me to join the committee. Houdini selected his volunteers, me included. I feigned surprise, smiled at my date, and joined the stage.

Houdini invited the committee to inspect the cell, but asked me to stay with him. He had a special task in mind for me. I was invited to sit down on the stage and place my own feet in the stocks that Houdini would use. I sat down, and quickly found my feet encased in wood. While the stocks were being clamped in place, Houdini asked, "Tell me, whom are you attending tonight's performance with?"

I mentioned my date.

Houdini asked her to raise her hand. On seeing her, Houdini turned to me and inquired, "Is this your wife?"

"No, it's our first date," I responded.

"I would say there are no chains on you, but given current circumstances, that would not be accurate, would it?"

This by-play made the audience laugh, and brought attention back to the stocks. For try as I might, I could not remove my ankles from their confinement. By this time, the rest of the committee had completely inspected the torture cell, and I was then released from my confinement. We all started to leave the stage, but Houdini stopped me.

"Sir, you are not free yet," he joked.

I was asked to sit in the chair next to the ax.

Houdini then took my place in the stocks. He was hoisted upside down into the air, and positioned directly over the water cell. He then looked at the audience, and asked them to follow my lead in holding their breath when he cued me.

With that said, Houdini swung his arms around. He breathed in deeply once, and exhaled. He did it again, and then again. The third time he pointed at me, and I gave the signal for everyone in the theater to hold their breath.

Houdini was then dropped into the water cell. It happened so quickly that I thought he might hit his head on the bottom. Almost immediately, a canopy was placed in front of the water cell, and Houdini was gone from sight.

With everybody holding his or her breath, the only sound in the theater was the orchestra playing a mournful "Asleep in the Deep."

Thirty seconds passed. Some members of the audience exhaled.

Forty-five. More gave up, including my date.

One minute. I could hold no more. The silence was so tense you could almost hear it.

One minute fifteen. I caught my date's eyes and we both smiled nervously.

One minute thirty. The silence was turning to desperation. Someone in the audience screamed, "There must be something wrong. Get him out of there."

One minute forty five. By now, even the assistants were nervous.

One minute fifty five.

Two minutes.

Enough was enough. One of the assistants headed toward the canopy while the other grabbed for the ax. But before they reached the canopy, Houdini, smiling, came crashing through it. Well, the tension had built so high that the applause was deafening. Once the applause finally subsided, Houdini climbed on top of the tank and splashed his feet in the water. As the curtain closed, he shouted to me, "You're free now." He then turned and waved to my date, who was by now very impressed with her new suitor.

And now it's 1966, 52 years to the day after that night, the night we met, and 50 years after our marriage, and in front of all of our children, our grandchildren, and all of our friends, I offer this toast to you, my darling Clara, "happy anniversary. This was no escaping you."

> "Wherever you direct their attention,
> the audience will look there." —DR. HARLAN TARBELL[1]

The Show Biz Training techniques in this chapter are based on the following Learnertainment Principles:

Principle 8: Stage the performer—Orchestrate every detail of the environment.
Principle 5: Direct attention—Suggest the outcomes you expect.

Other Learnertainment Principles applicable to this chapter are:

Principle 1: Make it fun—Create an atmosphere of playfulness.
Principle 2: Layer meaning—Present your message on several levels.

PERSONALITY

The theater lobby looked inviting. The popcorn smelled and tasted delicious. The seats were comfortable. The overture was intriguing. Excitement was building. Then the moment arrived. The performer stepped on stage. Crawled would be a better word for it. The magician offered a perfunctory nod toward the audience, and began. The illusions were performed as if they might not work. The dialog was delivered to no one in particular. The jokes sounded flat. It was obvious that the performer did not want to be there. Suddenly, neither did the audience.

Entertainment requires personality. All the solid writing, meticulous planning, and incessant rehearsal cannot deliver an effective performance. A personality is required. Without a solid performer, a performance is doomed.

**CUE CARD: Entertainment
is personality driven.**

In Chapter 4, we discovered that our brains constantly scan the horizons for threats. We also determined that much of the processing that our brains do is subconscious, and that negative emotion lurks just below the surface of our consciousness, waiting for a reason to panic.

We all pick up signals from other people. These signals suggest everything we need to know about each other. This is especially true in entertainment. A performer may be standing in front of thousands of people, but each individual within that thousand feels a personal connection from the performer.

Entertainment depends on that connection. Magic, for instance, is very much a confidence art. People believe in the miracles because the performer believes, and they trust the performer. The performer sets the tone; the audience responds. Emotions are contagious, and people will mimic the emotions suggested to them.[2] In discussing magic, Dariel Fitzee expanded on this theme:

> **"The spectator sees the magician himself. He is aware of the performer's appearance, his dress, his features, and his posture. He is conscious of the type of person he seems to be, of his style of talking, of his apparent educational background. He even realizes something of the performer's disposition. Yet much of this information comes to the spectator subconsciously. The mind has a way of putting together clues from here and there, clues which definitely establish this performer as an individual. It is an automatic process, the details of which the spectator is totally unaware."[3]**

From a learning perspective, Renate Nummela Caine and Geoffrey Caine concurred: "Students respond to subtle stimuli, including all the small signals that show what the teacher is really thinking and feeling."[4]

Although the spectators may be consciously unaware of the performer's personality, attitude, education, posture, and other attributes, the performer must be completely aware of these factors. They direct the performance.

When all possible external preparation has been done, the self remains. So, the self must be practiced too. Some areas that require focus are:

- ▶ Finding a persona

- ▶ Communicating effectively

- ▶ Conquering stage fright

- ▶ Using a mike

FINDING A PERSONA

Charlie Chaplin, speaking about his start in movies, said, "Little as I knew about movies, I knew that nothing transcended personality."[5] Chaplin was correct. The face you wear on stage is a major part of your appeal.

If you expect people to pay attention to you, they must have a reason to do so. As magician Bruce Posgate says, "You must be different from the man on the street."[6] Because you are in the front of the room, you are expected to be different. You must give them a reason to listen to you. If you cannot give the learners a reason to pay attention to you, they won't.

Entertainers achieve this distinction by drawing on their own personalities. As Fitzee described it:

> **"To achieve distinct individuality as a magician it is necessary that you be distinguished from the rank and file. The distinguishing marks are entirely due to the combination of features which are exclusively your own. It this combination is pleasing to others, you have a pleasing personality. If this combination is superlatively [original emphasis], you are on your way to stardom."[7]**

Sometimes referred to as charisma, this individuality is the ability to command attention because of who the audience perceives you are. Although this discussion deals with the audience's perception of you, it is, more often than not, a true characterization, with all your faults and attributes publicly on display.

This leads to a dilemma. Do you masquerade as someone else on stage, or do you allow your personality to come through, warts and all? Bruce Posgate may have the best advice: "Why not just be yourself? It's more fun! It is much easier and needs no effort. Just be yourself with a friendly smile on your face. If you adopt the attitude, 'We're all in this together so let's have a lot of fun' you will have your audience with you, all the way."[8]

Funnyman Steve Allen backed this position when he said, "Your stage self should be very close to your actual social self."[9] Being yourself has a number of distinct advantages:

▶ You'll be more genuine with the audience, and they'll sense it.

▶ You'll never have to remember what you character would do. You already know the answer.

▶ You won't have to learn a fake bio. Your character already has one: yours.

▶ Your genuineness will make it easier to direct the audience's attention toward the goals you have set.

Exposing your inner self in front of strangers can be frightening. It's easy to think, "What if they don't like me?" It's harder to realize that they will like you, but only if they see you as a real person.

Standing naked in front of your learners implies showing your faults. We are all multi-faceted. We all have faults. It is not necessary to present all of you to the audience, just those parts of you that you wish to share. But, those parts you do share must be genuine. They must be the real you.

A place to start is in examining your personality traits. Do so by making a list of the various facets of your personality. Then, determine which of those traits you wish to display, and which you choose to downplay. Table 12-1 has been created to assist with this task.

It is important to be brutally honest with yourself. Your audience doesn't care about niceties. If you ignore one of your personality quirks, it won't go away. Your learners will find it anyway. As Bob Vincent explained:

> **"You are actually being auditioned by them each and every show. The minute you appear in view on stage, several hundred eyes and ears are examining you, *very carefully* [original emphasis]. All of your assets and liabilities become apparent immediately. If you're an egotist it shows! If you have no depth of emotion it shows!! and [sic] if your sole purpose for being on stage is to make money and only please yourself, and not the audience, that shows too."**[10]

The result would be a lack of confidence in you as the instructor. Magician Max Dessoir, in speaking about this subject, said: "The conjurer must inspire confidence in order to be believed, and to win from the start the sympathy of the public, so that the audience, without exception, will be willing to follow the intentions of the artist."[11]

With a firm grasp on the personality traits you intend show the audience, you should next mold those traits into a base character you can comfortably maintain throughout the performance. Dessoir continued:

> **"Character shows up in mannerisms, dress, conduct, beliefs, attitudes, manner of talking, manner of walking, grooming, personal appearance, reaction under stress and in many other ways. Character is revealed best by an individual's reactions to impediments, obstacles, stresses, emotions**

ATTRIBUTES EVALUATION WORKSHEET

Part 1
Circle the attributes that people describe you as having. Next, underline the attributes you believe that you have.

Adaptable	Easygoing	Nurturing	Responsive
Adventurous	Efficient	Objective	Restless
Aggressive	Empathetic	Observant	Sensitive
Alert	Energetic	Opinionated	Serious
Analytical	Enterprising	Orderly	Skeptical
Autonomous	Enthusiastic	Organized	Sociable
Caring	Expressive	Original	Speculative
Challenging	Factual	Outgoing	Spontaneous
Charming	Fair	Outspoken	Strategic
Clever	Firm	Patient	Structured
Committed	Flexible	Perceptive	Supportive
Compassionate	Forceful	Precise	Sympathetic
Concerned	Friendly	Personable	Tactful
Conscientious	Gentle	Persuasive	Talkative
Controlled	Harmonious	Playful	Theoretical
Cooperative	Idealistic	Pleasant	Thorough
Creative	Imaginative	Popular	Tolerant
Critical	Impersonal	Practical	Tough
Curious	Independent	Pragmatic	Traditional
Decisive	Individualistic	Private	Trusting
Deep	Innovative	Questioning	Understanding
Demanding	Inquisitive	Quick	Versatile
Detached	Inspirational	Realistic	Virtuous
Determined	Inventive	Reflective	Visionary
Devoted	Logical	Reserved	Vivacious
Diplomatic	Loyal	Resourceful	Warm
Direct	Modest	Responsible	Witty

Part 2
Based on the words you circled, list the attributes you want your learners to see, and those you wish to downplay.

I want the learners to see me as:

► _____

► _____

► _____

► _____

I do not want the learners to see me as:

► _____

► _____

► _____

► _____

▶ _____   ▶ _____
▶ _____   ▶ _____
▶ _____   ▶ _____
▶ _____   ▶ _____
▶ _____   ▶ _____
▶ _____   ▶ _____
▶ _____   ▶ _____
▶ _____   ▶ _____
▶ _____   ▶ _____
▶ _____   ▶ _____
▶ _____   ▶ _____
▶ _____   ▶ _____
▶ _____   ▶ _____
▶ _____   ▶ _____

Part 3

Based on the words that describe the way you want the learners to see you, write a statement that defines your on-stage personality.

My on-stage personality will be:

_____
_____
_____
_____
_____
_____
_____
_____
_____
_____

TABLE 12-1

and the like. Throughout your entire routine, this character must be maintained. Everything you do must be influenced and shaped by this character."[12]

To help shape your character, you should ask yourself the questions listed in Table 12-2.

Your character should only do those things that are a part of your natural makeup. The purpose in answering these questions is not to invent a new you, but rather to force conscious thought about every aspect of your being your present to your audience. Be a character. BE YOURSELF!

CUE CARD:
Be yourself on stage.

CONQUERING STAGE FRIGHT

Everyone is afraid of something, including me. Fortunately though, I have never been afraid of the stage. From the stage I can control the environment. Cocktail parties are another matter: all sorts of things can go wrong there!

But how do you overcome stage fright? The answer is simple. You overcome stage fright, and become confident on stage, by being on stage. The more stage experience you gain, the more confident you become, and the less anxiety you experience. Volunteer to assist fellow instructors as often as possible. Join a speakers club such as Toastmasters International. Take part in a community play. Speak out for a cause you believe in. Regardless of the forum you choose, get in front of people as often as possible. Soon, you'll gain confidence.

Although confident, you may never escape the pre-performance jitters. Even the most polished professionals experience some pre-performance apprehension. But they surmount it because they know their routine cold. They have already considered and prepared for every possible detail. As Fitzee explained:

"The best solution for the problem of being at ease is to be at ease. A thorough knowledge of your lines. A clear understanding of what you are to

---

CHARACTER EVALUATION WORKSHEET

Part 1

To determine what your character (your stage persona) will look like, answer the following questions:

▶ **How does my character stand?**

_____

▶ **How does my character walk?**

_____

▶ **How does my character talk?**

_____

▶ **How does my character dress?**

_____

▶ **How does my character relate to others?**

_____

▶ **How does my character display emotions?**

_____

▶ **How does my character respond to difficulties?**

_____

▶ **How does my character view him or her self?**

_____

Part 2

Given the descriptions you wrote in Part 1, write a brief stage persona description of your character.

_____
_____
_____
_____
_____
_____
_____
_____

TABLE 12-2

do and when you are to do it. Complete confidence in your ability to do the tricks you have selected. You can gain this knowledge through the fact that you have been over the act time after time—perfectly."[13]

It is normal to experience pre-performance anxiety. It may even be healthy. Nonchalance can breed sloppiness. It is the difference between excitement and fear. If you are afraid, then you have not rehearsed enough. If you are not excited, then you are not worthy of your audience. Once you begin, you will have little time for such self-serving emotions anyway. They will get lost in the adrenaline of the moment.

**CUE CARD: Stage fright is bad,
stage anxiety is good.**

A second method for combating stage fright is to focus on the word and not yourself. In the words of Bob Vincent: "In order to be truly involved deeply with the audience, you must not be conscious of 'self' and only be totally committed to the 'word.'"[14]

By the "word," Vincent means the material you are presenting. Once you become the message you wish to send, the performance is no longer about you. You transcend your own emotions and get lost in the word. Vincent added: "As a performer, you need to be absolutely sure of yourself when you walk on stage. For this reason, you need to completely forget about yourself, and make the total commitment to every sound that emanates from your lips, and every gesture that comes from your body."[15]

**CUE CARD: Become
one with your message.**

COMMUNICATING EFFECTIVELY

There are two ways in which a performer projects information, verbally, and nonverbally. We will discuss both, beginning with verbal communication.

Verbal Communication

The more obvious of the two communication methods is verbal. There are five factors to consider in verbal communication:

- ▶ Pitch
- ▶ Inflection
- ▶ Speed
- ▶ Cadence
- ▶ Volume

PITCH

The pitch of your voice is the basic sound your voice makes, and every voice is different. Vocal pitch is determined in part by a person's gender. A female voice is pitched an octave higher than a male voice. Beyond this difference, each person's voice has it's own comfortable pitch.

There is no specific advantage regarding pitch. Males with low, James Earl Jones style voices seem to be in demand for voice-over work. But low-pitched voices can put people to sleep. They can also be perceived as threatening. For instance, James Earl Jones was also the voice of *Star Wars*' Darth Vader.

Females with low-pitched voices are sometimes considered sultry. For example, in the film *Who Framed Roger Rabbit?* (1988), the character Jessica Rabbit was a femme fatale. To provide an air of sultry mystery, Kathleen Turner was cast for the role.

High-pitched voices, especially female voices such as Joan Rivers, have been successful too. Rivers has built a career out of gossip, with her line, "Can we talk?" High-pitched voices can also be perceived as anxious, excited, or nervous. In men, high-pitched voices can seem out of place. This has not, however, stopped Joe Pesci from building a highly successful career for himself in films such as *My Cousin Vinnie* (1992).

Most of us recoil the first time we hear our own voice broadcast back at us. Nevertheless, the pitch we hear on tape is the instrument we have to work with. Make the most of it. Breathe deeply, much as you would while lying in bed, to lower and add depth to your pitch, and vary the inflection, speed, cadence, and volume of your voice.

INFLECTION

The inflection of your voice is in many ways more important than your pitch. A monotone delivery will suggest boredom, and a fast, high-pitched delivery will suggest excitement or anxiety. You cannot significantly change the pitch you have, but you can vary your vocal inflection. Make your speech informal but energetic, and emphasize the key words in each sentence. Your speech pattern should imply that you are relaxed and have something interesting to say.

SPEED

The average person speaks at a rate of 125 to 180 words per minute.[16] Most people can process words at a rate of up to 500 words per minute.[17] This presents a verbal communications challenge. Your learners will be finishing your sentences in their heads before you do. Do not rush through your sentences to keep pace with your learners. Instead, speak the minimum number of words necessary to make your point. Script writing can help focus your words. In addition, make the inflection of your words interesting. Speak naturally, and emphasize key words. That way, your learners will focus both on what you say, and how you say it.

CADENCE

Each of us speaks in a rhythmic pattern. Professional speakers take their natural rhythmic patterns, and form them into memorable phrases. In the hands of an expert communicator, phrases sound lyrical and poetic. For instance, Winston Churchill rallied the British nation during its darkest World War II days, in part, because of the following speech. To help you spot the cadence structure, it has been laid out here as if in poem form:

> "We shall not flag or fail.
> We shall go on to the end.
> We shall fight in France,
> we shall fight on the seas and oceans,
> we shall fight with growing confidence and growing strength in the air,
> we shall defend our island, whatever the cost may be.

We shall fight on the beaches,
we shall fight on the landing grounds,
we shall fight in the fields and in the streets,
we shall fight in the hills;
we shall never surrender."[18]

Notice the sing-song approach of the words, created by the repeated cadences. The phrases are so well constructed that the words, even though they do not rhyme, seem like a poem. You could almost imagine those words as a song.

Abraham Lincoln had similar poetic abilities. Consider these excerpts from his Gettysburg Address:

"But in a larger sense, we can not dedicate
we can not consecrate
we can not hallow this ground.
It is rather for us to . . . highly resolve that this nation under God
shall have a new birth of freedom;
and that government of the people,
by the people,
for the people,
shall not perish from the earth."[19]

Note the same sing-song approach. The language sings, and became rightfully memorable.

Jesse Jackson offers an example from our own times. Much of his communication ability comes from the cadences he chooses, and the way he uses those cadences to make his point. During his 1984 presidential campaign, in a speech before the Democratic National Convention, he said the following:

Suffering breeds character.
Character breeds faith,
and in the faith will not disappoint.
Our time has come.
Our faith, hope, and dreams have prevailed.
Our time has come.
Weeping has endured for nights but that joy cometh in the morning.
Our time has come.

No grave can hold our body down.
Our time has come.
No lie can live forever.
Our time has come.
We must leave the racial battle ground
and come to the economic common ground
and moral higher ground.
America, our time has come.[20]

Obviously, speaking only in rhyme is neither possible nor desirable, but you should be aware of the natural cadences in your speech pattern, and capitalize on those phrases that roll lyrically off your tongue.

In addition, you should aggressively strive to rid your speech of annoying patterns such as "ummmm," "you know," "you guys," "it's like," and any other phrase you find yourself repeating often. They waste your learners' time, and your breath.

VOLUME

The best example of how not to speak was demonstrated by Ted Knight on the *Mary Tyler Moore Show*. Knight portrayed his character, Ted Baxter, as a pompous fool. One of the techniques Knight used to solidify this portrayal was overly projecting his voice. The resulting characterization made Baxter seem like a fool. Granted, a trainer must project enough volume to be heard. But the difference between being heard and appearing pompous is slight. Besides, if you don't hold some volume back, you'll have no more to give when you must emphasize a point.

A good mike can help. As we will soon discover, a mike allows you to talk in a normal manner and still reach your learners. When no mike is available to you, project just enough to reach every person in the room, but have pity on the people in the first row. Don't stand over them as you shout to the back of the room.

Vocal Bombast   By Millbower and Yager

Some people say I'm loud!?

LEARNING TO SPEAK

There is no substitute for practice. For inspiration, listen to old radiotapes of some of the world's great speakers. Comedians Jack Benny and Goucho Marx, moral leaders Martin Luther King Jr. and Billy Graham, and politicians Winston Churchill and Ronald Reagan provide excellent examples of well modulated tones. If you listen to performers closely, you will notice a pace to their delivery, with strategic pauses to emphasize key points.

Try delivering some speeches yourself. Record yourself delivering them. Then, play the recording back. Aggressively analyze your pitch, inflection, speed, cadence, and volume. Table 12-3 can help with that analysis. Then, rerecord yourself and repeat the process. With practice, you can deliver your words with such emotion and meaning that your learners will want to absorb your every nuance.

VOCAL AWARENESS TABLE

Use this table to gain an awareness of your vocal characteristics.

Pitch:

I believe my pitch is	Low	Medium	High

My pitch could be described as _____

Given my pitch, my character should be _____

Inflection:

My inflection is	Monotone	Varying	Energetic
I emphasize key words	Rarely	Sometimes	Often

To use inflection more effectively, I will . . .

_____

Cadence:

My cadence is	Nonexistent	Moderate	Lyrical
I speak memorable phrases	Rarely	Sometimes	Often

To use cadence more effectively, I will . . .

_____

Volume:

My volume is	Soft	Medium	Loud
I vary my volume	Rarely	Sometimes	Often

To use volume more effectively, I will . . .

_____

TABLE 12-3

Nonverbal Communication

A plumber knows how to use a snake, a firefighter knows how to use a ladder, and a carpenter knows how to use a hammer. To not know the tools of their trade would make them ineffective. The primary tool actors' use, just like instructors, is their bodies.

Your body is your tool. It gets you from place to place, it absorbs sensations around you so that your brain can make sense of the world, and it allows you to entertain. Every point you emphasize, everything you feel, in fact, your very relationship with the audience, is transmitted through your body. As Walt Disney said: "I have discovered that language has an autonomy. Every spoken word has its facial grimace, emphasizing the meaning."[21]

CUE CARD: What you think and feel is communicated through your body.

Every spoken word has a nonverbal component. It is not enough just to speak. You must also ensure that all the nonverbal signals you send align with what you say. The verbal content of your message accounts for only 7 percent of what people hear, and the tone of your voice adds another 38 percent. Body language, at 55 percent, adds the rest.[22]

Davidson and Cort applied this information to show biz when they said: "Your *body language* [original emphasis]—posture, stance, the position of your shoulders, arms and hands—says as much as [sic] to the audience as what you are singing. On stage, your body is an extension of your mind."[23]

In *Between One and Many*, Steven Byron and Michael Scott make much the same point about public speaking:

> "Audience members use appearance to initially make judgments about a speaker's level of attractiveness. The consequences of this judgment are far reaching for speakers. Research tells us that speakers perceived as attractive by audience members also are perceived as smart, successful, sociable, and self-confident. As a result, speakers who fall into this category enjoy an audience whose initial impression of them is favorable."[24]

And Michael Lawlor and Peter Handley, in *The Creative Trainer*, focus the point on instructors:

"**Most trainers concentrate their attention on what they have to say, that is, on the verbal content of their lesson. Very few think about the way they say it or the use they make of their body while they are saying it. The result is that, although what they say may be understood, it will not be remembered. This is because it has not penetrated the so-called logical/critical and emotional barriers of their listeners.**"[25]

Next we examine several components of nonverbal communication, including:

► Gestures

► Stance

► Eye contact

► Clothing

GESTURES

In everyday life, people use gestures. Try talking on the phone or giving directions without using your hands and you will discover how important gestures are to your communication style. The same dynamic holds true on the stage.

Each stage gesture is a chance to support your point. Great performers know this, and make meticulous use of their bodies. When magicians rehearse for a performance, they work out every hand gesture. Only gestures that enhance the routine are kept. All extraneous gestures are abandoned.

Professional singers often can gesture with only one hand. The other is holding a mike. The gestures they make are carefully thought out. Each gesture enhances and emphasizes a point in the song. Most often, these gestures are also open handed with the palm facing toward the audience. Open hand gestures imply honesty and accessibility, whereas backhand gestures imply superiority and contempt. These gestures are usually avoided, unless they are required to make a point.

The size of your gestures also matters. Make your arm movement appropriate to the size of your classroom. If you are in an auditorium, expand the size of your gestures. If you are in a conference room, tone them down.

Great performers also keep their hands out of their pockets. The hands are too important for communication to be locked up in such a manner. In addition, hands placed in pockets suggest a lack of openness or confidence. The resulting bulges also make the performer look chunky.

As part of your rehearsal regimen, stand in front of a mirror and observe what your hands do as you talk. Look for unnecessary actions and negative connotations in your

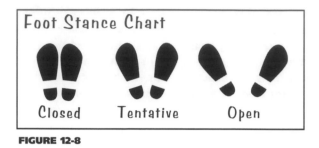

FIGURE 12-8

hand movements. Once you find those weaknesses, learn how to control them, lest they control you.

STANCE

Like gestures, your stance suggests either openness or inaccessibility. Professional entertainers rarely turn their back on the audience. They half turn. They stand up straight. A magician cannot slouch. That posture would imply a lack of confidence that could destroy the illusion. Their posture is a three-quarters stance, with both feet firmly planted a few inches apart, and with their toes pointed outward toward the audience. The entire stance indicates confidence and accessibility.

You should face the audience at all times. If circumstances require you to turn your back, turn only halfway. Don't simultaneously talk and write on an easel. Write first, then talk. Stand up straight. Use the three-quarter stance as displayed in Figure 12-8. Demonstrate to the audience, via your posture, that you are proud of what you have to share, and are open to their participation.

EYE CONTACT

Magic great Dr. Harlan Tarbell once advised magicians, "The audience follows your eyes."[26] It's true. Magicians rely extensively on eye movement to point the audience away from the illusion's mechanics. A simple look is often enough to allow a magical switch to occur. In this same manner, when during a musical performance the spotlight moves from one performer to another, the other performers will turn and look at the performer being spotlighted. This tells the audience where their focus should be. In addition, a performer who will not look at the audience has a more difficult time building rapport. To the audience, the behavior implies that they are not important. A breaking off of eye contact with the audience severs the magical electricity that runs between the performer and the audience.

In the learning environment, your eyes can have a similar effect. They help you connect with your trainees. They tell your learners that you care about them. Maintain eye contact. Do not look away or turn your back. "Talk to your audience not the screen. If you maintain eye contact with the participants they are encouraged to pay attention."[27]

Just as a singer turns toward the soloing performer, you should watch your own videos. Yes, I mean that video you have seen 40 times and can't bear to see again. In Chapter 10, I shared my desire to never play "Proud Mary" again. Yet, I would gladly perform it if the audience wanted it. Furthermore, I would smile at them as I did it. That video is your "Proud Mary." Watch it with your learners. When you turn your eyes away from it, you are suggesting that it doesn't warrant your attention. If it isn't good enough for you, how can you expect them to watch it?

In large venues, it may not possible to make eye contact with every member of your audience. Instead, focus on a few individuals who are looking at you and then expand your circle. If you look in the general direction of all the audience members, it will appear that you are making eye contact with each individual.

Finally, use the whole stage. Don't forget those learners who are seated on your least favored side. They deserve your attention too. If you can't remember to work both sides, set your stage in such a way as to force you to use all of it.

CLOTHING

Earlier in this chapter, we discussed the need to become a personality. One of the major factors performers use to aid their personality is the clothing they choose to wear. This is especially evident in Madonna's career. The singer changed her clothing with virtually every album of new material. This gimmick kept her ahead of the times, and even set off fashion trends. The same is true in the magical arts. Older style magicians performed in a tuxedo. With the advent of the hippie 1960s, that style looked dated. To create a hipper image, magician Doug Henning dressed in tie-dyed shirts and blue jeans. As a result, he enjoyed considerable career success. In the 1970s, another magician entered the public arenas. David Copperfield looked both romantic and debonair. His wardrobe was more elegant than Henning's and he too enjoyed much career success.

The goal of clothing should be to present a professional image. Knowing what you want your character to be, dress in ways that complement your character. For example, I know that I look formal and somewhat stuffy, so in intimate training sessions, for college classes, and when speaking to people younger than myself, I do not wear a tie. In this way, I make myself more accessible. On the other hand, when I am involved in a full-blown presentation, I dress businesslike, and quite conservatively. This allows me, as we discussed in the section on comedy in Chapter 5, to play stuffy for laughs.

You should also avoid carrying loose change in your pockets. Great performers separate their stage clothes from their daily wear. The chances of needing money or an ID on

HOW DO I LOOK EVALUATION WORKSHEET

Step 1

To determine how you look on stage, score your effectiveness on the following items by placing an "X" in the appropriate box on each line, with "1" representing the worst possible rating, and "7" representing the best. Skip those items that do not apply to you.

Rating	1	2	3	4	5	6	7
Shirt							
Pressed							
Clean							
Not faded							
Tasteful							
Pants							
Pressed							
Clean							
Not faded							
Tasteful							
Tie							
Clean							
Hangs straight							
Unstained							
Shoes							
Polished							
Laces not frayed							
Don't squeak							
Pockets							
No loose items							
No bulges							
Jewelry							
Understated							
Unscratched							
Not tainted							
Hair							
Combed							
Neat							
Nails							
Clean							
Polished							
Trimmed							
Make-up							
Understated							
Perfume/cologne							
Faintly present							

Step 2

Now that you have scored your effectiveness in each item, connect the Xs. Once you have connected the Xs, turn the worksheet onto its left side to view the resulting graph.

My three greatest strengths:	My three greatest areas of opportunities:
1. _____	1. _____
2. _____	2. _____
3. _____	3. _____

As a result of this worksheet, I will:

_____

_____

_____

_____

TABLE 12-4

stage are slim. Most performers keep their pockets clear of these items. This allows for freer movement and a better looking, bulgeless body form, and prevents extraneous pocket noise.

You should also pay special attention to the color of the stage around you, especially in larger venues. If you are dressed in the same basic color as the background, your learners may lose sight of you. Likewise, try not to clash with the background. Choose your attire for the day with an eye to the environment you will be performing in.

Finally, use Table 12-4 to help you evaluate the message your clothing sends about you.

USING A MIKE

Novice performers are often afraid of the microphone. Sometimes, this fear is due to stage fright. Other times it's a lack of confidence. More frequently, it's simply an unfamiliarity with microphone technique. The first two reasons are dealt with in the sections on building a persona and conquering stage fright. We will deal with mike techniques now. For the truth is that a mike is a performer's best friend, and once you know some basic mike techniques, you can use it to great advantage.

A mike allows you to speak at a comfortable volume level, with a natural tone, and still be heard. It saves wear on your voice—and this is the amazing part—places a manifestation of you at the learners' sides. It can build intimacy with each member of the audience, even those furthest away from the stage.

Instructors most often use two common types of mikes, hand-helds and clip-ons (often called lavalieres). We will discuss both next.

Hand-held Microphones

The most common type of hand-held microphone is the Shure model SM58. The 58 is an all-around workhorse. You see it on television, in night clubs, and on the stage. Its draw is its versatility. It is equally adapt at picking up a singer's inflection as a speaker's whisper. Better yet, it is nearly indestructible. The 58 is so prevalent that many club vocalists carry their own.

Cord Confinement   By Millbower and Yager

What do we do now?

Regardless of its advantages, the 58 has a mike cord that comes out of its back, and connects to a public address system (PA). This cord provides a temptation that some vocalists can't resist: wrapping themselves up in it. Many performers become so engaged in the mike cord that they become one with it, sometimes even blending into the mike stand to the point that they are all but invisible. Wrapping yourself in a mike cable is counterproductive. To the audience, this behavior suggests insecurity, and it makes communication more difficult. Most people would find it difficult to hold a conversation without using their hands, and yet the mike wrappers willingly confine their own hands in an inanimate object. It is a waste of an important resource: your body.

If you find yourself in a situation in which you must use a mike with a cord, ignore the cord. Forget it exists. Keep your body and your free hands free. Wrap yourself in the audience, not the mike cord.

To become comfortable with a corded mike, walk around your home with a mike in your hand while dragging the cord behind you. Basketball players, to become comfortable with ball handling, walk, eat, sit, and sleep with a basketball. They handle the basketball until it becomes an extension of their being. The same dynamic is true with a mike. Hold it, walk with it, become one with it. Make it what it is, an extension of you, not your master.

In addition to keeping the mike cord away from your body, you should also keep the mike out of your face. When you hold the mike, aim it at your chin, and talk over the top of it. If you can't place two fingers between the mike and your chin, you are holding it too closely.

A second type of hand-held mike is wireless. The techniques for using it are the same as with a corded mike. In addition, if you have trained yourself properly to ignore the mike cord, you won't miss the cord when you use a wireless mike. Your audience will never see you grasping at the air as you subconsciously reach for an invisible mike cord.

Clip-on Microphones

Perhaps the most common type of microphone is the lavaliere lapel mike. This mike has great pickup when placed properly on a speaker's body. Clip the mike to your clothing about three inches below your chin, and pointed straight up at your mouth.

Some clip-ons are wireless. They have a length of cord that extends from the mike to a transmitter, usually worn on the belt. I usually run the cord under my shirt to my belt. In the one instance where I neglected to do this, one of my hands caught the cord and pulled the mike off of my suit jacket. I have found that by placing the cord under my shirt, I avoid the problem completely. One additional factor for women to consider is the clothing you will perform in. Remember to wear an outfit that you can clip the transmitter to. Otherwise you will be forced to hold the transmitter.

Some clip-ons have a cord that attaches to a PA. If you are uncomfortable with this leach, you audience will notice. Before you place yourself in that situation, practice walking around while dragging a cord. For those readers with small children, pretend the cord is a child tugging at your leg.

Volume Levels

When you check the mike levels exercise caution. A mike in an empty room sounds completely different than a mike in a room full of learners. Sound waves tend to bounce around empty rooms. As a result, the room may have an echo. Your tendency will be to turn the mike down. When your learners are in the room, their bodies will absorb some sound waves. You will find that you need higher volume levels than it seemed were necessary during your empty room test.

Feedback

One of a facilitator's nightmare scenarios is the situation where all the learners are holding their ears because of mike feedback. Although invisible, sound waves constantly bounce around a room. If you've ever heard an echo in your bathroom, or in the mountains, you have heard sound waves echoing back at you. Feedback occurs when a PA system picks up its own amplified sound, creating a loop of sound waves. Fortunately, there is an easy solution. Don't stand in front of the speakers.

In conclusion, know where the speakers are. Become comfortable dragging a mike cord behind you. Don't hide behind the mike stand. Above all else, become one with your mike. Control it, lest it control you.

CUE CARD: Control your mike, lest it control you.

IN CONCLUSION

In the last several chapters, we have explored techniques largely drawn from the magical arts. We discovered the techniques magicians use to set the stage, and to stage themselves. We learned that the successful performer is able to weave those techniques together into a cohesive whole that captures and maintains the spectators' attention.

Unfortunately for magicians, they deal in false reality. The spectator's attention must be clearly focused where the magician wants it, and away from those items that, if seen in their true light, would destroy the illusion. As Sharpe explained: "The conjurer's aim should be to ensure a clear perception of the train of events which constitute the illusion, but a misperception of the technical details by which the illusion is accomplished."[28]

In a like manner, the successful instructor presents an environment in which the train of events is clear and focused on the learning goal, and in which the technical details escape attention. Although learning is not deception, it should be magical.

---

[1] Tarbell, Dr. Harlan (1927). *Tarbell Course in Magic.* New York: Louis Tannon Magic Routines.

[2] Hatfield, Elaine, Cacioppo, John T., Rapson, Richard L., and Hatfield, Cacioppo (1994). *Emotional Contagion (Studies in Emotional and Social Interaction).* Cambridge, UK: Cambridge University Press.

[3] Fitzee, Dariel (1975). *Magic by Misdirection.* Pomeroy, OH: Lee Jacobs Productions.

[4] Caine, Renate Nummela, and Caine, Geoffrey (1991). *Making Connections: Teaching and the Human Brain.* Parsippany, NJ: Dale Seymour Publications.

⁵ Johnson, Bruce "Charlie" (1988). *Comedy Techniques for Entertainers: Charlie's Comedy Creation Course.* La Crosse, WI: Visual Magic.

⁶ Posgate, Bruce (1961). *Kid-Show Showmanship.* Colon, MI: Abbott's Magic.

⁷ Fitzee, Dariel (1943).

⁸ Posgate, Bruce (1961). *Show Business Is Two Words.* Studio City, CA: Main Track Publications.

⁹ Allen, Steve, with Wollman, Jane (1998). *How to Be Funny: Discovering the Comic You.* Amherst, MA: Prometeus Books.

¹⁰ Vincent, Bob (1979).

¹¹ Dessoir, Max (1893). The psychology of Legerdemain. *The American Journal of Psychology,* Vol. VI.

¹² Fitzee, Dariel (1943).

¹³ Ibid.

¹⁴ Vincent, Bob (1979).

¹⁵ Ibid.

¹⁶ Bedrosian, Maggie (1994). *Speak Like a Pro: When What You Say Can Mean Millions.* Rockville, MD: BCI Press.

¹⁷ Byron, Steven R, and Scott, Michael D. (2000). *Between One and Many: The Art and Science of Public Speaking.* Mountain View, CA: Manfield.

¹⁸ *Webster's Dictionary of Quotations* (1992). New York: Smithmark.

¹⁹ Thomas, Benjamin (1952). *Abraham Lincoln: A Biography.* New York: Alfred A. Knopf.

²⁰ Jackson, Jesse (1984). Democratic National Convention Prime Time Speech.

²¹ Smith, Dave (2001). *The Quotable Walt Disney: It Was All Started by a Mouse.* New York: Hyperion.

²² Lawlor, Michael, and Handley, Peter (1996). *The Creative Trainer: Holistic Facilitation Skills for Accelerated Learning.* London: McGraw-Hill.

²³ Davidson, John and Casady, Cort (1979).

²⁴ Byron, Steven R, and Scott, Michael D. (2000).

²⁵ Lawlor, Michael, and Handley, Peter. (1996).

²⁶ Tarbell, Dr. Harlan (1927).

²⁷ Munson, Lawrence S. (1992). *How to Conduct Training Seminars: A Complete Guide for Training Managers & Professionals,* 2nd edit. New York: McGraw-Hill.

²⁸ Sharpe, Sam H. (1988). *Conjurers' Psychological Secrets.* New York: Hades Publications.

CHAPTER THIRTEEN

FINALE

Welcome to a Bess Tess Story

HARRIET AND THE HOUSEKEEPERS: SCENE FOUR

The "A Bess–Tess Story" was the breakthrough that Harriet needed. From that idea sprang the rest of her decisions. She created a story for both Tess and Bess. She made it humorous but relevant. Music would set the scene, magic would capture attention, and props would bring Bess and Tess to life.

Her preparation took a week, but when the day came, she was ready. As the housekeepers approached the room, she had confidence. She knew her "A Bess–Tess Story" would work.

In the room she had an instrumental version of *The Brady Bunch* theme song playing. While the song played, she also ran an electronic presentation she had prepared. The presentation asked asbestos related quiz questions, and then displayed the answers. Along one wall she had set up an almost museum-like display table. Prominently displayed were several items, including a pipe wrapped in insulation, a banana, a ceiling tile, a hat, some dry spackling, a toy car, a shingle, an extension cord, a lollypop, and a floor tile. As the housekeepers entered the room, she asked each one to select one item from the table, and take it to her seat.

When the electronic presentation and the music ended, and the housekeepers had gathered, she started. "Good morning and welcome. We are here today to talk about . . ."

With that, she sounded a toy siren she had placed in the front of the room.

". . . Asbestos," she continued. Some of the housekeepers began to groan, but she stopped them. "Don't worry," she explained. "This class will be different."

"Today, I intend to help you discover what type of," she sounded the siren again, "asbestos materials you may encounter at work, give you some important information, and answer any questions you might have. To do that, I need your help with this story," she said.

Harriet displayed the "Role Play Extravaganza" cartoon.

"Now, I realize that volunteering can be a nerve-wracking experience. I promise not to film it."

That got a laugh. Everyone relaxed a little. "Would someone be willing to play Bess? And Tess?"

With the laugh still in their minds, two women came forward. Harriet took a minute to give both them wardrobe props: a pair of nerdy glasses for Bess and a cigarette prop with an overly long holder for Tess, and then they began.

She displayed a storybook. "I have a really hot story for you today." With that, she opened up her magical prop, Hot Book. It shot flames six inches into the air and immediately got everybody's attention.

"This is the story of two sisters, Bess and Tess," she continued. "In other words, it's 'A Bess–Tess Story.'"

With that, she restarted the Brady Bunch theme music, and keyed her electronic presentation to display the appropriate lyrics. She then invited everyone to sing along.

It's a story, of an older sister,
Who was happy doing just what she was told,
By the name of Bess she's known as the "Best" girl,
Yes, she was made of gold.

It's a story, of a second sister,
Who was busy causing problems that's for sure,
Although her name was Tess the "T" stood for trouble,
No, she was not demure.

Then one day when both sisters got employment,
And they knew that it was more than just for glory,
That the two of them should work the same department,
That's how we begin this Bess Tess story.

The Bess Tess story,
The Bess Tess story,
That's the way we will begin this Bess Tess story.

"Bess and Tess were twins." She stopped and looked at the two housekeepers, who were obviously not twins. One was Jamaican and the other Swedish. "As you can tell, they look exactly alike. But in reality, they were as different as different could be."

"Bess was a true talent. Her family joked that she had been called 'Bess' because the 'B' stood for 'best.'"

She turned to the "Bess" performer and asked him to demonstrate some "best" attitude.

They all cheered as Bess strutted her stuff.

"On the other hand, Tess was a rebel. In fact, her family joked that she was named 'Tess' because 'T' stood for trouble. And trouble she was." She turned to the 'Tess' performer without saying anything. The housekeeper knew what to do. She snarled trouble as she puffed on her prop cigarette. The housekeepers reacted to Tess, some with boos and some with cheers.

"Both sisters went to work in a housekeeping department, much like this one, in an older building, much like ours. The first day on the job, Bess and Tess were required to watch the company's mandatory Asbestos Awareness training video. Coincidentally, the housekeepers in the class looked a lot like all of you."

Harriet asked the two participants to return to their seats and had the class watch the video. To emphasize its importance, she watched it too.

When the video ended, Harriet continued, "Bess paid close attention to the video." She then turned to the housekeeper playing Bess, and asked, "You were paying attention, weren't you? . . . Say yes!"

Bess agreed.

"Tess paid no attention whatsoever to the video." She looked at the Tess performer.

"Not one word!" the Tess performer replied.

"Bess and Tess then settled into their jobs. Oh, Tess complained a little, but they both enjoyed what they were doing. And then, one day, an amazing coincidence occurred. Both Bess and Tess encountered the same situation. . ."

With that, Harriet threw two globs of white fibers off the display table, actually torn apart cotton balls, and onto the floor.

". . . white fibers loose on the floor."

"Both women bend in close to look at these fibers."

She repeated the line, until both volunteers left their seats to look at the fibers.

They both said, almost in unison, "Look at what we have here. I better do something about this."

Of course, the line wasn't said in unison, but Harriet led a round of applause for them anyway.

Next, Harriet divided the room into two teams, one side with the Bess performer as its group leader, and the other assigned to Tess.

"Now, if you remember, Bess paid attention to the video, so she knew exactly what to do. On the other hand, Tess did not remember." She displayed a multiple-choice slide. "What did Bess and Tess do? Did they. . .

A. Sweep it up with a broom and dustpan.
B. Vacuum it.
C. Ignore it.
D. Call their manager.

She instructed the Tess group to choose the worst possible option, and the Bess group the best. She gave them 45 seconds, the length of her musical selection, to determine an answer. As they worked, she played a short instrumental version of *The Brady Bunch* theme. When the music stopped, she asked them what they had decided.

The Tess group chose answer "C, Ignore it" as their answer. The Bess group chose "D." After she heard the answers, she went back to her book and said, "Let's see what Tess and Bess did."

"Tess never considered calling her manager. It was in her rebel nature to take care of it herself. She had a pan and broom nearby, so she swept the fibers up."

The "Tess" performer came back to the front of the room and swept the white fibers up.

"Meanwhile, Bess was taking a different tack. She called her manager for help."

With this, Harriet selected a "manager" from the class, and placed a gaudy "manager" tie on the housekeeper. She then gave the "manager" a script to read from.

The manager performer read, "Bess, thanks for bringing me in on this one. We don't know what these fibers are. They could contain. . ."

Harriet sounded her warning alarm again.

". . .Asbestos," he continued. "Let's call in some asbestos removal experts."

"And, that is the appropriate answer. Call the experts."

Harriet led a round of applause for the manager's decision and invited the manager back to her seat. She then continued through a series of questions based on the asbestos awareness video. She kept the mood light, but focused on content. She quizzed them on other reaction scenarios, the different types of asbestos, and the health effects of asbestos related illnesses.

When they had completed the quiz, she thanked them, and reminded them that they each had picked up a prop when they entered. She asked them each individually to showcase their prop and indicate whether or not the material their prop represented was likely to contain asbestos.

Once they had all done so, and she knew that they had absorbed the lesson, she announced that the class was almost over, except for two pieces of information. She asked them first to complete their class evaluations. While the learners completed their evaluations, she brought the Bess and Tess performers into the hallway. She gave them both props, and asked them to prepare for the finale.

"As you know, Bess handled asbestos in the correct manner, where Tess did not. We'd like to conclude with a look into the future that faced Bess and Tess." With that, she reintroduced Tess. The housekeeper playing Tess re-entered the room wearing a terrible looking white hair wig, a shawl, and leaning on a cane as if she were an old, unhealthy lady. She coughed and shuffled her feet as she walked. In contrast, Bess bounced into the room, full of energy and looking the same as before.

Harriet had the two stand side-by-side, facing the housekeepers. She then said, "Because Bess didn't smoke, and handled asbestos properly, she lived a long life. Meanwhile Tess, who had inhaled asbestos fibers, had breathing problems. Those problems were compounded by her smoking habit."

"But, the story didn't have to end this way. For, this is a made-up story and the ending is in your hands. In this case, the "T" in Tess actually stood for Terrific. She did pay attention during her asbestos awareness class, and because she knew her smoking put her at greater risk, she was even more careful around potential asbestos situations." Harriet instructed the Tess performer to remove her shawl and wig. "As a result," she continued, "both women stayed safe around asbestos, and they lived happily ever after."

Harriet then presented both with Asbestos Achiever's certificates. As the class applauded the two performers, she joined in with a series of short siren blasts. She then concluded the class with a reprise of the Bess–Tess song.

It's a story, a made-up story,
Of two sisters who worked safely every day,
By the name Bess and Tess, they were the "Best" girls,
Yes, they were safe in every way.

The Bess–Tess story,
The Bess–Tess story,
That's the way we all will end this Bess–Tess story.

With the song complete, Harriet distributed the required legal information and dismissed the class.

Harriet was pleased with the class results. The evaluations indicated that the housekeepers enjoyed the class. Better yet, the knowledge retention quiz had demonstrated that they absorbed the content. Harriet thought the *matter had ended there, but a week later, a card appeared on her desk. It was from the housekeepers. In it, they thanked her for taking the time to make the class interesting. But the best part was the way they had all signed their names. For, as a part of their signatures, each one had added a new middle name, "Bess."*

"Do things and make things which give pleasure to people in new and amusing ways." —WALT DISNEY[1]

IN REVIEW

We have come a long way in our journey through Show Biz Training. Act One, "The Info-fog," focused on the need for Show Biz Training techniques. In Chapter One, "The Distracted Learner," we discovered the info-fog our learners face, and the factors that have caused its existence. Next, in Chapter Two, "The World is a Stage," we determined that stories have always been with humans, and that those stories evolved into the entertainment giant we confront today. In Chapter Three, "Let Me Entertain You," we examined the ways in which various entities—advertising, news, business, sports and edutainment— have all used entertainment to increase the effectiveness of their messages.

With all those factors in mind, we next, in Chapter Four, "Learnertainment," over-viewed the ways in which the human brain functions. A special emphasis was focused on the role of survival and emotion, and how they interact with each other. We next explored Giorgi Lozanov's Suggestopedia and its attempt to reach the deep recesses of the brain through relaxed joy. Finally, and most importantly, we examined the Learnertainment Chain and saw how entertainment directly related to human brain processing. We then were introduced to the eight Learnertainment Principles:

Principle 1: Make it fun—Create an atmosphere of playfulness.
Principle 2: Layer meaning—Present your message on several levels.
Principle 3: Cue the audio—Add the auditory signal to the visual.
Principle 4: Evoke emotion—Engage your learners emotionally.
Principle 5: Direct attention—Suggest the outcomes you expect.
Principle 6: Stage the environment—Orchestrate every detail of the environment.
Principle 7: Use mnemonics—Provide visual learning cues.
Principle 8: Stage the performer—Orchestrate every detail of your performance.

Through those principles, we explored the entertainment arts. We learned the tools that comedians, musicians, and magicians use and discovered ways to apply those tools to the learning environment.

Principle 1: Make It Fun— Create an Atmosphere of Playfulness

Act Two, "Lessons from Entertainment," overviewed three major show biz elements: comedy, music, and magic.

In Chapter Five, "Lessons from Comedy," we learned the benefits of humor. We examined the joke structures comedians use. We also discovered that people who laugh together become a community, and that an atmosphere of playfulness unleashes positive emotions that make learning memorable.

Principle 2: Layer Meaning— Present Your Message on Several Levels

In "Lessons from Comedy," we also discovered that comedy works because it presents information on more than one level. It forces a learner to walk all the way around a subject. It generates an understanding deeper than what would be possible with traditional lecture-based methods.

Principle 3: Cue the Audio— Add the Auditory Signal to the Visual

In Chapter Six, "Lessons from Music," we learned, through movie music, about the auditory signal. We focused on a case study, the extinction of silent films. From that case study, we determined that the auditory signal was too powerful a tool to overlook. We also examined some templates for applying music to the learning environment.

Principle 4: Evoke Emotion— Engage Your Learners Emotionally

Music also taught us how critical emotion is in creating a whole experience. We examined the wholeness that music adds to an environment, from shopping centers to the local cinema. In addition, we learned that emotional signals are more likely to be remembered by our brain, and thus aid retention.

Principle 5: Direct Attention—
Suggest the Outcomes You Expect

From magic, in Chapter Seven, "Lessons from Magic," we discovered the power of direction to point the learners toward the outcomes we want them to achieve. We discovered that magicians cheat nature by redefining the events that occur around them. Suggestion was examined at length as a tool for directing learners toward positive outcomes.

Principle 6: Stage the Environment—
Orchestrate Every Detail of the Environment

In Act Three, "Stagecraft," we explored the particulars of stagecraft, beginning with Chapter Eight, "The Stage." It found us examining the details of the environment that must be in place for magicians and other performers to deliver flawless entertainment. We examined the possible seating arrangements, and their advantages and disadvantages. The elements of the stage were then examined. We looked at the effects of lighting and scenery. We even considered ways in which all five senses might be employed to stage the environment.

Principle 7: Use Mnemonics—Provide Visual Learning Cues

Next, in Chapter Nine, "Props," we examined the usefulness of props in the learning environment. We discovered that visual representations save explanatory time, and that props can serve as visual memory cues. To help us determine appropriate prop usage in the learning environment, we concluded the chapter with an examination of the OFF-BEAT™ Prop Selection Matrix.

Principle 8: Stage the Performer—
Orchestrate Every Detail of Your Performance

In Chapter 10, "The Script," and Chapter 11, "Rehearsal," we focused on the performer and continued examining the environment as we learned how entertainers prepare for a performance by scripting and then rehearsing the material scripted. We discovered that entertainment's Three-Act Structure is applicable to the learning environment, and that scripting has distinct advantages. We then we discussed the correct rehearsal steps. Chapter Twelve, "The Performer," helped us evaluate our own performance abilities. We looked at our personality traits, our vocal projection ability, our posture and our clothing, and we discussed microphone usage.

Bad News   By Millbower and Yager

I'm sorry to say our class is over.

Copyright © 2002 Stylus Publishing, LLC. Reprinted by permission from Cartoons for Trainers, Stylus Publishing, Sterling, VA.

Finally, at the beginning of this chapter, we saw an example as Harriet applied Show Biz Training to her asbestos awareness class. In the process, she created an enjoyable experience that increased learner retention.

We are almost done. There is one matter we should, however, discuss before we wrap this production. That subject is one every show biz professional wants to avoid, but never ever escapes: the critics.

HANDLING THE CRITICS

Every show biz performance has its critics; yours will too. Expect objections, especially from those locked in the pre-info-fog world. More importantly, address these objections in your lesson plan. The most likely complaints will be:

- ▶ "This is a gimmick!"
- ▶ "Fun detracts from learning!"
- ▶ "My employees will never go for this!"
- ▶ "Our instructors aren't skilled in these techniques!"
- ▶ "There are logistic challenges!"
- ▶ "This will cost more!"
- ▶ "We're sending a message that we're not serious!"

"This Is a Gimmick!"

Traditionally minded thinkers may denigrate Show Biz Training as "gimmicky." My emphatic and immediate answer is: "Exactly!" It is gimmicky. But so is advertising. And television. And the movies. And edutainment. Gimmicks abound in our society. They exist, not for the sake of a gimmick, but because they help communicators cut through the info-fog.

In *The Entertainment Economy,* Michael Wolf proclaimed, "Generic experiences will find it harder to attract consumers, while constantly refreshed ones will succeed."[2] Although Wolf was discussing the use of entertainment techniques in business, the point is equally valid in the learning environment. A generic classroom environment will find itself increasingly at risk from both a learning and a financial standpoint.

"Fun Detracts from Learning!"

There are two replies to this objection:

▶ Fun makes learning more palatable.

▶ The medium is not the message.

FUN MAKES LEARNING PALATABLE

The truth is, you can have fun while you learn, and as we discovered in Chapter Four, Show Biz Training helps people relax so that they can learn. The Learnertainment Chain can serve as a presentation aid if you need to make this point.

THE MEDIUM IS NOT THE MESSAGE

Joseph Pine and James Gilmore warned in *The Experience Economy:* "It's easy to conclude that shifting to staged experiences simply means adding entertainment to existing offerings. That would be a gross understatement. Staging experiences is not about entertaining customers, it's about *engaging* them."[3]

Good entertainments provide confectionery enjoyment. Entertainments with little content are like cotton candy: tasty when eaten, but lacking in nutritional value. The entire James Bond series can be viewed in this context. Although I am a fan of these films, I must admit that the only one who gets taught a lesson is the villain.

Great entertainments do more; they also teach. Because they teach, they seem to have more staying power than the confections. There is, so to speak, more meat on the bone. Two films that teach and entertain are *Beauty and the Beast* (1991), with its message that beauty comes from within, and *Forrest Gump* (1994), demonstrating that behavior matters more than intelligence.

The question therefore is really one of balance, and a proper balance is critical. When using magic, for instance, the surprise value can overwhelm the learning focus. Learners may begin focusing on the secret of the illusion, and ignore its meaning.

Beauty and the Beast displays the necessary balance. When an audience first begins viewing the film, they may be taken in with the breathtaking animation. But soon, the equally breathtaking story takes hold, and the technique is forgotten. The technique becomes a means, rather than the message.

Show Biz Training should not be the focus of your instruction. If you add it as sugar, not nutrition, it will detract from the learning process. Learnertainment cannot substitute for meaningful content. The Show Biz Training techniques you use should not determine your learning points. The learning points should determine the Show Biz Training techniques you use.

CUE CARD: Show Biz Training should not be the focus of your instruction.

"MY EMPLOYEES WILL NEVER GO FOR THIS!"

It is true that some audiences will be less receptive to Show Biz Training than others, but no audience is immune to laughter. I have personally witnessed hardened classrooms come to life when Show Biz Training confronted the negative emotions within the learners. Show Biz Training techniques are uniquely equipped to replace those negative emotions with positive, joyful emotions. The end result is engaged learners and increased retention.

In situations in which you perceive resistance, introduce the techniques slowly. Allow your learners time to grow comfortable in your classroom. As their negative emotions dissipate, add more Learnertainment. Eventually, even hardened skeptics will begin to enjoy themselves. After all, "I'm not going to have a good time" is not a sustainable attitude when confronted with laughter.

"OUR INSTRUCTORS AREN'T SKILLED IN THESE TECHNIQUES!"

Instructors who use Show Biz Training must possess, in addition to facilitation and communication skills, comedic timing. They must be able to use props. They will be required to learn magic tricks. And, they will have to know when to use them, and when not to use them.

These are unavoidable facts. But, imagine how much more professional you and your colleagues will become. In addition to the solid knowledge of the content you already possess, you will also develop the presentation professionalism that Show Biz Training techniques entail. Regardless, the world is moving in entertainment's direction. We will all likely be forced to embrace Learnertainment, regardless of our wishes.

"THERE ARE LOGISTIC CHALLENGES!"

As we have discovered, live entertainment is complicated. It involves much more than standing in front of a room and placing overheads on a projector. The props and magic will need to be stored somewhere.

There will also be more materials to transport. Easel pads, classroom supplies, and laptops are difficult enough to negotiate. Instructors who use Show Biz Training techniques will also have props, magic, and music recordings to lug around. Fortunately, many props and illusions pack flat. Other items can easily be stored in small bins. And all these materials can be transported with a small handcart.

Finally, classroom facilitation itself may be a challenge. CD players, overhead projectors, and temperamental laptops can already wreak classroom havoc. Props, magic, and music recordings add to the logistics that must be managed in a classroom. The scripting and rehearsal process can help in this regard. The more you can commit your performance to procedural memory, the easier these details become. Besides, technology has evolved to the point where you can integrate the music and video clips you need directly into your computer presentation.

"THIS WILL COST MORE!"

Show Biz Training does cost money. It costs more in two different ways:

► Show Biz materials are expensive.

► Labor costs will increase.

MATERIALS ARE EXPENSIVE

When you purchase a magic illusion, you are purchasing its secret, and those secrets are expensive. Magic is intentionally priced high enough to prevent the general public from discovering the secret of the trick. This cost is really in your best interest. Just as you want your learners to focus on the message and not the illusion, you also don't want someone disrupting the class to share the illusion's secret. The costs associated with magic prevent this from happening.

Props can be costly or not, depending on the prop itself, and where you shop for it. A situation I experienced is instructive. I purchased a fake cell phone through a reputable magician's supply company for $20.00. Three days later, I went to the local Wal-Mart and found an equivalent item in the closeout bin for $1.99. Aggressive toy store shopping will be your best cost containment procedure.

Musical material can also be expensive. It's not that the music itself is costly. Rather, the rights to use the music can add cost. Regardless, it is better to pay a little more in up-front costs. The cost of a copyright infringement lawsuit is even more prohibitive. The appendix lists suppliers of royalty-free music, as well as comedy, props, and magic suppliers.

LABOR COSTS WILL INCREASE.

Learning Show Biz Training techniques will take time. So will script writing. And rehearsal. And classroom setup and pack up. All of these incidentals add labor costs. But, these additional costs will be offset by increased effectiveness. By documenting the increased effectiveness of Show Biz Training, you can validate the extra costs.

"WE'RE SENDING A MESSAGE THAT WE'RE NOT SERIOUS!"

For some people, the motive behind this objection may be related to their image of professionalism. They may regard themselves as having a serious purpose, and fear that "frivolous" behavior will undercut their message. The position reminds me of the aristocrat in the Stan Freberg Sunkist commercial we overviewed in Chapter Three, "Let Me Entertain You." The actor's portrayal was stuffy. He warned in advance that he wouldn't like the fruit. When he discovered, much to his surprise, that the fruit was "quite good," he dropped his primary complaint and switched to another objection.

Likewise, image-motivated objections will surface as one point, and then another. In the classroom, our professional self-image is important only as it affects our learners' abilities to learn. Ironically, the application of Learnertainment is likely to improve our image with the very people we most need to impact, our learners.

Taken as a whole, these challenges do not add up to an argument for the exclusion of Show Biz Training. They do, however, suggest the need for careful planning and application. But I wouldn't expect anything less from a Show Biz professional.

CUE CARD: Show Biz Training requires careful planning and application.

QUESTIONS TO CONSIDER

I would like to close by posing two questions:

▶ Is your learning so enjoyable that you could charge admission?

▶ Would you give a ticket to your training to someone you liked and admired?

If you answered "No" to either of these questions, how do you think your learners feel? And, what are you going to do about it?

YOU'RE THE STAR: BREAK A LEG!

Assuming that you answered, "I'm going to add Show Biz Training techniques to my classroom," I'd like to leave you with an old show biz term. It stems from a medieval belief in sprites that enjoyed causing trouble. What made the sprites doubly problematic was the belief that if the sprites heard you ask for something, they would make the opposite happen. Just in case the sprites were listening, people would wish each other bad luck. (In fact, this is Chapter Thirteen for that very reason.) Although people no longer fear the sprites, show biz performers are notoriously suspicious. So in keeping with the show biz tradition you are about to enter, break a leg![4]

**CUE CARD:
Break a leg!**

1 Smith, Dave (2001). *The Quotable Walt Disney: It Was All Started by a Mouse.* New York: Hyperion.

2 Wolf, Michael J. (1999). *The Entertainment Economy: How Mega-Media Forces Are Transforming Our Lives.* New York: Random House.

3 Pine II, Joseph B., and Gilmore, James H. (1999). *The Experience Economy.* Boston, MA: Harvard Business School Press.

4 <http://members.aol.com/MorelandC/HaveOriginsData.htm>

COMEDY

Offbeat Training
329 Oakpoint Circle
Davenport, FL 33837
(407) 256-0501
<www.offbeattraining.com>

Cartoons for Trainers
Lenn Millbower & Doris Yager
Stylus Publishing, LLC.
<www.styluspub.com>

MAGIC AND PROP RESOURCES

Magic Supply Companies

Professional magicians purchase their illusions and props through magic dealers. These dealers do not know the needs of trainers, and cannot be expected to answer training-related questions. They are, however, expert magicians, and excel in answering questions directly related to the illusions they sell.

Hank Lee's Magic Factory
PO Box 789
Medford, MA 02155
(800) 874-7400/(617) 482-8749
<www.magicfact.com>

Abbott's Magic
124 St. Joseph St.
Colon, MI 49040
(800) 92-MAGIC/(616) 432-3235

Louis Tannen, Inc.
24 West 25th St., 2nd Floor
New York, NY 10010
(212) 929-4500
<http://www.tannenmagic.com>

Training Supply Companies

Although they do not specialize in magic, two training supply companies sell magic illusions. Because their primary market is on the needs of trainers, these companies can address training related questions with greater specificity than the magic supply companies. They also offer a wide variety of props.

Creative Presentation Resources
P.O. Box 180487
Casselberry, FL 32718
<www.presentationresources.net>

The Trainer's Warehouse
89 Washington Ave
Natick, MA 01760
(800) 299-3770
<www.trainerswarehouse.com>

Tool Thyme for Trainers
4108 Grace King Place
Metairie, LA 70002
(504) 887-5558
<www.tool-trainers.com>

Novelty Suppliers

Novelty suppliers do not cater to the needs of trainers, but occasionally stock items that are useful for training. Also, because these suppliers must appear to a wider audience than the training community, expect to see odd, tasteless, exotic, and sometimes erotic items in their catalog. Hundreds of these suppliers are listed on the Internet. Below are a few resources.

The Gag Works
PO Box 1293
Los Alamitos, CA 90720
<http://www.gagworks.com>

Incredible Gifts
1746 B Berkeley
Santa Monica, CA 90404
(800) 982-5992
<www.IncredibleGifts.com>

Fun Ideas
P.O. Box 5472
Lighthouse Point, FL 33074
(877) 665-4438
<www.funideas.com>

Music Suppliers

Most music suppliers do not offer royalty-free music. Insure you know the legal usage parameters of the music you select. An asterisk after the supplier's name indicates that the music they offer is fully licensed.

Offbeat Training Tunes*
329 Oakpoint Circle
Davenport, FL 33837
(407) 256-0501
<www.offbeattraining.com>

MediaRider.com*
2376 Summerwind Place
Carlsbad, CA 92008
(760) 730-7480

Phillips Classics
PolyGram Classics & Jazz
825 Eighth Ave, 26th Floor
New York, NY 10019
<www.philclas.polygram.nl>

Time Warner
5300 Warner Blvd
Burbank, CA 91505

Narada Productions, Inc.
4650 N. Port Washington Road
Milwaukee, WI 53212
(414) 961-8350
<www.narada.com>

Steven Halpern's Inner Peace Music
PO Box 2644
San Anselmo, CA 94979
(800) 909-0707
<www.innerpeacemusic.com>

Trainer Sounds
Performance Insights
1615 Highway 184
Ghent, KY 41045
<www.offbeattraining.com>

The Music Bakery
7522 Campbell Rd., #113-2
Dallas, Texas, 75248
(800) 229-0313
<www.musicbakery.com>

Network Music LLC*
15150 Avenue of Science
San Diego, California 92128
(800) 854-2075
<www.networkmusic.com>

The Classical Archives*
<www.classicalarchives.com>

Files in PDF format of the Show Biz Training Templates on pages 338–359 are available at www.amacombooks.org/showbiztraining

JOKE CREATION TEMPLATE

Part 1: How To Write a Joke

1. Identify the subject you wish to joke about (class introductions).
2. List every idea you can think of that relates to that subject (family, family members, brothers and sisters, half brothers and sisters/occupations, magician sawing a woman in half).
3. Group related ideas (half brothers and sisters/sawing a woman in half)
4. Identify two ideas that fit together but have alternative meanings (half brothers and sisters could be siblings or part of a magician's sawing-in-half trick).
5. Write an *Introduction* (student introductions during the first day of class).
6. Select one of the ideas to be your *Surprise* (half brothers and sisters).
7. Add *Detail* that obscures the other idea (father's occupation is as a magician, his favorite trick is sawing a woman in half).
8. Set up the surprise (any brothers and sisters?).
9. Try your joke out on people, and keep tweaking it until it gets a favorable response.

Part 2: Structure Template:

1. *Introduction.*
   Introduce the subject.

   _____

2. *Detail.*
   Provide additional detail.
   ▶ *Detail 1.*

   _____

   ▶ *Detail 2.*

   _____

   ▶ *Detail 3.*

   _____

3. *Surprise.*
   Conclude with a surprise ending.

   _____

Part 3: Structure Analysis:

1. *Introduction.*

   Is the Introduction brief?

   _____

   Is it easily comprehensible?

   _____

   Is the subject introduced in a way that builds curiosity?

   _____

2. *Detail.*

   Do the details build curiosity?

   _____

   Do they add tension?

   _____

   Is the tension sustained as long as possible?

   _____

   Do the details effectively hide the   rise?

   _____

4. *Surprise.*

   Does the ending release the tension?

   _____

   Does it fit the *Introduction*?

   _____

   Does it fit the *Detail*?

   _____

   Is the ending different from the expected conclusion?

'PUNNISH'MENT ANALYZER

Part One: How To Write a Pun:

1. Identify the subject of your pun (Communication).
2. List every idea you can think of that relates to that subject (electronic communication, Internet, intranet, LAN).
3. Select ideas from the list that could have alternate meanings, or are similar to other words. (What could "LAN" mean? What if the problem was related to Australia? Could it then be the "LAN" down under?).
4. Write the *Surprise* (the LAN down under).
5. Write an *Introduction* (a company was having customer service problems).
6. Add *Detail* that sets up the *Surprise* without giving it away (traveled to Australia where computer communications had been upgraded, the Australian branches intranet became the model).
7. Try your pun out on people, and keep tweaking it until it gets a groan.

Part 2: Pun 2: Pun template:

1. *Introduction.*
   Introduce the subject.

   _____

2. *Detail.*
   Provide additional detail.
   ▶ *Detail 1.*

   _____

   ▶ *Detail 2.*

   _____

   ▶ *Detail 3.*

   _____

3. *Surprise.*
   Select a surprise ending.

   _____

Part 3: Pun analysis:

1. *Introduction.*
   Is the Introduction brief?

   _____

   Is it easily comprehensible?

   _____

   Is the subject introduced in a way that builds curiosity?

   _____

2. *Detail.*
   Do the details build curiosity?

   _____

   Do they add tension?

   _____

   Is the tension sustained as long as possible?

   _____

   Do the details effectively hide the surprise?

   _____

4. *Surprise.*
   Does the pun release the tension?

   _____

   Does it fit the *Introduction*?

   _____

   Does it fit the *Detail*?

   _____

   Is the ending different from the expected conclusion?

OVERTURE PLACEMENT ANALYZER

Use this matrix to determine the effectiveness of the overture music you select.

Step 1: Select the overture music.
Begin brightly, with a fanfare or other attention getting device.

    Selection 1: _____

Transition through the other major musical themes.

    Follow-up selections: _____

The quietest point is placed in the center.

    Midpoint selection: _____

Build to a rousing conclusion.

    Concluding selections: _____

Step 2: Evaluate the music for effectiveness.

Does the music:	Yes	No
▶ Immediately capture attention?	_____	_____
▶ Set the mood of the training?	_____	_____
▶ Match the style of the presentation to follow?	_____	_____
▶ Establish a positive learning environment?	_____	_____
▶ Sound familiar to the learners?	_____	_____
▶ Directly relate to the subject at hand?	_____	_____
▶ End with a fast, upbeat pace?	_____	_____
Total Score (7 maximum)	_____	_____

The higher the Yes column score, the more effective the overture will be.

LEITMOTIF PLACEMENT ANALYZER

Use this matrix to determine the effectiveness of the leitmotifs you select.

Step 1: Select leitmotifs.

1. List the major themes of your learning environment.

    Theme 1: _____

    Theme 2: _____

    Theme 3: _____

    Theme 4: _____

    Theme 5: _____

2. What songs (or sound effects) relate to those themes?

    Theme 1: _____

    Theme 2: _____

    Theme 3: _____

    Theme 4: _____

    Theme 5: _____

3. Where can you place those songs (or sound effects) in the context of your instruction?

    Theme 1: _____

    Theme 2: _____

    Theme 3: _____

    Theme 4: _____

    Theme 5: _____

Step 2: Evaluate the music for effectiveness.

Do the letimotifs you selected: Yes   No

► Align with the class content?   _____   _____
► Communicate information about their assigned situation?   _____   _____
► Help the learners connect to the assigned situation?   _____   _____
► Make an emotional connection with your learners?   _____   _____

The higher the Yes column score, the more effective the leitmotif will be.

GAME SHOW MUSIC PLACEMENT ANALYZER

Use this matrix to aid you in selecting appropriate game show music.

Introducing the game show

Selection: _____

Does the music	Yes	No
► Exhibit high energy?	_____	_____
► Hype the activity?	_____	_____
► Relate to the subject matter?	_____	_____

Displaying the prizes

Selection: _____

Does the music

► Display a light up-tempo feel?	_____	_____
► Have no vocals?	_____	_____
► Stay in the background?	_____	_____

Seeking and introducing game show players

Selection: _____

Does the music

► Display high energy?	_____	_____
► Create a sense of movement?	_____	_____
► Create a sense of excitement?	_____	_____

Asking questions

Selection: _____

Does the music

► Have no vocals?	_____	_____
► Heighten tension?	_____	_____
► Stay in the background?	_____	_____

Timing answers

Selection: _____

Does the music

► Play in short segments?	_____	_____
► Length match the timed length required?	_____	_____
► Have no vocals?	_____	_____

Conducting lightning rounds

Selection: _____

Does the music   Yes   No

- ► Play in short musical segments?   _____   _____
- ► Keep the energy level focused?   _____   _____
- ► Keep the momentum moving forward?   _____   _____

Thanking the players

Selection: _____

Does the music

- ► Display high energy?   _____   _____
- ► Repeat the players' introductory music?   _____   _____
- ► Create a sense of movement?   _____   _____

Concluding the activity

Selection: _____

Does the music

- ► Display high energy?   _____   _____
- ► Relate to the subject matter?   _____   _____
- ► Conclude on a positive note?   _____   _____

                              Total score (24 maximum)   _____   _____

The higher the Yes column score, the more effective the overture will be.

ATMOSPHERIC MUSIC ANALYZER

Use this matrix as an aid in selecting appropriate atmospheric music.

To enhance feelings of happiness:
▶ **Fast music with high rhythmic activity; short, quick notes**

Selection 1: _____

Selection 2: _____

Selection 3: _____

To encourage sadness:
▶ **Slow music with low rhythmic activity**

Selection 1: _____

Selection 2: _____

Selection 3: _____

To build excitement:
▶ **High rhythmic activity**

Selection 1: _____

Selection 2: _____

Selection 3: _____

To create a feeling of calm:
▶ **Slow, minor key music; low rhythmic activity**

Selection 1: _____

Selection 2: _____

Selection 3: _____

To encourage better moods:
▶ **Fast, major key music**

Selection 1: _____

Selection 2: _____

Selection 3: _____

To overcome boredom:
▶ **High rhythmic music**

Selection 1: _____

Selection 2: _____

Selection 3: _____

BACKGROUND MUSIC ANALYZER

Use this matrix as an aid in selecting appropriate background filler.

Part 1: The need for music

Are your learners:

	Yes	No
▸ Involved in a group discussion?	_____	_____
▸ Involved in a paired discussion?	_____	_____
▸ Reflecting on a subject?	_____	_____
▸ Working privately, on solo activities?	_____	_____
▸ Practicing creative visioning?	_____	_____

If you answered "Yes" to any of these questions, background music would be effective.

Part 2: Selecting appropriate music

Is the music you would like to use:

	Yes	No
▸ Slow	_____	_____
▸ Reflective	_____	_____
▸ Melodic	_____	_____
▸ Nonvocal	_____	_____
▸ Instrumentally light	_____	_____

If you answered "Yes" to all of these questions, you chose an effective selection.

REPETITIVE TASK MUSIC ANALYZER

When selecting music for repetitive tasks, answer the following questions:

	Yes	No
▸ Is the music steady in its rhythm?	_____	_____
▸ Can you walk to the rhythm of the music?	_____	_____
▸ Can you perform the repetitive task to the music?	_____	_____
▸ If the music has lyrics, will the learners be able to sing them?	_____	_____
▸ Can the lyrics be rewritten to correspond with the repetitive task?	_____	_____
▸ Do you have the ability to speed up the music as task skills increase?	_____	_____
▸ If the music is sped up, does it still sound acceptable?	_____	_____

If you answered "Yes" to all the questions, the music is appropriate for repetitive tasks.

REVIEW ENHANCING MUSIC ANALYZER

When selecting music for reviews, answer the following questions:

	Yes	No
▶ Is the music steady in its rhythm?	_____	_____
▶ Can you easily walk in rhythm to the music?	_____	_____
▶ Does the rhythm of the music pulse once or less per second?	_____	_____
▶ Is the music devoid of lyrics?	_____	_____
▶ Does the music maintain a steady volume level?	_____	_____
▶ Is the music steady in its instrumentation?	_____	_____
▶ Does the music tend to make you feel sad?	_____	_____
▶ When you play the music, does it fade into the background?	_____	_____
Total (8 maximum)	_____	_____

The higher the Yes column score, the more effective the music usage will be.

POP MUSIC PLACEMENT ANALYZER

Step 1: Use the following questions to select a pop song.

▶ What is the purpose for using a pop song?

_____

▶ What pop songs will best serve that purpose?

1. _____

2. _____

3. _____

Step 2: Use the following questions to determine the most appropriate pop song.

	Yes	No
▶ Do you want the learners to focus on the song?	_____	_____
▶ Can you easily walk or sway in rhythm to the music?	_____	_____
▶ Do the song's lyrics relate to your class subject matter?	_____	_____
▶ Do you know the meaning of the song's lyrics?	_____	_____
▶ Is the meaning of the song's lyrics consistent with your message?	_____	_____
▶ Will your learners positively relate to the song?	_____	_____
▶ Will the use of the song be inoffensive?	_____	_____
▶ Do you have the legal rights to use the song?	_____	_____
Total (8 maximum)	_____	_____

The higher the Yes column score, the more effective a pop song will be.

MUSICAL DIFFICULTIES AVOIDANCE ANALYZER

Use the following questions to avoid some of the difficulties associated with music.

	Yes	No
▸ Is your usage of music less than 40% of total class time?	_____	_____
▸ When you use music, do you have specific reasons for doing so?	_____	_____
▸ Is your placement of music integrated into the whole?	_____	_____
▸ Is the music usage appropriate to the learning situation?	_____	_____
▸ Is your music selection based on need, not on favoritism?	_____	_____
▸ Does your music match the cultural norms of your learners?	_____	_____
▸ Are the song's lyrics appropriate to the learning situation?	_____	_____
▸ If using songs with lyrics, do you want the song to be noticed?	_____	_____
Total (8 maximum)	_____	_____

The higher the Yes column score, the more you will avoid difficulties associated with the use of music.

CLASSROOM SHOW READINESS FORM

Part 1: Outside the Classroom

The approach to the classroom	Yes	No	Corrective Action to Take:
▶ Is the hall carpet/flooring clean?	_____	_____	_____
▶ Are the walls dirty?	_____	_____	_____
▶ Are all posted signs neat and orderly?	_____	_____	_____
▶ Do posted signs undercut your message?	_____	_____	_____
▶ Can the hallway be more inviting?	_____	_____	_____
▶ Can the hall support your content?	_____	_____	_____

The classroom door

	Yes	No	
▶ Are old notices taped on the door?	_____	_____	_____
▶ Is the door dirty?	_____	_____	_____
▶ Will the door stay open if you need it to?	_____	_____	_____
▶ Does the door squeak?	_____	_____	_____
▶ Can the door be more inviting?	_____	_____	_____
▶ Can the door support your content?	_____	_____	_____

Part 2: Inside the Classroom

At first glance	Yes	No	Corrective Action to Take:
▶ Does the room look inviting?	_____	_____	_____
▶ Can you make it more inviting?	_____	_____	_____
▶ Can the room support your content?	_____	_____	_____

The stage

	Yes	No	
▶ How can the platform be more inviting?	_____	_____	_____
▶ How can the platform support your content?	_____	_____	_____

The room

	Yes	No	
▶ Is the lighting adequate?	_____	_____	_____
▶ Are the walls clean?	_____	_____	_____
▶ Is the floor clean?	_____	_____	_____

▶ Is the room cluttered? _____ _____ _____

▶ Does the room smell pleasant? _____ _____ _____

▶ Is the temperature comfortable? _____ _____ _____

▶ Will sound travel well? _____ _____ _____

▶ Can the room be more engaging? _____ _____ _____

The seating

▶ Are the seats comfortable? _____ _____ _____

▶ Is the seating arrangement appropriate? _____ _____ _____

▶ Can the stage be seen from every seat? _____ _____ _____

▶ Are the tables clean? _____ _____ _____

▶ Do the chairs and tables wobble? _____ _____ _____

The scenery

▶ Can you decorate the room? _____ _____ _____

▶ Will the decorations support your content? _____ _____ _____

Lighting

▶ Will your face be lit? _____ _____ _____

▶ Will the learners see their notes? _____ _____ _____

FIVE-SENSES ENHANCEMENT FORM

Use this form to enhance the classroom environment through the five senses.

Sight

▶ What visuals are present in the classroom?

_____

_____

▶ What visuals should be present in the classroom?

_____

_____

▶ How can you add those visuals?

_____

_____

Smell

▶ What odors are present in the classroom?

_____

_____

▶ What odors should be present in the classroom?

_____

_____

▶ How can you add those odors?

_____

_____

Touch

▶ What touchable items are present in the classroom?

_____

_____

▶ What touchable items should be present in the classroom?

_____

_____

► **How can you add those touchable items?**

_____

_____

Taste
► **What tastes are present in the classroom?**

_____

_____

► **What tastes should be present in the classroom?**

_____

_____

► **How can you add those tastes?**

_____

_____

Hearing
► **What sounds are present in the classroom?**

_____

_____

► **What sounds should be present in the classroom?**

_____

_____

► **How can you add those sounds?**

_____

_____

THE OFFBEAT PROP PLACEMENT MATRIX™

Use this matrix to determine the effectiveness of the props you select.

The props you select should be:	Yes	No

Original
- ▶ Will the usage place the prop in an original situation? _____ _____
- ▶ Will the placement surprise your audience? _____ _____
- ▶ Will the prop connect with your learners in unexpected ways? _____ _____
- ▶ Will the connection create a mnemonic learning tool? _____ _____

Fascinating
- ▶ Will the prop command your learners' attention? _____ _____
- ▶ Will the learners want to know more about it when they see it? _____ _____
- ▶ Will the prop have no apparent connection to the subject? _____ _____
- ▶ Will the learners attempt to guess the connection? _____ _____

Fun
- ▶ Will the prop bring forth a feeling of fun? _____ _____
- ▶ Will it encourage an environment of playfulness? _____ _____
- ▶ Will it evoke a feeling of positive emotion? _____ _____
- ▶ Will the usage be humorous? _____ _____

Build Upon
- ▶ Will the prop usage build upon what has already occurred? _____ _____
- ▶ Will the usage fit naturally within the flow of instruction? _____ _____
- ▶ When the usage is revealed, will it add value to the subject? _____ _____
- ▶ Will the prop provide a bridge to the next topic? _____ _____

Elaborate
- ▶ Will the prop usage add new insight into the subject? _____ _____
- ▶ Will it say visually what you are communicating verbally? _____ _____
- ▶ Will it add a holistic layer of meaning? _____ _____
- ▶ Will the learners comprehend the subject more completely as a result of the usage? _____ _____

Appropriate
- ▶ Is the prop usage appropriate to the learners? _____ _____
- ▶ Will the prop meet the learners' cultural expectations? _____ _____
- ▶ Will the prop engage the learners at their intellectual level? _____ _____
- ▶ Will the learners understand the meaning of the prop? _____ _____

Tasteful
- ▶ **Will the prop be inoffensive to the learners?** _____ _____
- ▶ **Will they react positively to the usage?** _____ _____
- ▶ **Can potential problems be addressed in advance?** _____ _____
- ▶ **Will the usage cause your organization any legal challenges?** _____ _____

Total Score (24 maximum) _____ _____

The higher the Yes column score, the more effective the prop usage will be.

MATERIALS LIST FORM

Use this form to compile a list of all needed materials.

Prologue needs:

▶ **Props**

_____

_____

▶ **Participant materials**

_____

_____

▶ **Presentation materials**

_____

_____

Act One materials needed:

▶ **Props**

_____

_____

▶ **Participant materials**

_____

_____

▶ **Presentation materials**

_____

_____

Act Two materials needed:

▶ **Props**

_____

_____

▶ **Participant materials**

_____

_____

► **Presentation materials**

_____

_____

Act Three materials needed:
► **Props**

_____

_____

► **Participant materials**

_____

_____

► **Presentation materials**

_____

_____

REHEARSAL QUESTIONS TO ASK

Here are some theatrical-based rehearsal questions. Use them to help you plan your performance.

The script:
▶ **What is the message of the script?**

_____

_____

▶ **What is the point of view of each character?**

_____

_____

▶ **How does that point of view support the message of the script?**

_____

_____

▶ **How can the performers convey the point of view of their characters?**

_____

_____

▶ **What costume will best support the point of view of each character?**

_____

_____

The props:
▶ **What prop needs to be in what spot at what moment?**

_____

_____

▶ **Where should the prop be placed before the time it is needed on stage?**

_____

_____

▶ **How do I get the prop on stage? Off stage?**

_____

_____

▶ **Where should it be placed afterwards?**

_____

_____

The performers:
▶ **Who walks where, when?**

_____

_____

▶ **Where should each performer stand at any given moment?**

_____

_____

Other:
▶ **What lighting will best support the script?**

_____

_____

▶ **What music will best support the script? When should it be cued?**

_____

_____

Act *n.* One of the major divisions of a play.

Ad-lib *v.* To improvise and deliver in an extemporaneous manner.

Amphitheater *n.* An oval or round structure having tiers of seats gradually rising outward from the performance area.

Backlight *n.* Backlight separates the foreground from the background.

Bits of Business *n.* A small routine within a performance designed to gain laughs.

Close-up *abj.* A form of magic that occurs directly in front of spectators without the separation that a stage provides.

Cue Card *n.* A large card containing cues and held off-camera for the benefit of performers.

Delivery *n.* The inflections, mannerisms, and other characteristics a performer uses to communicate a message.

Fill *n.* Fill lighting is used to compensate for the shadows created by key lighting.

Follow Spot *n.* A spotlight that swivels so that the operator can follow the performer as the performer moves around the stage.

Foreshadow *v.* To present an indication or suggestion of events that will occur later in the performance.

Fourth Wall *n.* The stage; performers are said to "break the fourth wall" when they talk to the audience or walk into the audience from the stage.

Framing (To Frame) *adj.* To place actions within a context.

Gel *n.* A material placed in front of stage lights to alter the color of the lights.

House Lights *n.* The lighting over and around the audience.

Illusion *n.* An erroneous perception of reality presented as fact by a magician.

Infotainment *n.* Information packaged and presented with entertainment techniques.

Key *adj.* Key lighting is the principle illumination for a stage.

Levitate *v.* To rise or cause to rise into the air and float in defiance of gravity.

Mark *n.* A piece of tape on a stage that indicates the precise location where a performer should stand.

Misdirection *n.* To point the audience's attention away from critical activity.

Monologue *n.* A series of jokes delivered by a comedian.

Overture *n.* A musical composition intended to introduce the performance that follows.

Patter *n.* The words a magician speaks while performing an illusion.

Plot *n.* The main story points of a performance.

Pratfall *n.* A fake fall executed by a comedian to elicit laughs.

Prop *n.* Any article a performer holds during a performance.

Pun *n.* A play on words that results in the creation of wit.

Punch Line *n.* The climax of a joke.

Scenery *n.* The features of the setting in which a performance occurs.

Sight-line *n.* The line at the edge of a stage that separates what an audience can and cannot see.

Sitcom *n.* A comedy in which the humor comes about as a result of the situations the characters find themselves in.

Stage *n.* A raised platform on which a performance is delivered.

Stage Lighting *n.* Lighting focused on the raised platform where a performance is delivered.

Take *n.* The repeated acting out of a scene in a performance.

Technicians *n.* The single most important person in a performance, charged with ensuring the success of the technical aspects of the performance.

Teleprompter *n.* A machine placed next to a camera that scrolls the text a performer reads while looking at the camera.

Three-quarters *adj.* A stance in which the performer faces the audience while placing one shoulder forward.

Theater-in-the-round *n.* A performance in which the audience fully surrounds the performer.

Up-tempo *adj.* A musical selection with a fast beat.

Voice-over (Talk-over) *n.* The vocal track of narration that runs over an image.

INDEX

ABOUT LENN MILLBOWER

Through 30 years of extensive study and hands-on experience, Lenn Millbower has discovered practical methods for combining music, entertainment, and learning to create interventions that are creative, meaningful, and fun. He is:

► The author of *Training with a Beat: The Teaching Power of Music*, the foremost book on the practical usage of music in learning situations (Stylus Publishing)

► The author of *Cartoons for Trainers*, a popular collection of 75 cartoons for every type of training situation (Stylus Publishing)

► The composer and musical arranger of *Game Show Themes for Trainers*, a CD of original music for trainers (Offbeat Training Tunes)

► An in-demand speaker, with successful presentations at ASTD International, International Alliance for Learning, International Society for Performance Improvement, and TechKnowledge conferences

► A Learnertainment specialist who as president of Offbeat Training™ is dedicated to helping organizations create learning environments that reach past the noise of daily life

> ► A dynamic instructional designer and facilitator, formerly with the Disney University and the Disney Institute, with years of experience in the training and development industry

> ► A respected liberal arts educator with experience teaching at all levels

> ► An accomplished arranger-composer skilled in the psychological application of music to enhance learning

> ► A popular entertainer with vast performance experience, having traveled throughout the United States, Canada, and the Bahamas as a comedian, magician, and musician

Lenn Millbower received his BM in Composition from Berklee College of Music, and his MA in Human Resource Development from Webster University. He is a member of the International Alliance for Learning, the International Society for Performance Improvement, and ASTD.

CONTACT INFORMATION

Want more information about Offbeat Training™ techniques?
Want to contact Lenn Millbower?
Visit www.offbeattraining.com